Roy E. Myers
Mathematics Department
The Pennsylvania State University

Microcomputer Graphics

Addison-Wesley Publishing Company

Reading, Massachusetts • Menlo Park, California
London • Amsterdam • Don Mills, Ontario • Sydney

This book is in the
Addison-Wesley Microcomputer Books
Technical Series

Thomas A. Dwyer, Consulting Editor

Apple is a registered trademark of Apple Computer, Inc.

Library of Congress Cataloging in Publication Data

Myers, Roy E.
    Microcomputer graphics.

    (Addison-Wesley microbooks technical series)
    Includes index.
    1. Computer graphics.   2. Microcomputers—Programming.
I. Title. II. Series.
T385.M93   001.55'3   82-1661
ISBN 0-201-05092-7   AACR2

ISBN 0-201-05092-7

Fifth Printing, November 1983

ISBN 0-201-05092-7
EFGHIJKL-HA-89876543

Preface

Aristotle drew figures in the sand. Leonardo Da Vinci illustrated his studies of anatomy and engineering with ink drawings. Young children can express their emotions and ideas with pencil or crayon drawings before they can do so verbally. Whatever the medium, the value of visual images has long been recognized. "A picture is worth a thousand words."

Now, at a time when computers are controlling the functions of automobiles, stereo sound systems, and space satellites, it would be surprising if computers were not used in the development and display of graphic images. Applications of computer graphics range from video games, to computer assisted design, to the display of images received from Voyager 2 as it passed by Saturn.

Work in computer graphics began in the 1950s. While major advances have been made since then, few people have been able to use computer graphics. For years the cost of equipment has kept graphics out of reach of most computer users. But now a new day has arrived. A microcomputer graphics system can be purchased for a few thousand dollars. Businesses, educational institutions, and individuals are finding that computer graphics is accessible, and that it can be useful, interesting, challenging, and fun.

While the graphics systems associated with low-cost microcomputers are far from the state of the art, they provide reasonable images in a reasonable time for a programmer of modest talents. More sophisticated graphics systems have capabilities which microcomputers do not provide. In order to achieve quality images, the microcomputer programmer must compensate for the limitations of the graphics hardware and the graphics language.

It is the intention of this book to provide the mathematical and programming techniques that are central to microcomputer graphics. The mathematical processes described are applicable to any computer system. The programs provided are written in BASIC for use on the Apple II; many may be adapted for use with other languages and microcomputers.

No attempt has been made to teach programming in BASIC. It is assumed that the reader is familiar with the language, and has access to the Applesoft^{tm} BASIC Programming Reference Manual and the Apple II Reference Manual. While example programs assume a 48K system with a disk drive, most can be modified to run on smaller systems. Apple II users without disk drives should find no difficulty in adapting the programs to cassette tape storage. On Apple II computers where memory capacity is limited to the point of providing only one high resolution graphics page, the replacement of HGR2 with HGR: POKE − 16302,0 will make most programs function properly.

The program examples are written to illustrate graphics techniques, not programming techniques; they are not intended to be model programs. The astute programmer will find ways to improve the execution time and to make the programs more "elegant." All programs have been tested and checked for errors. If one does not perform as described, it's more than likely a typing error.

ACKNOWLEDGEMENTS

A person working alone learns very little. It is through our contact with others that we gain the most. In realizing this I recognize that I have benefitted greatly from my association with Herb McKinstry, a good friend who is very generous with his time and talents. His comments, and those of Tom Dwyer, were very useful to me. Recognition is also due Neal, Alice, Karen, Glenn, and Linda for providing motivation and inspiration. Karen assisted in the preparation of materials. Karen and Alice helped with the proofreading.

Contents

Programs

Part I

Introduction

Chapter 1
The World Of Microcomputer Graphics

The phrase "computer graphics" does not have the same meaning to all persons. To some, it brings to mind a video arcade game; to others, a flight simulator for training aircraft pilots. To an architect, computer graphics provides a means of planning and displaying drawings for the design of a building. An engineer might use computer graphics to design and analyze an electrical circuit or a bridge.

The uses of computers for graphics purposes are many and varied. It is the intent of this book to consider the mathematical components and programming techniques necessary to generate graphics images on a low-cost microcomputer. The Apple II is used as the basis of discussion and all examples are written in Applesoft BASIC. In this chapter, we will consider example programs that illustrate both the capability of the computer and the programming processes that are described in later chapters.

RASTERS AND PIXELS

The Apple uses a *raster* display. This means simply that the display screen consists of a collection of horizontal lines (the *rasters*), and each raster line is made up of dots called *pixels*. In the Apple's high resolution graphics mode, there are 192 raster lines, each containing 280 pixels. The raster lines are numbered from 0 to 191; the pixels within each line are numbered from 0 to 279. Each pixel is thus identified by two numbers: the number of the raster line, and the number of the pixel within the line. Images are generated on the graphics screen by turning pixels on and off.

At the heart of a raster scan computer graphics language must be the ability to turn on individual pixels (i.e., to plot points). In Applesoft the HPLOT command performs this duty. HPLOT X,Y will turn on the pixel in the X position of raster line Y. For example, HPLOT 0,0 will turn on the dot in the top left corner of the screen; HPLOT 279,191 will turn on the dot in the bottom right corner. Dots in any position on any line are easily controlled in this way.

While most of the images we will be generating consist of more than a few individual dots, our first example program develops an image using only the HPLOT command.

Program 1.1: SPACE

```
1   REM PROGRAM 1.1 (SPACE)
2   REM PLOTS RANDOMLY SELECTED POINTS
10  HOME : HGR : HCOLOR= 3
20  FOR I = 1 TO 100
30 X = RND (1) * 279:Y = RND (1) * 191
40  HPLOT X,Y
50  NEXT I
```

In this program, "stars" are plotted in positions randomly selected by line 30, providing a new "star scene" each time the program is run.

Program 1.2: BOUNCING BALL

As a second example of a program based primarily on the HPLOT command, consider the following simulation of a bouncing ball:

```
1   REM PROGRAM 1.2 (BOUNCING BALL)
2   REM SIMULATES A BALL BOUNCING OFF FLOOR AND
    WALLS
10  DX = 4:X = 8:Y = 0:A = 2:V = 0
20  HOME : HGR
30  HCOLOR= 2: HPLOT 2,0 TO 2,133 TO 266,133
    TO 266,0
40  HCOLOR= 3: HPLOT X,Y: HPLOT X + 1,Y
50  IF Y = 132 THEN V = - V: IF V = 0 THEN V =
    - 20
60  IF X > 263 THEN DX = - DX
70  IF X < 6 THEN DX = - DX
80  V = V + A
90  HCOLOR= 0: HPLOT X,Y: HPLOT X + 1,Y
100 Y = Y + V:X = X + DX
110  GOTO 40
```

The "ball" is provided by line 40. In order to increase the visibility of the ball, two dots are plotted side-by-side. Line 30 provides "walls" and a "floor" for the ball to bounce against. As the ball moves, the horizontal movement is controlled by a constant velocity DX; the vertical movement is controlled by a variable velocity V, together with a constant acceleration A. The "movement" of the ball is simulated by plotting a dot in white (line 40), then erasing it by plotting the same dot in black (line 90). The position X,Y of the dot is changed (line 100) and the ball is plotted in the new position. "Bounces" off the walls and floor are controlled by lines 50 through 70. To maintain the action, line 50 accelerates the ball when its bounce is low (Y = 132 and V = 0). The ball will continue to bounce until interrupted by CTRL-C or RESET.

NOTE: In this chapter, the example programs use techniques which will be described in later parts of the book. Don't be concerned about programming details yet. Enjoy the graphics.

Program 1.3: SPACE SHIP

The program below draws a child's version of a space ship.

```
1    REM PROGRAM 1.3 (SPACE SHIP)
2    REM USES HPLOT TO DRAW ELEMENTARY SHAPES
10   HOME : HGR2 : HCOLOR= 3
20   HPLOT 120,170 TO 120,50 TO 140,20 TO 160,50
     TO 160,170
30   HPLOT 160,120 TO 180,170 TO 100,170 TO
     120,120
```

Programs of this sort are valuable for establishing a working understanding of the graphics screen. A rough line drawing on a page of graph paper will provide a model from which to write the program (see Figure 1.1).

We turn now to some "designer" programs.

Program 1.4: MOIRE

```
1    REM PROGRAM 1.4 (MOIRE)
2    REM DRAWS OVERLAPPING RANDOM PATTERNS
10   HGR2 :A = 5
20   X1 = RND (1) * 279:Y1 = RND (1) * 191
30   C = C + 1: IF C = 8 THEN C = 0
40   HCOLOR= C:Y = 191
```

(continued)

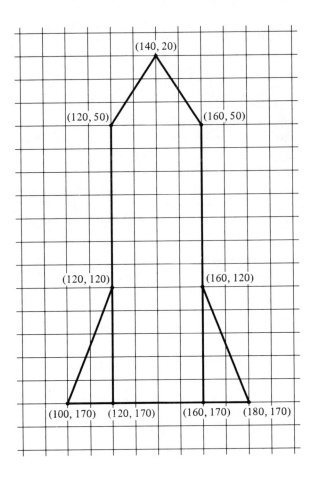

Figure 1.1

```
50   FOR  X  =  0  TO  279  STEP  A
60   HPLOT  X,191  TO  X1,Y1  TO  279  -  X,0
70   NEXT  X
80   FOR  Y  =  0  TO  191  STEP  A
90   HPLOT  279,191  -  Y  TO  X1,Y1  TO  0,Y
100   NEXT  Y
110   FOR  I  =  1  TO  500:  NEXT  I
120   IF  PEEK  (  -  16384)  =  155  THEN  POKE
      -  16368,0:  TEXT  :  HOME  :  END
130   GOTO  20
```

Press ESC to end the program

Color anomalies built into the Apple often result in pleasing effects, as illustrated in the MOIRE program. The effects seen here will be considered more carefully in the next chapter. For the present, enjoy the designs.

Line 20 determines a random "center" for the design. This program draws consecutive designs over one another, changing colors between designs (line 30,40). Line 110 provides a brief pause to allow time to view a pattern before drawing over it. Line 120 provides something new, an exit; pressing ESC will end the program. There will be more on this technique in Chapter 2.

Program 1.5: COLORED LINES

This program is briefer, and simpler in design.

```
1    REM  PROGRAM  1.5  (COLORED  LINES)
2    REM  RANDOMLY  DROPS  COLORED  LINES  ON  THE
     SCREEN
10   HGR2
20   X1  =  RND  (1)  *  279:Y1  =  RND  (1)  *  191
30   X2  =  RND  (1)  *  279:Y2  =  RND  (1)  *  191
40   C  =  C  +  1:  IF  C  =  8  THEN  C  =  0
50   HCOLOR=  C
60   HPLOT  X1,Y1  TO  X2,Y2
70   GOTO  20
```

Lines 20 and 30 select random end points for line segments drawn by line 60. Different colors are used in drawing consecutive line segments.

Program 1.6: CURVE

So far, our examples have used points and straight line segments. These are the components of all graphics images. We are able to draw curves and surfaces only by approximating them with straight line segments. The following example illustrates the technique:

```
1   REM PROGRAM 1.6 (CURVE)
2   REM STRAIGHT LINES - - > CURVE
10  HGR2 : HCOLOR= 3
20  FOR Y = 0 TO 191 STEP 4
30  HPLOT 0,Y TO 279 * Y / 191,191
40  NEXT Y
```

Clearly, only straight line segments are plotted (line 30). The image generated yields an approximation of a curve in the same manner as "string sculpture."

Program 1.7: CIRCLE

Circles can be generated through several techniques; some are considered in Chapter 5. The one used here is the fastest of those we will discuss. The significance of SC, CX, CY will be explained in Chapter 4.

```
1   REM PROGRAM 1.7 (CIRCLE)
2   REM CIRCLE GENERATOR
10  DT = .1:C = COS (DT):S = SIN (DT)
20  SC = 1.16:CX = 140:CY = 96
30  HGR2 : HCOLOR= 3
40  X = 0:Y = 80
50  HPLOT SC * X + CX,Y + CY
60  FOR I = 1 TO 63
70  T = X * C - Y * S:Y = Y * C + X * S:X = T
80  HPLOT TO SC * X + CX,Y + CY
90  NEXT I
```

Program 1.8: RING

An elaboration of the CIRCLE program yields a colorful spiral circular band. Again, tricks are used which will be explained later.

```
1   REM PROGRAM 1.8 (RING)
2   REM DRAWS A COLORFUL CIRCULAR BAND
10  DT = .1:C = COS (DT):S = SIN (DT)
20  SC = 1.16:CX = 140:CY = 96
30  HGR2 : HCOLOR= 3
40  X = 0:Y = 80
```

```
50   HPLOT SC * X + CX,Y + CY
60   FOR J = 1 TO 20
70   FOR I = 1 TO 63
80 T = X * C - Y * S:Y = Y * C + X * S:X = T
90   READ CL: POKE 28,CL: IF CL = 255 THEN
     RESTORE
100  HPLOT TO SC * X + CX,Y + CY
110  NEXT I
120  Y = Y - 2: NEXT J
130  DATA 42,85,127,128,170,213,255
```

Program 1.9: ARTIST'S AID

The last of our initial examples is also the most complex. This program will allow you to interact with the computer via the keyboard to generate designs.

A rotating cursor (a line segment) is used to color portions of the screen. The cursor is placed in one of three modes by pressing C, D, or E. In the C (cursor) mode, the cursor rotates and is barely visible. If you press D (draw), line segments are drawn in each position occupied by the cursor. In the E (erase) mode, black line segments are drawn in cursor positions, effectively erasing portions of the screen (since the background color is black).

The color used for the D (draw) mode is controlled by pressing keys 1, 2, 3, 4, 5, or 6. The colors obtained are those identified in the Applesoft Reference Manual, page 89.

The size of the cursor may be increased by pressing L (lengthen) and decreased by pressing S (shorten). To change the length quickly, press L or S and hold down REPT simultaneously.

Finally, the point around which the cursor rotates may be changed by pressing the keys I, J, K, or M. The effects are:

I   Move UP

J   Move LEFT

K   Move RIGHT

M Move DOWN

Holding down I, J, K, or M, together with the REPT key, allows rapid change of position.

The program makes use of a convenient tool called a shape table. In this example, a simple shape table is identified in lines 10 through 40. The shape is the rotating cursor. The size, rotation, color, and location of the shape then are changed by the program. Shape tables are discussed in the Applesoft Reference Manual (Chapter 9). We consider them in Appendix 2.

```
1   REM PROGRAM 1.9 (ARTIST'S AID)
2   REM PROVIDES PAINTBRUSH UNDER KEYBOARD
    CONTROL
10  POKE 768,1: POKE 770,4
20  POKE 771,0: POKE 772,4
30  POKE 773,0
40  POKE 232,0: POKE 233,3
50  HGR : POKE - 16302,0:C = 3:S = 25:
    X = 140:Y = 96
60  FOR I = 1 TO 64
70  A = PEEK ( - 16384): POKE - 16368,0
80  IF A = 155 THEN TEXT : HOME : END
90  IF A = 177 THEN C = 1
100 IF A = 178 THEN C = 2
110 IF A = 179 THEN C = 3
120 IF A = 180 THEN C = 4
130 IF A = 181 THEN C = 5
140 IF A = 182 THEN C = 6
150 IF A = 202 THEN X = X - 1: IF X < 0
    THEN X = 279
160 IF A = 203 THEN X = X + 1: IF X > 279
    THEN X = 0
170 IF A = 201 THEN Y = Y - 1: IF Y < 0
    THEN Y = 191
180 IF A = 205 THEN Y = Y + 1: IF Y > 191
    THEN Y = 0
190 IF A = 211 THEN S = S - 1: IF S < 1
    THEN S = 1
200 IF A = 204 THEN S = S + 1
210 IF A = 195 THEN F = 0
220 IF A = 196 THEN F = 1
230 IF A = 197 THEN F = 2
240 IF A = 200 THEN HGR2
250 HCOLOR= C: ROT= I: SCALE= S
260 IF F = 0 THEN HCOLOR= 3: XDRAW 1 AT X,Y:
    XDRAW 1 AT X,Y: GOTO 300
270 DRAW 1 AT X,Y
280 IF F = 1 THEN 300
290 HCOLOR= 4: DRAW 1 AT X,Y
300 NEXT I
310 GOTO 60
```

Be careful when typing this program. Some typing errors will result in ?SYNTAX ERROR, but others simply will cause the program to behave strangely.

When you have finished typing the program, type RUN and press RETURN. The screen will turn black and a flickering, rotating wand will appear near the center of the screen.

To control your cybernetic paintbrush:

- Press D to indicate that you want to draw.

- Press K and the REPT key simultaneously for about two seconds (this will paint a broad stroke to the right).

- Press key 5 to change color.

- Paint a sweeping stroke downward by pressing M and REPT together.

- Press C to cease drawing. The cursor will be visible, but will not paint its trail as it rotates.

- Press I and REPT together to move to the left.

- Press S and REPT simultaneously to shorten the cursor.

- Now press D to resume drawing.

Let your imagination and creative abilities take over. When you want to quit this program, press ESC. The program will return to the text page and will END.

If you want to return to the graphics page to admire your creation, *don't* type HGR. This will return to the high resolution graphics page, but will erase it immediately. Instead, type:

```
POKE -16297,0: POKE -16302,0: POKE -16304,0:
POKE -16300,0
```

If the image is one you want to save for display at a later time, it may be saved on a disk. First, decide on a NAME for the picture, then type:

```
BSAVE NAME, A$2000, L$2000
```

Then, any time you want to show this picture, type:

```
HGR: POKE -16302,0: PRINT CHR$(4); "BLOAD NAME,
A$2000"
```

SUMMARY

The intention of this chapter has been to provide short examples of programs that generate graphics images. While the programs are not very sophisticated, several make use of methods which may not be immediately clear. These techniques are explained in the chapters that follow. As you progress through the book, these programs should become transparent. You soon should be able to improve on them.

1. Several programs given in this chapter use the RND command. You might reasonably expect this command to yield random numbers when used. Actually, the numbers provided start through the same sequence every time the computer is turned on. As a result, the "random" designs generated by several of the programs really are predictable. To randomize the starting point in the sequence of random numbers, insert the following routine in Programs 1.1, 1.4, and 1.5.

```
3 TEXT: HOME
4 PRINT "WHEN READY, PRESS ANY KEY TO START"
5 IF PEEK (-16384)>127 THEN POKE -16368,0:
  GOTO 10
6 X=RND (1)
7 GO TO 5
```

Program lines 5 through 7 will continue to take numbers from the sequence of random numbers used by the computer until a key is pressed. Since the timing of the keypress is unpredictable, the numbers obtained by later use of RND will not predictable. The use of PEEK (−16384) and POKE −16368,0 are discussed in Chapter 2.

2. Graphics displays may be enlivened by sounds. Since the Apple has a speaker, why not use it? The bouncing ball of Program 1.2 will have an audible bounce if line 50 is modified in this way:

```
50 IF Y=132 THEN S=PEEK (-16336)+ PEEK (-16336):
   V=- V: IF V=0 THEN V= - 20
```

3. To gain familiarity with the graphics screen, draw some simple shapes like the space ship in Program 1.3, such as your initials or name, scenery (mountains, trees), houses, city skyline, and so forth. First, draw the image on graph paper, then translate the points and lines to a program to draw the image on the graphics screen.

4. Try some variations on Program 1.4. Line 10 defines A to be 5. This controls the density of the lines that generate the random images. Rewrite line 10 to define A = 3, 4, 6, or 7.

5. If you are tiring of typing the programs, note that a disk is available which contains all the programs given in this book. See the order card in the back of this book.

Part II

The Computer

Chapter 2

Graphics Characteristics of the Apple II

MEMORY ALLOCATION AND USAGE

Graphics output of the Apple II is really a display of the contents of a section of the computer's memory. Because of this characteristic, we begin our consideration of Apple II graphics with a study of the allocation and usage of memory. While the user may make some changes in the way memory is used by the computer, standard usage is shown by the memory map in Figure 2.1. Memory addresses are given in both hexadecimal (with "$" prefix) and decimal.

> **NOTE:** Throughout this chapter, brief examples are given that illustrate the principles under discussion. It is best to have an Apple II at hand to try the examples as you read.

An Apple II with 48K RAM has an additional 16K ROM, giving a total of 64K units of memory. While K is sometimes read as 1000, in computer work it represents 1024. Thus 48K means 48(1024) = 49152, and 64K represents 64(1024) = 65536. This may seem like a strange number of memory units to have available, but that is because we are more accustomed to decimal than to binary numbers. Remember, the computer is a binary machine, and 65536 in binary is 1000000000000000, which is not such an inconvenient number (except for its size).

Each unit of memory (a byte) holds eight bits of information. The information in a bit may be either a 0 or a 1. The location of a byte in memory is called its address. An address and its contents may be identified in decimal, binary, or hexadecimal (hex) notation. For example, if

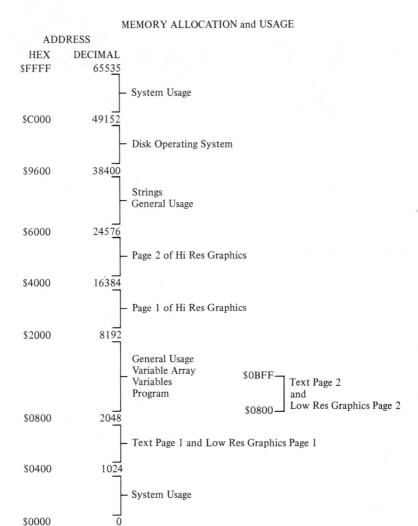

Figure 2.1

memory location 5005 contains the number 65, there are three ways to picture this unit of memory:

0001001110001101	01000001	5005	65	138D	41
in binary notation		in decimal notation		in hex notation	

In general, we will refer to addresses in either decimal or hexadecimal notation. While binary is used internally by the computer, it is too bulky for us to use consistently.

The 65536 memory locations are numbered consecutively from 0 through 65535 in decimal. In hex, the numbering is $0 through $FFFF. When discussing a memory location such as $1B82 (7042), frequently we will refer to $1B (27) as being the "high order byte" and $82 (130) as being the "low order byte" (7042 = 27 × 256 + 130).

NOTE 1: While there is little likelihood that the number 1B might be misread as a decimal number, a number like 82 might be intended as a decimal or as a hex number. It is necessary to have a means of distinguishing hex and decimal numbers. Since decimal notation is solidly entrenched in our language, we will not tamper with it, but will specially designate the hex notation. There are three common ways of doing this: $1B_{16}$, 1BH, or $1B. We're using the third form, since it is the one used in the Apple manuals.

NOTE 2: A more complete discussion of decimal and hexadecimal notation is included in Appendix 1.

Memory locations $400 (1024) through $7FF (2047) are used for two purposes: text display, and low resolution graphics. When it is in the TEXT mode, the computer interprets the contents of these memory locations as text and displays 24 lines, each having 40 character positions. When it is in the GR mode, the computer interprets the contents of memory locations $400 through $7FF as graphics-plus-text and displays four lines of text at the bottom of the screen and a 40 × 40 graphics matrix at the top.

Memory locations $800 (2048) through $BFF (3071) also may be used for text or graphics display, but Applesoft programs usually reside in this area. Techniques for using memory locations $800 through $BFF as a second text or graphics page will be given later, under Page 2 of Text.

Memory locations $2000 (8192) through $3FFF (16383) usually are used for high resolution graphics, page 1. When it is in the HGR mode, the computer will display a 280 × 160 graphics matrix and four lines of text at the bottom of the screen. The four lines of text are the last four lines of Text Page 1 ($400–$7FF).

A second page of high resolution graphics is available in memory locations $4000 (16384) through $5FFF (24575). When it is in the HGR2 mode, the computer interprets this area of memory as a 280 × 192 graphics matrix, with no text display.

It is possible to display high resolution graphics page 2 with text at the bottom of the screen. The text will be drawn from the last four lines of text page 2 ($800–$BFF). It also is possible to display high resolution graphics page 1 with no text at the bottom of the screen. In this case, the graphics display provides a 280 × 192 matrix. Similarly, low resolution graphics pages 1 and 2 each may be displayed with or without text. Techniques for effecting these modes are described below under Soft Switches.

MEMORY ADDRESSING FOR DISPLAY PURPOSES

Memory locations $400 through $7FF are used for text display and for low resolution graphics page 1, but the addressing structure is not as might be expected. Figure 2.2 illustrates the pattern of addressing this area of memory for use as a text page.

The label shown in Figure 2.2 may be printed by the commands

```
10 TEXT: HOME: VTAB 6: PRINT TAB (18); "TEXT"
20 PRINT TAB(15); "ADDRESSING"
```

or by the commands

```
10 TEXT:HOME
20 FOR ADDR=1681 TO 1684
30 READ X: POKE ADDR,X
40 NEXT ADDR
50 FOR ADDR=1806 TO 1815
60 READ X: POKE ADDR,X
70 NEXT ADDR
80 DATA 212, 197, 216, 212
90 DATA 193, 196, 196, 210, 197, 211, 211, 201,
   206, 199
```

Figure 2.3 shows the addressing pattern when memory locations 1024 through 2047 are used as a low resolution graphics page. Figure 2.4 shows the addressing of high resolution graphics page 1. High resolution graphics page 2 has a similar structure.

To obtain the memory address corresponding to a particular text screen location, add the row and column address codes. (Note that the column address is 1 less than the column number.) For example, to locate the address of the block containing the letter "X"; add the row address, 1664, and the column address, 19, to obtain 1683. The "R", with row address 1792 and column address 17, has memory address 1792 + 17 = 1809.

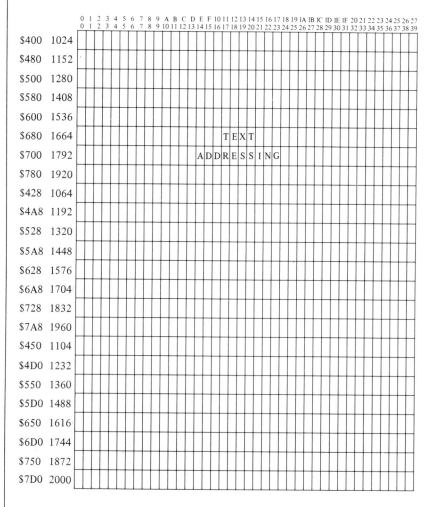

Figure 2.2. Addressing the TEXT Screen

To obtain the address of a particular screen location, add the corresponding row and column address codes. For example, to locate the address of the shaded block; add the row address code, 1664, and the column address code, 25, to obtain 1689. Address 1689 controls two blocks. The color of the upper block is determined by the contents of the lower nybble of address 1689; the lower block is controlled by the contents of the upper nybble. (A nybble is four bits, or half a byte.)

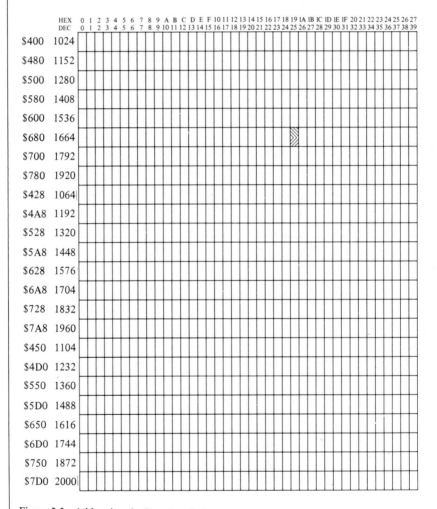

Figure 2.3. Addressing the Low Resolution Graphics Screen

Each block shown contains 8 bytes. The sum of the row address code and the column address code gives the address of the uppermost byte in a block. The addresses of the subsequent 7 bytes can be obtained by successive addition of 1024.

The addresses of the eight bytes in the shaded block are

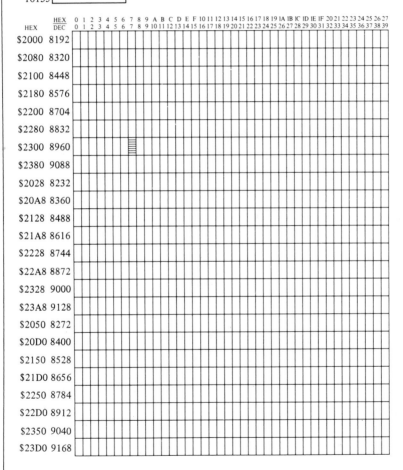

Figure 2.4. Addressing the High Resolution Graphics Screen

TEXT

Using the BASIC language command POKE, we may illustrate the screen addressing structures. A POKE stores a number in a specified memory location. For example, POKE 1390,25 stores the number 25 in memory location 1390. If the computer is using the TEXT mode for display purposes, the visible effect of this POKE would be to place an inverse (black on white) letter Y in position 31 of line 19. The inverse Y appears because the code for inverse Y is a decimal 25 (See ASCII Screen Character Set in the Apple II Reference Manual, page 15). The location of the inverse Y on the screen is determined by the addressing structure of the text screen (see Figure 2.2). To place a flashing Y (ASCII character code 89) directly above the inverse Y, we would POKE 1262,89. To place a normal (white on black) Y below the inverse Y, POKE 1518,217.

NOTE: If the above commands are executed consecutively, the scrolling of the screen may change the effective locations. To observe the effect described above, type:

```
TEXT: HOME: POKE 1390,25:POKE 1262,89:
POKE 1518,217 (RETURN)
```

GR

If the computer is in the GR mode, the interpretation of memory contents is handled quite differently. The display consists of a 40 × 40 graphics matrix with four lines of text at the bottom of the screen. The contents of one memory location controls the color of two graphics blocks, one stacked above the other. The color of the upper block is determined by the number in the lower nybble of the memory location; the color of the lower block is determined by the number in the upper nybble. Here are some examples to show how it works:

Since decimal 25 is equivalent to $19, POKE 1390,25 will place a magenta (color code 1) block under an orange (color code 9) block. Location 1390 controls screen blocks (30,36) and (30,37), so block (30,36) will be orange and block (30,37) will be magenta.

For a second example, note that decimal 89 is equivalent to $59 and memory location 1262 controls the contents of low resolution blocks (30,34) and (30,35). Thus, POKE 1262,89 will color block (30,34) orange and block (30,35) gray. Similarly, POKE 1518,217 will color block (30,38) orange and block (30,39) yellow.

HGR

If the computer is in the HGR or HGR2 mode, the image shown on the screen is almost a bit-by-bit display of the contents of part of the computer's memory. We may use the addressing pattern shown in Figure 2.4 and the POKE command to illustrate this graphics display.

When in the HGR mode, the top left screen position is controlled by memory location $2000 (8192). In fact, the first seven bits of memory location 8192 are displayed as the first seven dots on the topmost line of the HGR display screen. Bit 1 controls the leftmost dot, bit 2 controls the second dot, and so forth. Bit 8 is not displayed, but is used to control color (for details, see Apple Reference Manual, page 19).

As an example, assume location 8192 contains the number 18 (to assure this, POKE 8192, 18). The binary representation of 18 is 00010010. Since the graphics display shows the bits in reverse order, dots 2 and 5 should be ON and the others should be OFF.

Figure 2.5

The following program will illustrate a means of controlling the bit pattern display.

Program 2.1: BIT PATTERN

```
1    REM PROGRAM 2.1 (BIT PATTERN)
2    REM PLACES THE LETTER A ON THE HI RES SCREEN
10   DATA 8,20,34,34,62,34,34
20   HOME : HGR : VTAB 21
30   FOR I = 8192 TO 14366 STEP 1024
40   READ X
50   POKE I,X
60   INPUT K$
70   NEXT I
80   END
```

Each time you press RETURN an additional byte of the letter will be added.

The FOR loop beginning in line 30 references memory locations 8192, 9216, 10240, 11264, 12288, 13312, and 14366. The contents of these memory locations are displayed below one another at the top left corner of the screen. As a result of the loop in lines 30 through 70, the contents of these memory locations will be as follows:

Memory Location	Bit Pattern (reversed)		Display
	Decimal	Binary	
8192	8	0001000	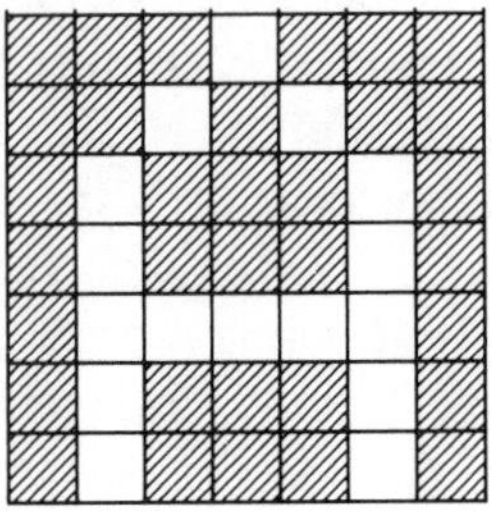
9216	20	0010100	
10240	34	0100010	
11264	34	0100010	
12288	62	0111110	
13312	34	0100010	
14336	34	0100010	

Figure 2.6

As the contents of these memory locations are displayed on the screen, they create the image of the letter "A."

The discussion above suggests a means by which text may be displayed on the graphics screen easily. More detail will be given in Chapter 3. For the present, we will identify procedures that define additional characters.

Map the character or symbol on a grid; 7 × 7 works well. For example, to obtain the letter "Z," convert each of the bit patterns to a number code, as has been done in Figure 2.7. Then POKE the bit pattern into memory. Memory locations may be identified from Figure 2.4.

To continue the example, we may display the symbols "A" and "Z" side-by-side in the top left corner of the screen using Program 2.2.

Program 2.2: BIT PATTERN CHARACTERS

```
1   REM PROGRAM 2.2 (BIT PATTERN CHARACTERS)
2   REM PLACES LETTERS A AND Z ON THE HI RES
    SCREEN
```

| | Bit Pattern (reversed) | |
| Display | Binary | Decimal |

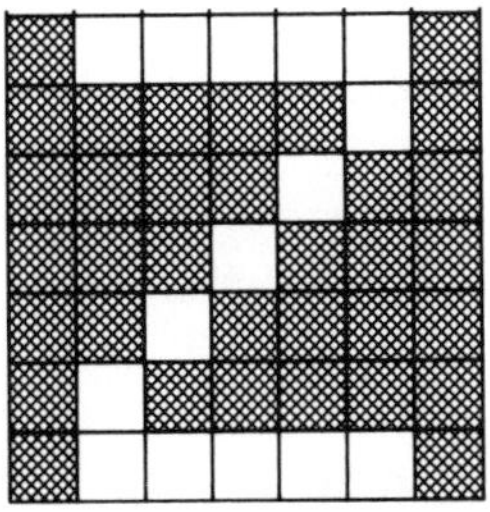

Binary	Decimal
0111110	62
0100000	32
0010000	16
0001000	8
0000100	4
0000010	2
0111110	62

Figure 2.7

```
10    HOME  :  HGR  :  VTAB 21
20    DATA  8,20,34,34,62,34,34            ⎫
30    FOR  I  =  8192  TO  14366  STEP  1024  ⎬  Letter  A
40    READ  X                             ⎭
50    POKE  I,X
60    NEXT  I
70    DATA  62,32,16,8,4,2,62             ⎫
80    FOR  I  =  8193  TO  14367  STEP  1024  ⎬  Letter  Z
90    READ  X                             ⎭
100    POKE  I,X
110    NEXT  I
120    END
```

NOTES AND SUGGESTIONS

Write a program that displays a short word, or your initials, on the graphics screen. First map the characters on graph paper.

COLORS

It is not our intention to dwell on the characteristics of color graphics display on the high resolution screen, but it is necessary to be aware of one significant restriction. Not every block can be plotted in every color. To illustrate, run Program 2.3.

Program 2.3: COLOR PROBLEM 1

```
1    REM PROGRAM 2.3 (COLOR PROBLEM)
2    REM PLOTTED LINES ARE NOT VISIBLE
10   HOME : HGR : VTAB 21
20   HCOLOR= 2
30   FOR I = 2 TO 5
40   HPLOT 7 * I,10 TO 7 * I,30
50   NEXT I
60   END
```

Note that while four vertical lines are requested by the program, only two are visible on the display screen. This is because color 2 (blue) may be drawn only in even numbered columns. Similar restrictions are placed on the other colors (except black and white). Colors 1 and 5 may be drawn in odd numbered columns; colors 2 and 6 may be drawn in even numbered columns. Only black and white are available in all columns.

To guard against drawing vertical colored lines in positions where they are not visible, double-drawing may be used: If a program generates coordinates (X,Y1), (X,Y2) to be used in a command

```
HPLOT X,Y1 TO X,Y2
```

add the command

```
HPLOT X+1,Y1 TO X+1, Y2
```

Program 2.4: PROBLEM WITH MIXED COLORS

Another color problem is illustrated in Program 2.4. Try it.

```
1    REM PROGRAM 2.4 (PROBLEM WITH MIXED COLORS)
2    REM PLOTTING OVER BACKGROUND COLOR
10   HOME : VTAB 21: HGR : HCOLOR= 2
20   HPLOT 0,0
30   CALL 62454
40   HCOLOR= 5
50   HPLOT 1,1 TO 100,100
60   END
```

Set screen color to blue (HCOLOR=2)

The colors available on the Apple are coded as follows:

0—BLACK 1	4—BLACK 2
1—GREEN(variable)	5—variable
2—BLUE(variable)	6—variable
3—WHITE 1	7—WHITE 2

Colors 1, 2, 5, and 6 are variable, depending on the adjustment of the color controls on the display monitor.

When mixing colors on a screen image, it is safest to select from colors 0, 1, 2, and 3, or from colors 4, 5, 6, and 7. In Program 2.4, we selected the color blue (line 10), which we then used as the background color (lines 20, 30). When color 5 is used to draw a diagonal line (line 50), the mix of colors results in an image which is either distracting or pleasing, depending on the effect you are seeking.

RESOLUTION

The term "resolution," when applied to the graphics screen, refers to the number of blocks in the grid used for graphing. The HPLOT X,Y command accepts integer values of X between 0 and 279, and integer values of Y between 0 and 191. For this reason, the high resolution graphics screens are said to have a resolution of 280 × 192, providing 53760 blocks, or pixels, in the graphics grid.

There is reason to contest this statement of resolution. Most Apple graphics programmers discover at an early stage that not every block can be plotted in every color. This is noticed in the execution of commands such as

```
HGR: HCOLOR=1: HPLOT 20,10 to 20,100
```

The intended vertical line does not appear on the screen. In fact, the resolution available for color plotting is not 280 × 192, but rather 140 × 192.

Many black and white lines also have an effective 140 × 192 resolution. To illustrate, try the commands

```
HGR: HCOLOR=3: HPLOT 10,10 to 100,100
```

While we might hope that the resulting line would be "thin" (one dot thick), this is not the case. Without clearing the screen, try

```
HCOLOR=0: HPLOT 9,10 TO 99,100
```

Clearly, the earlier line was "wider" than necessary.

On the other hand, much better resolution may be attained for black and white images.

Program 2.5: HIGHER RESOLUTION

To show that greater resolution may be achieved, try Program 2.5.

```
1   REM PROGRAM 2.5 (HIGHER RESOLUTION)
2   REM DISPLAYS 14 DOTS PER BYTE
10  HOME : HGR
20  FOR I = 1 TO 14
30  READ X
40  POKE 14800,X
50  VTAB 22: PRINT I
60  FOR J = 1 TO 500: NEXT J
70  NEXT I
80  DATA 1,129,2,130,4,132,8,136,16,144,32,160,
    64,192
```

Note DATA is paired, with difference of 128. Bit patterns differ only in high bit

Watch carefully when the program is run. You should be able to distinguish a sequence of 14 dots displayed as a result of changing the contents of a single byte. Since the graphics screen is 40 bytes wide, we have an implied resolution of 560 × 192.

The point of the foregoing discussion is that the Apple II high resolution mode is not always as good as 280 × 192, nor need it be as poor as 280 × 192 (for black and white plotting). The attainment of higher resolution clearly requires additional programming effort. That effort is not a focus of this book. The interested reader should consult the references given at the end of this chapter.

WHAT IS A LINE?

Dictionary definitions are not always applicable to the situations we face in daily life. Such is the case when we consider the interpretation of "line" as an image on a graphics screen. Theoretically, a line has a width, or thickness, of measure zero. In the graphical representation of a line, pixels are either ON or OFF. Since the dimensions of a pixel are not zero, the representation of a line has nonzero thickness. Further, pixels are neatly arranged in rows and columns. When diagonal lines are drawn, the results may be distinctly nonlinear.

As an illustration, consider the line of Figure 2.8. If we turn ON each pixel the line passes through, the image of the line will have a distinct stair-step appearance.

The Applesoft command HPLOT X1,Y1 TO X2,Y2 will result in a stair-step "line," similar to the one shown in Figure 2.8.

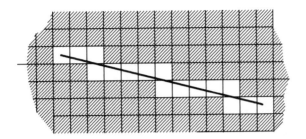

Figure 2.8

The way in which a line is defined also will affect its image. When drawing a line, Applesoft must determine which pixels should be turned ON. As a result of the calculations used, the direction in which a line is defined becomes important. Try the following:

```
HGR: HCOLOR=3:HPLOT 10,10 TO 100,90
```

A diagonal line is drawn. Now, without clearing the screen, try:

```
HPLOT 100,90 TO 10,10
```

Watch carefully. Although the same line is requested the image is slightly different. This is due to the reversed orientation. To see this in a different way, try the following:

```
HGR: HCOLOR=3: HPLOT 10,10 TO 100,90
HCOLOR=0: HPLOT 100,90 TO 10,10
```

While the second drawing of the line, in black, should have erased the white line, some traces remain.

The differences caused by line orientation usually are not important. However, on occasion, attention to such detail may be important in obtaining satisfactory images.

HCOLOR SETTINGS

Before using any plotting commands it is necessary to specify the area of memory to be used for plotting (HGR or HGR2), and the color to be used for plotting (HCOLOR = C, where C = 0, 1, 2, 3, 4, 5, 6, or 7). Once HCOLOR is specified, it remains set, through HPLOTs and

HPLOT TOs, until the next HCOLOR = statement. However, whenever HCOLOR is specified it must be followed by the HPLOT command, *not* HPLOT TO. The reason is this: When the statement HPLOT TO X,Y is executed, the color most recently used for plotting is retained. On the other hand, HPLOT X,Y always uses the color specified by the most recent HCOLOR = statement.

It would be convenient to be able to change colors in the midst of several HPLOT TO X,Y statements without inserting an HPLOT X,Y to reset HCOLOR. By circumventing the standard Applesoft procedures, we can accomplish this.

Memory location 228 ($E4) contains the color code of the most recently specified HCOLOR, while memory location 28 ($1C) contains the color code of the most recently plotted HCOLOR. If we change the contents of memory location 28 (with a POKE statement), we can fool Applesoft into changing colors.

Program 2.6: HCOLOR SETTINGS

To illustrate, try the following:

```
1   REM PROGRAM 2.6 (HCOLOR SETTINGS)
2   REM CONVENTIONAL COLOR CONTROL
10   HOME : VTAB 21: HGR : HCOLOR= 2
20   HPLOT 20,20 TO 50,75
30   HCOLOR= 3
40   HPLOT TO 100,10
50   HPLOT 10,100 TO 200,150
60   END
```

Note that specifying a new color in line 30 has no effect until line 50, when an HPLOT statement recognizes the new color. For comparison, try the following program.

Program 2.7: IMPROVED HCOLOR CONTROL

```
1   REM PROGRAM 2.7 (IMPROVED HCOLOR CONTROL)
2   REM SETTING HCOLOR WITH POKES
10   HOME : VTAB 21: HGR : HCOLOR= 2
20   HPLOT 20,20 TO 50,75
30   POKE 28,127: REM COLOR CODE OF HCOLOR=3
40   HPLOT TO 100,10
50   HPLOT 10,100 TO 200,150
```

Note that the change of color in line 30 had effect in line 40 (when Applesoft thought the most recently plotted HCOLOR was 3), but that line 50 changes the color back to the color specified in the most recent HCOLOR = statement.

To use this procedure it is necessary to have the color codes of the HCOLORs available for plotting:

HCOLOR	Color Code	Color
0	0	Black
1	42	Green
2	85	Blue
3	127	White1
4	128	Black2
5	170	variable
6	213	variable
7	255	White2

The technique described here was used in the Program 1.8 in Chapter 1 to change the plotting color through a sequence of values.

SOFT SWITCHES

When the command HGR is used in a program, it has several effects. Among them are:

1. Display high resolution graphics page 1;

2. Clear high resolution graphics page 1 to black;

3. Identify high resolution graphics page 1 as the area to be used for subsequent plotting.

There are times when one would want to display the contents of a graphics page without erasing it, or flip between two graphics pages. Special effects, especially animation, may be provided by displaying page 1 while drawing on page 2, then flipping to display page 2 while drawing on page 1, and so forth. These types of demands cannot be met with the HGR, HGR2 commands.

Control over display modes is available through the use of "soft switches," eight memory locations accessed through software. It is useful to think of these as four switches:

1. A text-graphics switch;

2. A full screen-mixed screen switch;

3. A page 1-page 2 switch;

4. A high resolution-low resolution switch.

Each switch controls only the specified mode of display. BASIC commands control several switches at a time. For example, HGR will set switch 1 to graphics, switch 2 to mixed screen, switch 3 to page 1, and switch 4 to high resolution. The command GR is different in that it sets switch 4 to low resolution. (Note: Each of these commands performs duties in addition to setting the switches.)

Independent control of each of the four switches is available through the use of the POKE command, as suggested in Table 2.1.

Table 2.1

Switch	Effect	BASIC Command
1	GRAPHICS mode	POKE −16304,0
	TEXT mode	POKE −16303,0
2	FULL SCREEN text or graphics	POKE −16302,0
	MIXED graphics and text	POKE −16301,0
3	PAGE 1	POKE −16300,0
	PAGE 2	POKE −16299,0
4	LOW RESOLUTION	POKE −16298,0
	HIGH RESOLUTION	POKE −16297,0

Each switch may be pushed (POKEd) to either of its two possible positions. It remains there until pushed (POKEd) to the other position.

Since the four switches may be controlled independently, it would seem that 16 possible display modes are available. This is not the case, however. When switch 1 is in the text position (POKE −16303,0), changes in switches 2 or 4 have no visible effect.

There are, in fact, ten observably different display modes, as Table 2.2 shows.

Table 2.2

Mode	Basic Commands
TEXT, page 1	POKE −16303,0: POKE −16300,0
TEXT, page 2	POKE −16303,0: POKE −16299,0
Low resolution graphics, page 1, full screen	POKE −16298,0: POKE −16304,0 POKE −16300,0: POKE −16302,0
Low resolution graphics, page 1, mixed screen	POKE −16298,0: POKE −16304,0 POKE −16300,0: POKE −16301,0
Low resolution graphics, page 2, full screen	POKE −16298,0: POKE −16304,0 POKE −16299,0: POKE −16302,0
Low resolution graphics page 2, mixed screen	POKE −16298,0: POKE −16304,0 POKE −16299,0: POKE −16301,0
High resolution graphics, page 1, full screen	POKE −16297,0: POKE −16304,0 POKE −16300,0: POKE −16302,0
High resolution graphics, page 1, mixed screen	POKE −16297,0: POKE −16304,0 POKE −16300,0: POKE −16301,0
High resolution graphics, page 2, full screen	POKE −16297,0: POKE −16304,0 POKE −16299,0: POKE −16302,0
High resolution graphics, page 2, mixed screen	POKE −16297,0: POKE −16304,0 POKE −16299,0: POKE −16301,0

Changing from one display mode to another requires changing only the switches that must be affected. For example, to change from full screen high resolution graphics page 1 to full screen high resolution graphics page 2, only switch 3 need be changed (POKE −16299,0). To change from full screen high resolution graphics page 1 to mixed screen high resolution graphics page 1, only switch 2 need be changed (POKE −16301,0).

Program 2.8: FLASHING X AND SQUARE

Program 2.8 illustrates one type of effect available through the use of the soft switches.

```
1 REM PROGRAM 2.8 (FLASHING X AND SQUARE)
2 REM ILLUSTRATES USE OF SOFT SWITCHES
10 HGR : HCOLOR= 3
20 HPLOT 90,40 TO 190,40 TO 190,160 TO 90,160 TO
   90,40
30 HGR2
```

(continued)

```
40  HPLOT  90,40  TO  190,160:  HPLOT  190,40
    TO  90,160
50  FOR  I  =  1  TO  100
60  FOR  J  =  1  TO  50:  NEXT  J          Set display
70  A  =  1  -  A                              switch
80  POKE  -16299  -  A,0
90  NEXT  I
```

The process described above allows for the display of images on either of the two graphics pages, but does not permit easy modification of the images. A more pleasing effect may be provided by modifying the images on the graphics pages while the display is showing text, or another graphics page. The soft switches allow control over the display mode, but have no effect on the graphics page used for drawing.

Memory location $E6 (230) is used to identify the graphics page to be used for drawing. If page 1 is to be used, the location will contain $20 (32); if page 2 is to be used, the location will contain $40 (64). Since the contents of $E6 (230) may be controlled independently of the display mode, it is possible to prepare one page for display while displaying the other page.

Program 2.9: ANIMATED SQUARES

Program 2.9 illustrates the process of preparing a graphics page for display while displaying another.

```
1    REM  PROGRAM  2.9  (ANIMATED  SQUARES)
2    REM  ILLUSTRATES  ANIMATION  TECHNIQUES
10   HGR  :  HGR2
20   A  =  1:B  =  -1:C  =  2:D  =  1
30   FOR  I  =  1  TO  20              Set drawing
40   FOR  J  =  1  TO  2                  page
50   POKE  230,32  *  J
60   A  =  A  +  B
70   HCOLOR=  0
80   HPLOT  140  -  A,96  -  A  TO  140  +  A,96  -  A
     TO  140  +  A,96  +  A  TO  140  -  A,96  +  A
     TO  140  -  A,96  -  A
90   A  =  A  +  C
100   HCOLOR=  3
110   HPLOT  140  -  A,96  -  A  TO  140  +  A,96  -  A
     TO  140  +  A,96  +  A  TO  140  -  A,96  +  A
     TO  140  -  A,96  -  A
```

```
120   POKE - 16299 - D,0
130   D = 1 - D
140   NEXT J,I
160   B = -B:C = -C
170   GOTO 30
```

Set display switch

Program 2.9 should result in the display of a growing, then shrinking, square. The alternation of growing and shrinking phases will continue until interrupted by CTRL-C or RESET.

Within the program, line 50 identifies the graphics page on which drawing is to take place. Note that drawing always takes place on the page not being displayed. Lines 60 through 80 erase the square previously drawn on the graphics page (by drawing it in black, the background color). Lines 90 through 110 draw a new square in a larger or smaller size. Line 120 then flips the display switch to show the newly drawn square. The program then continues, erasing and drawing on the undisplayed graphics page.

MEMORY MOVE

There are a number of reasons for moving data from one area of memory to another. Our main interest is with graphics. Since Apple II graphics display is really a display of memory contents, moving memory (in the sense of moving the contents of memory) has the effect of moving the data that represents a graphic image.

> **NOTE:**   The phrase "moving memory" is a conventional, but not an accurate, description of the effect we are pursuing. We will actually be COPYing data from one area of memory to another.

One method of moving data from one area of memory to another is to use the BASIC commands PEEK and POKE. PEEK reads the contents of a specified memory location, while POKE stores a value in a memory location. Thus the command

```
POKE 9, PEEK (8)
```

reads the contents of location 8 (PEEK (8)) and stores it in location 9. The contents of location 8 are not affected.

Using PEEKs and POKEs, the contents of any section of memory may be copied to any other area. For example, the following will copy

the contents of high resolution graphics page 2 to high resolution graphics page 1.

```
110 FOR I = 8192 TO 16383
120 POKE I, PEEK(8192 + I)
130 NEXT I
 .
 .
 .
```

The only criticism of the above procedure is that it is much too slow.
Fortunately, a machine level program to do the same thing is available
to the user. A BASIC program may access the machine level MOVE
program by first providing the following initialization:

```
POKE 768,160: POKE 769,0
POKE 770,76: POKE 771,44
POKE 772,254
```

Then, each time the contents of an area of memory are to be copied to a
new area, it is necessary to identify:

1. The beginning address of the SOURCE (section to be copied);

2. The ending address of the SOURCE;

3. The beginning address of the DESTINATION (section to receive the
    data).

Then CALL 768 will implement the MOVE program.

Each of the three addresses to be identified must be given in two
stages. The high and low bytes of the addresses must be stored for access
by the MOVE program as follows:

Location	Contents
60	Low byte of beginning SOURCE address
61	High byte of beginning SOURCE address
62	Low byte of end of SOURCE address
63	High byte of end of SOURCE address
66	Low byte of beginning DESTINATION address
67	High byte of beginning DESTINATION address

For example, the following program will initialize the MOVE program, copy the contents of high resolution graphics page 2 onto high
resolution graphics page 1, then copy the contents of memory locations
$6000 through $7FFF onto high resolution graphics page 2.

Program 2.10: MEMORY MOVE SUBROUTINE

```
1    REM PROGRAM 2.10 (MEMORY MOVE SUBROUTINE)
2    REM NOT A DISPLAY PROGRAM
10   REM INITIALIZE
20   POKE 768,160: POKE 769,0
30   POKE 770,76: POKE 771,44
40   POKE 772,254
50   REM PAGE 2 TO PAGE 1
60   POKE 60,0: POKE 61,64
70   POKE 62,255: POKE 63,95
80   POKE 66,0: POKE 67,32
90   CALL 768
100   REM PAGE 3 TO PAGE 2
110   POKE 60,0: POKE 61,96
120   POKE 62,255: POKE 63,127
130   POKE 66,0: POKE 67,64
140   CALL 768
```

The PEEK and POKE method of copying data may be a simpler routine to put into a BASIC program, but the initialization and calling of the machine level MOVE program is much faster in execution.

The use of the MOVE program requires one caution: if the beginning of the destination lies within the source, part of the source will be written over before it has been copied. This effect usually would be one to avoid. However if it is intended to duplicate a pattern repeatedly, we might over-write the source intentionally. Program 2.11 asks for a name, prints it at the top of a clear screen, then copies it over the rest of the page.

Program 2.11: NAME COPIER

```
1    REM PROGRAM 2.11 (NAME COPIER)
2    REM USES MEMORY MOVE TO DUPLICATE A STRING
10   POKE 768,160: POKE 769,0
20   POKE 770,76: POKE 771,44
30   POKE 772,254
40   TEXT : HOME
50   INPUT "YOUR NAME, PLEASE";A$
60   HOME : PRINT A$
70   L = LEN (A$) + 1
80   POKE 60,0: POKE 61,4
90   POKE 62,255 - L: POKE 63,7
100   POKE 66,L: POKE 67,4
110   CALL 768: WAIT -16384,128
120   HOME
```

Pause until a key is pressed; then clear screen

ADDITIONAL GRAPHICS PAGES

In Program 2.10 above, the contents of locations $6000 through $7FFF are copied onto high resolution graphics page 2. There is little reason for doing this unless a high resolution picture has been stored in locations $6000 through $7FFF. There are three ways of getting a picture in $6000 through $7FFF:

1. Load it from disk (BLOAD PICTURE, A$6000);

2. Draw it on high resolution page 1 or 2, then copy it to $6000-$7FFF;

3. Draw directly on "high resolution page 3" ($6000-$7FFF).

Option 3 is easily implemented from BASIC and is illustrated in Program 2.12. You must identify "page 3" as the area to be used for drawing (POKE 230,96), clear the screen to black (CALL 62450), and then proceed with normal plot commands. As long as we are expanding the number of graphics pages, why not add a "page 4"? Memory locations $8000 through $9FFF could be used for drawing purposes, except for the fact that DOS overlaps this area. Clearing this "Screen," or drawing on it, will erase or disable part of DOS. In preparation for this, line 100 disconnects DOS. As a result, at the end of the program, it will be necessary to reboot the system.

"Page 5" of high resolution graphics ($A000-$BFFF) can be used in the same manner as "page 4."

When using "page 4" or "page 5," it is necessary to avoid having strings stored there. Since strings are usually stored just under HIMEM, (just below DOS), one solution is to set HIMEM to 8191 early in the program.

```
1 HIMEM: 8191
```

This will cause strings to be stored just below high resolution graphics page 1.

Program 2.12: ADDITIONAL GRAPHICS PAGES

```
 1   REM PROGRAM 2.12 (ADDITIONAL GRAPHICS PAGES)
 2   REM DRAWS, DISPLAYS 4 PAGES OF GRAPHICS
10   TEXT : HOME : HCOLOR= 3
20   POKE 768,160: POKE 769,0
30   POKE 770,76: POKE 771,44
40   POKE 772,254
50   POKE 230,64: CALL 62450
60   HPLOT 140,10 TO 140,180
```

clear screen indicated by location 230 then draw there

```
70    POKE 230,96: CALL 62450
80    HPLOT 120,10 TO 120,180
90    HPLOT 160,10 TO 160,180
100   IN# 0: PR# 0
110   POKE 230,128: CALL 62450
120   HPLOT 110,10 TO 110,180
130   HPLOT 140,10 TO 140,180
140   HPLOT 170,10 TO 170,180
150   POKE 230,160: CALL 62450
160   HPLOT 110,10 TO 110,180
170   HPLOT 170,100 TO 10,100 TO 110,10
180   PRINT "THIS PROGRAM WILL DISPLAY ONE OF
      FOUR": PRINT
190   PRINT "HIGH RESOLUTION IMAGES": PRINT
200   PRINT "PRESS KEYS 1, 2, 3 OR 4 TO SEE
      THEM": PRINT
210   PRINT "PRESS 'ESC' TO END THE PROGRAM":
      PRINT
220   PRINT "PRESS 'RETURN' TO RETURN TO THIS
      MENU"
230   POKE -16297,0: POKE -16302,0
240   VTAB 18: GET A$: PRINT :X= FRE (0)
250   IF ASC (A$) = 27 THEN TEXT : HOME :
      PRINT "DOS IS DEAD!": END
260   IF ASC (A$) = 13 THEN POKE -16303,0:
      GOTO 240
270  A=VAL (A$): ON A GOTO 290,340,390,440
280   GOTO 240
290   POKE -16304,0
300   POKE 60,0: POKE 61,64
310   POKE 62,255: POKE 63,95
320   POKE 66,0: POKE 67,32
330   CALL 768: GOTO 240
340   POKE -16304,0
350   POKE 60,0: POKE 61,96
360   POKE 62,255: POKE 63,127
370   POKE 66,0: POKE 67,32
380   CALL 768: GOTO 240
390   POKE -16304,0
400   POKE 60,0: POKE 61,128
410   POKE 62,255: POKE 63,159
420   POKE 66,0: POKE 67,32
430   CALL 768: GOTO 240
440   POKE -16304,0
450   POKE 60,0: POKE 61,160
460   POKE 62,255: POKE 63,191
470   POKE 66,0: POKE 67,32
480   CALL 768: GOTO 240
```

Clear screen indicated by location 230 then draw there

Move pages 2, 3, 4, 5 to page 1

Program 2.12 illustrates the use of the soft switches in combination with the ability to draw on portions of memory other than high resolution pages 1 and 2. Of course, images drawn on "page 3," "page 4," or "page 5" will not be visible unless moved to pages 1 or 2.

The exit (line 250) is a cold exit, with DOS inoperative. Replacing line 250 with

```
250 IF ASC(A$) = 27 THEN TEXT: CALL 50688
```

will result in rebooting the disk upon exit, assuming that the disk controller is in slot 6.

PAGE 2 OF TEXT

The Apple II provides a means of displaying a second text page (POKE $-16303,0$: POKE $-16299,0$), but does not make it easy to write on this text page. While our primary interest is in high resolution graphics, the ability to display text on page 2 is valuable, especially since mixed-text-and-graphics on high resolution page 2 will draw its text portion from text page 2.

The first problem associated with the use of text page 2 is that it resides in a portion of memory (\$800–\$BFF) usually used for Applesoft BASIC programs. In order to use text page 2 in a BASIC program, it is necessary to locate the program in some other area of memory. This is easily done. Memory locations \$67 (103) and \$68 (104) contain the low and high bytes, respectively, of the address of the beginning of the Applesoft program in effect. Thus location 103 usually contains \$01 (1) and location 104 usually contains \$08 (8). (While the area of memory reserved for the program begins at \$800, location \$800 will contain a zero; the program actually begins at \$801.)

If a BASIC program is to use text pages 1 and 2 and high resolution graphics pages 1 and 2, the first large block of memory available for locating the program begins at \$6000 (24576). If we wish to enter or load a program at that address we must set the contents of 103 and 104 to \$01 (1) and \$60 (96) respectively (24576 = 96 × 256). We must also enter the beginning-of-program code (0) at location \$6000 (24576). To enter a program at this location, we could type:

```
POKE 103,1
POKE 104,96
POKE 24576,0
NEW
```

then begin typing the new program.

To load and run a program at this location, we could type:

```
POKE 103,1
POKE 104,96
POKE 24576,0
RUN PROGRAM
```

The above four lines may be typed from the keyboard, be part of an Applesoft program, or be EXECed from a text file.

Having identified a means of placing the BASIC program out of the way of text page 2, we turn to the problem of writing on this text page. There are two ways of doing so:

1. Printing on text page 1, as usual, then using the machine level MOVE program to copy the contents of text page 1 onto text page 2; or

2. Printing directly on text page 2.

In order to use the second method, it is necessary to identify page 2 as the area to be used for printing. Memory location $29 (41) normally contains numbers between 4 and 7, identifying 1024 memory locations between $400 and $7FF as the part of memory used for storing text or low resolution graphics. Loading $29 with 8, 9, 10, or 11 will cause this location to point to $800 through $BFF. Printing then will be directed to page 2. Unfortunately, location $29 is reset to a value between 4 and 7 each time a RETURN is encountered (at the end of each line of a BASIC program). Thus location $29 must be set immediately before each PRINT to page 2. Program 2.13 illustrates the method.

Program 2.13: TWO PAGES OF TEXT

```
1    REM PROGRAM 2.13 (TWO PAGES OF TEXT)
2    REM ILLUSTRATES PRINTING, DISPLAYING PAGE TWO
     OF TEXT
3    REM BE SURE TO SET PROGRAM POINTERS
4    REM AT LOCATIONS 103,104
5    REM BEFORE LOADING OR TYPING THIS PROGRAM
10   HOME : VTAB 10
20   FOR I = 2048 TO 3071: POKE I,160: NEXT I
30   POKE -16299,0
40   SPEED= 55
```

(continued)

```
50   POKE 41, PEEK (41) + 4: PRINT "WE ARE NOW
     PRINTING ON PAGE 2."
60   POKE 41, PEEK (41) + 4: PRINT "GET READY FOR
     A CHANGE TO PAGE 1."
70   FOR I = 1 TO 1000: NEXT I
80   POKE -16300,0: VTAB 10
90   PRINT "WE ARE NOW PRINTING ON PAGE 1."
100   PRINT "WE WILL DISPLAY EACH OF THE TWO"
110   PRINT "TEXT PAGES REPEATEDLY"
120   PRINT "WHILE COUNTING FROM 1 TO 40"
130   SPEED= 255
140   FOR J = 1 TO 20
150   POKE -16299,0
160   VTAB 18: POKE 41, PEEK (41) + 4:
      PRINT 2 * J - 1
170   FOR I = 1 TO 1000: NEXT I
180   VTAB 18: PRINT 2 * J
190   POKE -16300,0
200   FOR I = 1 TO 1000: NEXT I
210   NEXT J
```

Print immediately after setting pointer (41)

NEGATIVE IMAGES

An Apple high resolution graphics image is a display of the bit patterns of the numbers contained in a block of the computer's memory. When an image is being displayed, a pixel which is turned ON corresponds to a bit which contains a 1. If a pixel is turned OFF, the corresponding bit contains a 0.

If the contents of the high resolution graphics memory locations are systematically changed, the displayed image will be changed. The negative, or complement, of an image will result if all of the ON pixels are turned OFF and all of the OFF pixels are turned ON. To cause this change, bit contents must be changed: 0s must replace 1s and 1s must replace 0s. This may be accomplished, for the first page of high resolution graphics, by

```
FOR I = 8192 TO 16383: POKE I, 255 - PEEK(I):
NEXT I
```

or, for the second page of high resolution graphics,

```
FOR I = 16384 TO 24575: POKE I, 255 - PEEK(I):
NEXT I
```

PROGRAMMING AIDS

READING THE KEYBOARD

Interactive programs accept user input by using either the INPUT or the GET statement. When either of these is used the computer will wait for user input before continuing with calculation or display of results. There are occasions when we might prefer to have program execution continue until a specific key, say ESC, is pressed. This was the case in Program 1.4. Rather than forcing a halt in the graphics display while awaiting user input, the program looks regularly at the contents of memory location −16384 (PEEK(−16384)). This memory location receives the result of any keypress. If ESC is pressed [PEEK(−16384) = 155], the program is ended (line 120). Otherwise, program execution continues. (For a list of ASCII keycodes, see the Apple II Reference Manual, page 7.)

Program line 120 takes care of one other detail. When a key is pressed, the appropriate code is stored in memory location −16384 and is retained there. When the results of the keystroke are read, the command POKE −16368,0 "clears the keyboard strobe," preparing to receive a new keystroke.

Program 1.9 provides another example of keyboard input without the use of INPUT or GET statements. Line 70 reads the keyboard; the result of a keypress, analyzed in lines 80 through 240, is used to control the behavior of the program.

LONG PROGRAMS

If strings of dots start creeping across the graphics screen during program execution, or if the end of a program disappears suddenly, it may be that your program is too long. The strings of dots may be the visible effect of variables being stored in the part of memory which is used for high resolution graphics display. If program storage requires more memory than is available between $800 and $1FFF, then an HGR command within the program will erase the end of the program.

Prevention of these problems is fairly easy. At any stage of entering a program, or after it is loaded from disk,

```
PRINT PEEK(175) + 256 * PEEK(176)
```

will give the address of the memory location which contains the end of the Applesoft program. This address must be sufficiently below 8192 (the beginning of high resolution graphics page 1) to allow room for storage of the variables defined in the program. If it appears that insufficient room is available, take one of the following precautions:

1. Store variables above the graphics page. To do this, define LOMEM equal to 24576 (to put variables above high resolution graphics page 2) or 16384 (to put variables above high resolution graphics page 1, but in page 2). The value of LOMEM must be established early in the program; for example,

```
1 LOMEM:24576
```

2. Store the program and variables above the graphics pages. This part of the computer memory frequently goes unused. The area normally used for program storage lies between 2048 ($800) and 8191 ($1FFF). There are about 6000 bytes of memory there. However, between the second page of graphics and DOS, there are nearly 14000 bytes of memory in a 48K RAM system. Locate long programs there. The process to be followed is the same as described earlier, under Text Page 2.

NOTES AND SUGGESTIONS

1. The Apple Reference Manual is one of the best references for information on memory usage. Related articles frequently appear in magazines such as the *Apple Orchard, MICRO,* and *Nibble.* Articles specific to higher resolution graphics have appeared in *Apple Orchard,* Vol. 1, No. 2, and Vol. 2, No. 1. An excellent reference to memory organization is What's Where in the Apple by W. F. Luebbert.

2. Modify Program 1.9 to respond to

S (save current image on page 2 of high resolution graphics). Use the memory move subroutine.

T (display the image which is on high resolution graphics page Two). Use the POKEs for Soft Switches.

O (display the image which is on high resolution graphics page One). Use the POKEs for Soft Switches.

R (recopy image from page 2 to page 1). Use the memory move subroutine.

Each of S, T, O, and R should cause automatic transfer to the C (cursor) mode.

With these keys recognized by the program, it will be possible to:

1.   Save partially completed images on page 2, while drawing will continue on page 1;

2.   Compare further work (on page 1) with an earlier effort (on page 2);

3.   Return to an earlier version if later work is not satisfactory.

3.   Write a FLASHER program, which draws an image on page 1 of high resolution graphics, places its negative (complement) on page 2, then flips the display switch between page 1 and page 2 so that the original and its negative are alternately displayed. It will be necessary to place a counting loop (FOR I = 1 to 50:NEXT I) between successive POKEs of the display switch in order to waste a little time. Otherwise the display screen will not be able to keep up with the computer output.

4.   For the FLASHER program, arrange that all drawing and complementing occur while displaying the text page. Display the graphics pages only during the flashing part of the program. Allow exit from the flashing with the pressing of ESC.

5.   Write a program that will draw

• On page 2 of high resolution graphics, the outline of a house (stick figure style, no windows or doors);

• On page 3 of high resolution graphics, the above image, with windows, doors;

• On page 4 of high resolution graphics, the image on page 3, with an attached garage at the side;

• On page 5 of high resolution graphics, the image of page 4, with a tree (a triangle, Christmas tree style) beside the house.

When the drawings are complete, allow each of the images to be displayed on receiving a corresponding keypress (use the MOVE routine).

If you are more ambitious, use color graphics to add blue sky, sun, green grass, driveway, and so forth, to the various images; or provide a single view for each of the four seasons.

Chapter 3
TEXT on the Graphics Screen

Applesoft makes no provision for easy display of text on the graphics pages. It is possible to display graphics with four lines of text, but this is not entirely satisfactory. To be effective, labels should be capable of being positioned among graphic images. Two methods of providing text are presented below. Example programs are given which may be made more versatile to suit the needs of the user.

BIT PATTERN TEXT

The character set used on the TEXT page is given on page 14 of the Apple II Reference Manual. Each character consists of a pattern of white dots on a matrix of 8 × 7. An enlargement of the letter A is shown in Figure 3.1.

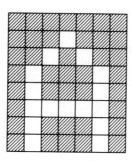

Figure 3.1

The high resolution graphics page, with a matrix of 280 × 192, may be divided into 8 × 7 blocks, resulting in 24 rows of 40 blocks each. A comparison with the dimensions of the TEXT page suggests a means for providing text on the graphics screen. A process for duplicating the text character bit patterns onto the graphics screen would provide labels as desired. Program 3.2 includes a subroutine that performs this duty. The development of the subroutine rests on a means of locating the specific byte of memory which corresponds to a desired screen location, and a means for placing the text character bit patterns on the screen.

CHARACTERS

It was pointed out in Chapter 2 that the high resolution graphics display is a map of the contents of a block of computer memory.

To illustrate, consider memory location 8192. This byte of RAM is displayed at the top left corner of the HGR screen. Assume that the byte contains the number 67 (POKE 8192,67). In binary notation, the number 67 is represented as 01000011. On the HGR screen the pattern will be reproduced, in reversed order, as:

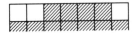

Figure 3.2

Note that HGR displays only the lower seven bits of the byte, with the low order bit first.

Similarly, if 8192 contains the number 87 (binary 01010111), the following bit pattern will appear at the top left corner of the HGR screen:

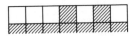

Figure 3.3

The block of eight bytes at the top left corner of the graphics screen are numbered as shown in Figure 3.4.

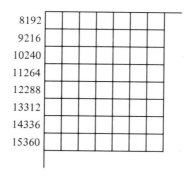

| 8192 |
| 9216 |
| 10240 |
| 11264 |
| 12288 |
| 13312 |
| 14336 |
| 15360 |

Figure 3.4

In order to print the symbol 4 at the top left corner of the screen, we will arrange for these memory locations to contain the bit patterns shown in Figure 3.5.

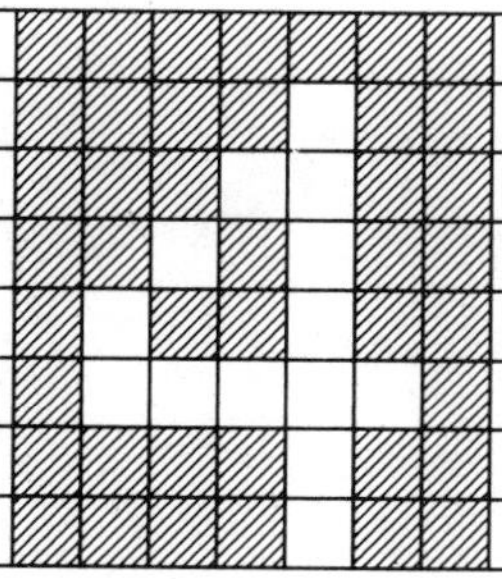

		BIT PATTERN (reversed)	
		Binary	Decimal
8192		0000000	0
9216		0010000	16
10240		0011000	24
11264		0010100	20
12288		0010010	18
13312		0111110	62
14336		0010000	16
15360		0010000	16

Figure 3.5

We can display the number 4 by the following sequence of commands:

```
HGR: POKE 8192,0: POKE 9216,16: POKE 10240,24:
POKE 11264,20: POKE 12288,18: POKE 13312,62:
POKE 14336,16: POKE 15360,16
```

In a similar fashion we could display other symbols, first drawing the bit pattern, converting the bit pattern from a binary code to a decimal number, then POKEing the bit pattern into the appropriate memory locations. An 8×7 pattern is the most easily addressed, but more elaborate symbols and patterns may be displayed as combinations of 8×7 blocks.

While any desired symbol may be displayed, the process is as yet rather inefficient. We lack a convenient means of accessing the bit patterns and displaying them on the screen. Several methods are available. Programs 3.1 and 3.2 approach the solution by means of an array AL%(I,J).

Since the standard Apple character set has 64 characters, each having an eight byte display pattern, the array is dimensioned AL%(64,8). If we number the characters in array so that the symbol 4 is the 20th character, we should expect to find:

$$AL\%(20,0) = 0$$
$$AL\%(20,1) = 16$$
$$AL\%(20,2) = 24$$
$$AL\%(20,3) = 20$$
$$AL\%(20,4) = 18$$
$$AL\%(20,5) = 62$$
$$AL\%(20,6) = 16$$
$$AL\%(20,7) = 16$$

The symbol 4 may be placed at the top left corner of the screen by:

```
HGR
FOR I = 0 TO 7
ADDR=8192 + I*1024
POKE ADDR, AL%(20,I)
NEXT I
```

Since the first 32 ASCII values do not correspond to the characters we normally would want to display, it is convenient to reference the array entries for a character K$ as:

```
AL%(CH,0)
```

through

```
AL%(CH,7)
```

where

```
CH = ASC(K$) - 32
```

One task remains: Identifying the screen locations at which the character should appear. At this point it would be well to review the screen addressing pattern used for high resolution graphics.

Figure 3.4 shows the addresses of the block of eight bytes whose contents are displayed at the top left corner of HGR. The addresses range from 8192 through 15360, in increments of 1024. Immediately below 15360, a second block of eight bytes begins, with an initial address of 8320. The addresses of the bytes in this block range from 8320 through 15488, in increments of 1024. Eight such blocks appear at the left of the upper third of the screen. The base address of block $I(0 \leq I \leq 7)$ is given by the formula:

```
BA = 8192 + 128*I.
```

Within each block, the eight bytes $J = 0, 1, 2, \ldots, 7$ may be addressed as:

```
BA + 1024*J
```

The middle third of the screen is addressed in a similar manner, but uses a reference of 8232 instead of 8192 (note that $8232 = 8192 + 40$). The lower third has the same structure, using an initial reference of 8272 (note that $8272 = 8192 + 2 \times 40$).

To identify the address of a memory location whose contents are displayed along the left side of the HGR screen, it is necessary to determine:

1. Whether the screen location is in the upper, middle, or lower segment;

2. The block desired within each segment;

3. The byte desired within each block.

In order to address the graphics screen for text purposes, we will be concerned most with steps 1 and 2, since each symbol will make use of all eight bytes within a block.

For convenience, the upper, middle, and lower third of the screen will be referred to as segments 0, 1, and 2 respectively. Similarly, the eight blocks within each third will be referred to as blocks 0 through 7 (top to bottom).

Program 3.2 uses HT and VT (as in HTAB and VTAB) to identify the screen location at which text is to be located. Considering VT first, note that:

VT = 1–8 identifies blocks in segment 0

VT = 9–16 identifies blocks in segment 1

VT = 17–24 identifies blocks in segment 2

As a result, the segment number, SE, may be identified by:

```
SE = INT((VT - 1)/8).
```

Within each segment it is necessary to identify the block (BL = 0 through 7) indicated by VT. To this end, note the following association between VT, SE, and BL:

VT	SE	BL	VT	SE	BL	VT	SE	BL
1	0	0	9	1	0	17	2	0
2	0	1	10	1	1	18	2	1
3	0	2	11	1	2	19	2	2
4	0	3	12	1	3	20	2	3
5	0	4	13	1	4	21	2	4
6	0	5	14	1	5	22	2	5
7	0	6	15	1	6	23	2	6
8	0	7	16	1	7	24	2	7

If Applesoft provided a MOD command, the block number could be calculated as BL = (VT − 1)MOD(8). With MOD missing, we have:

```
BL = VT - 1 - 8*INT((VT-1)/8)
```

The base address of each block may be calculated as:

```
BA = 8192 + 40*SE + 128*BL
```

Thus, we can identify:

```
BA = 8192 + 40*INT((VT-1)/8) +
     128*(VT-1 - 8*INT((VT-1)/8))
```

Having resolved the addressing of character positions along the left of the graphics screen, we now turn to the effect of HT. Happily, this is an easy task since the addresses of adjacent bytes along a horizontal line differ by 1. The byte identified by a specific VT and HT has base address:

```
BA = 8192 + 40*INT((VT-1)/8) +
     128*(VT-1 - 8*INT(VT-1)/8))+ HT - 1
```

This formula permits the identification of a block position by VT and HT (as in VTAB, HTAB) as a means to access the base address of the block. You should confirm its equivalence to the simpler formula:

```
BA = 8063 + 128*VT - 984*INT((VT-1)/8) + HT
```

IMPLEMENTATION

Having determined a method of placing characters at specific screen locations, we now turn to the provision of the bit patterns. The use of an array to store the bit patterns for symbols requires that the array be made available. Defining the elements of the array within the program requires a bulky addition to the user program. Accessing the array by means of a text file is time consuming and is wasteful of disk space. The approach used below, while unconventional, wastes little time or space.

Program 3.1 fills a two dimensional integer array AL%(I,J). An I (= 0 through 63) identifies each symbol K$ by ASC(K$) − 32. Each AL%(I,J) (J = 0 through 7) identifies one byte of the bit pattern of the character I. The DATA read into the array was identified by first drawing a character on an 8 × 7 matrix to establish the bit pattern, then converting the bit pattern from a binary to decimal code. When the array is filled, it is saved on disk as a binary file (line 90).

A few words about the saving of the array to disk: Memory locations 107 and 108 contain the address of the beginning of the array space (low order byte first). Memory locations 109 and 110 contain the address of the end of the array space. The array space is moved upward in memory as new variables (such as ADDR and LN) are defined, since simple variables are stored between LOMEM and the array space. It is thus important that the calculation of the beginning address (ADDR) and the length (LN) of the block of memory to be BSAVEd not result in moving the array, and that the array then be stored before any additional variables are defined. For this reason ADDR and LN are defined in line 10; the calculation in lines 70 and 80 will not disturb the array space.

Program 3.2 demonstrates the use of the array. It must be loaded from disk and stored in appropriate memory locations, and the array pointers must be properly set. To this end, ADDR, the destination of the array (which should follow the simple variables), is read in line 20 of Program 3.2. After the array has been loaded (line 30), the length of the BLOADed file is read from locations 43616 ($AA60) and 43617 ($AA61). Finally, the pointers to the end of the array space are set (lines 50, 60). The array is then ready for use.

Program 3.2 illustrates the use of the symbol-printing subroutine (lines 210–290). The subroutine receives a string ST$ and horizontal and vertical tab settings HT and VT. The string is then read, character by character, and the symbol bit patterns are POKEd into the calculated memory locations.

The subroutine may be used in graphics programs to place labels at specified locations on the high resolution screens. Before jumping to the subroutine, it is necessary to define the label (ST$) and the tab settings (HT, VT), In setting HT, be careful that the label not run off the right side of the screen. Otherwise, since the program will not provide a line feed, the end of the label may appear in surprising places. Similarly, check to assure that the values of HT and VT are in the proper ranges ($1 \leq HT \leq 40; 1 \leq VT \leq 24$).

Program 3.1: BIT PATTERN ALPHABET FILE

```
1     REM PROGRAM 3.1 (BIT PATTERN ALPHABET FILE)
2     REM SAVES AN ALPHABET FILE ON DISK
10    ADDR = 0:LN = 0
20    DIM AL%(64,8)
30    FOR I = 0 TO 63
40    FOR J = 0 TO 7
50    READ AL%(I,J)
60    NEXT J,I
70    ADDR = PEEK (107) + 256 * PEEK (108)
80    LN = PEEK (109) + 256 * PEEK (110) - ADDR
90    PRINT CHR$ (4); "BSAVE ALPHABET, A";
      ADDR;",L";LN
100   END
110   DATA 0,0,0,0,0,0,0,0: REM SPACE
120   DATA 0,8,8,8,8,8,0,8: REM !
130   DATA 0,20,20,20,0,0,0,0: REM "
140   DATA 0,20,20,62,20,62,20,20: REM #
150   DATA 0,8,60,10,28,40,30,8: REM $
```

```
160    DATA 0,6,38,16,8,4,50,48: REM %
170    DATA 0,4,10,10,4,42,18,44: REM &
180    DATA 0,8,8,0,0,0,0,0: REM '
190    DATA 0,8,4,2,2,2,4,8: REM (
200    DATA 0,8,16,32,32,32,16,8: REM )
210    DATA 0,8,42,28,8,28,42,8: REM *
220    DATA 0,0,8,8,62,0,0,0: REM +
230    DATA 0,0,0,0,0,8,8,4: REM ,
240    DATA 0,0,0,0,62,0,0,0: REM -
250    DATA 0,0,0,0,0,0,0,8: REM .
260    DATA 0,0,32,16,8,4,2,0: REM /
270    DATA 0,28,34,50,42,38,34,28: REM 0
280    DATA 0,8,12,8,8,8,8,28: REM 1
290    DATA 0,28,34,32,24,4,2,62: REM 2
300    DATA 0,62,32,16,24,32,34,28: REM 3
310    DATA 0,16,24,20,18,62,16,16: REM 4
320    DATA 0,62,2,30,32,32,34,28: REM 5
330    DATA 0,56,4,2,30,34,34,28: REM 6
340    DATA 0,62,32,16,8,4,4,4: REM 7
350    DATA 0,28,34,34,28,34,34,28: REM 8
360    DATA 0,28,34,34,60,32,16,14: REM 9
370    DATA 0,0,0,8,0,8,0,0: REM :
380    DATA 0,0,0,8,0,8,8,4: REM ;
390    DATA 0,16,8,4,2,4,8,16: REM <
400    DATA 0,0,0,62,0,62,0,0: REM =
410    DATA 0,4,8,16,32,16,8,4: REM >
420    DATA 0,28,34,16,8,8,0,8: REM ?
430    DATA 0,28,34,42,42,26,2,60: REM @
440    DATA 0,8,20,34,34,62,34,34: REM A
450    DATA 0,30,34,34,30,34,34,30: REM B
460    DATA 0,28,34,2,2,2,34,28: REM C
470    DATA 0,30,34,34,34,34,34,30: REM D
480    DATA 0,62,2,2,30,2,2,62: REM E
490    DATA 0,62,2,2,30,2,2,2: REM F
500    DATA 0,60,2,2,2,50,34,60: REM G
510    DATA 0,34,34,34,62,34,34,34: REM H
520    DATA 0,28,8,8,8,8,8,28: REM I
530    DATA 0,32,32,32,32,32,34,28: REM J
540    DATA 0,34,18,10,6,10,18,34: REM K
550    DATA 0,2,2,2,2,2,2,62: REM L
560    DATA 0,34,54,42,34,34,34,34: REM M
570    DATA 0,34,34,38,42,50,34,34: REM N
580    DATA 0,28,34,34,34,34,34,28: REM O
590    DATA 0,30,34,34,30,2,2,2: REM P
600    DATA 0,28,34,34,34,42,18,28: REM Q
```

(continued)

```
610    DATA 0,30,34,34,30,10,18,34: REM R
620    DATA 0,28,34,2,28,32,34,28: REM S
630    DATA 0,62,8,8,8,8,8,8: REM T
640    DATA 0,34,34,34,34,34,34,28: REM U
650    DATA 0,34,34,34,34,34,20,8: REM V
660    DATA 0,34,34,34,42,42,54,34: REM W
670    DATA 0,34,34,20,8,20,34,34: REM X
680    DATA 0,34,34,20,8,8,8,8: REM Y
690    DATA 0,62,32,16,8,4,2,62: REM Z
700    DATA 0,62,6,6,6,6,6,62: REM LEFT BRACKET
710    DATA 0,0,2,4,8,16,32,0: REM BACKSLASH
720    DATA 0,62,48,48,48,48,48,62: REM RIGHT
       BRACKET
730    DATA 0,0,8,20,34,0,0,0: REM ^
740    DATA 0,0,0,0,0,0,0,62: REM UNDERLINE
```

Program 3.2: BIT PATTERN TEXT FOR THE GRAPHICS PAGE

```
1    REM PROGRAM 3.2 (BIT PATTERN TEXT FOR THE
     GRAPHICS PAGE)
2    REM DEMONSTRATES PRINTING FOR THE GRAPHICS
     PAGE
10   ADDR = 0;LN = 0
20   ADDR = PEEK (107) + 256 * PEEK (108)
30    PRINT CHR$ (4);"BLOAD ALPHABET,A";ADDR
40   LN=256 * PEEK (43617) + PEEK (43616)
50    POKE 110, INT ((ADDR + LN) / 256)
60    POKE 109,ADDR + LN - 256 * INT ((ADDR + LN)
      / 256)
70    HGR : HOME : VTAB 21
80   VT = 5:HT = 5:ST$ = "BIT PATTERN TEXT FOR
     HGR"
90    GOSUB 210
100  VT = 7:HT = 5:ST$ = "PROVIDING TEXT,
     NUMBERS, AND SYMBOLS"
110   GOSUB 210
120  VT = 10:HT = 10:ST$ = "TRY IT!"
130   GOSUB 210
140  VT = 20:HT = 1:ST$ = "ENTER:"
150   GOSUB 210
160   INPUT "STRING ";ST$
170   INPUT "VTAB ";VT
180   INPUT "HTAB ";HT
190   GOSUB 210
200   END
```

```
210  BA  =  8063  +  128  *  VT  -  984  *
     INT  ((VT  -  1)  /  8)  +  HT
220    FOR  I  =  1  TO  LEN  (ST$)
230  CH  =  ASC  (  MID$  (ST$,I,1))  -  32
240    FOR  J  =  0  TO  7
250    POKE  BA  +  1024  *  J,AL%(CH,J)
260    NEXT  J
270  BA  =  BA  +  1
280    NEXT  I
290    RETURN
```

NOTES AND SUGGESTIONS

1. There are commercially available programs that make use of the bit-pattern approach to providing symbols for the graphics page. These typically come with several character sets and provide the capability of adding symbols considered useful by the user. The programs are written in machine language, and thus are much faster than the ones described above.

2. The subroutine of Program 3.2 may be modified to print labels vertically instead of horizontally. Make the following changes:

```
210    FOR  I  =  1  TO  LEN  (ST$)
220    BA  =  8063  +  128  *  VT  -  984  *
       INT  ((VT  -  1)  /  8)  +  HT
230  CH  =  ASC  (  MID$  (ST$,I,1))-32
240    FOR  J  =  0  TO  7
250    POKE  BA  +  1024  *  J,AL%(CH,J)
260    NEXT  J
270  VT  =  VT  +  1
280    NEXT  I
290    RETURN
```

You might find it useful to include two subroutines in a program, one for horizontal labels, and one for vertical labels.

3. Inverse printing may be achieved: replace line 250 of Program 3.2 with:

```
250  POKE  BA  +  1024*J,  255  -  AL%(CH,J)
```

4. If you want to have symbols printed upside down (why not?) try the following replacement for line 250:

```
250  POKE  BA  +  1024*J,  AL%(CH,7  -  J)
```

5. A line feed capability may be added to the subroutine of Program 3.2 by changing lines 210 through 290 to read as follows:

```
210   FOR I = 1 TO LEN (ST$)
220   BA = 8063 + 128 * VT - 984 *
      INT ((VT - 1) / 8) + HT
230   CH = ASC ( MID$ (ST$,I,1)) - 32
240   FOR J = 0 TO 7
250   POKE BA + 1024 * J,AL%(CH,J)
260   NEXT J
270   HT + HT + 1: IF HT = 41 THEN HT = 1:
      VT = VT + 1
280   NEXT I
290   RETURN
```

To protect against an inconvenient break in the middle of a word, you may add a loop which reads each word (characters between spaces), and measures its length. If a word length exceeds 40 − HT, it will not fit on the current line and a line feed is appropriate:

```
HT = 1:VT = VT + 1: GOTO ***
```

6. You may extend the array AL%(I,J) to include the lower case alphabet and any special symbols you want to have. If the array is dimensioned AL%(90,8), with entries Al%(64,J) through AL%(89,J) containing the bit patterns of the lower case alphabet, the existing subroutine will print the label "Lower" when provided with the string:

```
ST$ = "L" + CHR$(78) + CHR$(86) +
CHR$(68) + CHR$(81)
```

7. Numbers defined as part of a string, as in

```
ST$ = "X = 45"
```

are processed properly by the subroutine. To display a number X that is calculated within the program, use

```
ST$ = STR$(X)
```

8. Printing in HGR2 may be done just as efficiently. The address of the RAM location which corresponds to the top left corner of the screen changes from 8192 to 16384. The effect of this change is seen in line 210, which should (for HGR2) read:

```
210 BA = 16255 + 128 * VT - 984 *
INT ((VT - 1)/8) + HT
```

9. The program will not permit the input of certain symbols (such as "," from the keyboard. However, when the symbols are included in the definition of a string, such as:

```
ST$ = "A,B"
```

the subroutine will properly process the symbols.

SHAPE TABLE TEXT

Shape table graphics provides a second way of placing text on the graphics pages. With the expenditure of additional effort at the preparation stage, the user can have a symbol-manipulation tool that is in some ways more powerful and flexible than what is provided by bit patterns.

A shape table is a collection of predefined shapes, or graphic images, which may quickly be placed at specified locations on a high resolution graphics page. Accessing shapes for drawing is an easy process. Each shape is stored in coded form and identified by number. A shape may be displayed by specifying the shape number N and the desired screen location (X,Y), through either of the commands:

```
DRAW N AT X,Y
```

or

```
XDRAW N AT X,Y
```

While either DRAW or XDRAW will display a specified shape at a desired location, DRAW uses the most recently specified HCOLOR, while XDRAW displays a shape in the complement of the colors that currently are in the screen locations the shape is to occupy. As a result, consecutive XDRAWs cause the display, then erasure, of a shape. Further, since:

```
XDRAW N AT X,Y  (complement colors)
XDRAW N AT X,Y  (complement colors again)
```

results in complementing the complement of the colors originally found, the screen is returned to its original status.

Actually, the challenge associated with shapes is not in the drawing of a shape, but rather in the construction of the shape table. The Applesoft Reference Manual provides a description of shape tables and shows how to make one. While the process described there will allow the user to design and use shapes, it is a tedious and frustrating job. It is, in fact, the type of task that may effectively be handled by the computer. Shape table programs have been published in computer magazines, and several are commercially available. A listing of one is given in Appendix 2, along with a general discussion of shapes.

In this chapter, our interest in shape tables is for the display of text. We need a shape table in which the shapes are the standard text symbols. The user may wish to create a shape table for this purpose; however, Program 3.3 will enter a shape table containing the standard text page characters. The shapes are numbered by the ASCII character codes as follows:

Shape number of character K$ = ASC(K$) − 32.

Program 3.3: SHAPE TABLE ALPHABET FILE

```
1    REM PROGRAM 3.3 (SHAPE TABLE ALPHABET FILE)
2    REM SAVES A SHAPE TABLE ALPHABET ON DISK
10   FOR I = 24576 TO 25364
20   READ X
30   POKE I,X
40   NEXT I
50   PRINT CHR$ (4);"BSAVE SHAPE ALPHABET,
     A24576,L793"
60   END
70   DATA 63,0,128,0,134,0,142,0,157,0:
     REM                                 ----------
80   DATA 172,0,185,0,200,0,206,0,214,0
90   DATA 222,0,236,0,245,0,249,0,255,0
100  DATA 2,1,9,1,24,1,32,1,44,1:
     REM                             SHAPE TABLE
110  DATA 56,1,67,1,79,1,93,1,102,1
120  DATA 116,1,127,1,133,1,139,1,148,1
130  DATA 156,1,165,1,175,1,190,1,202,1:
     REM                             ADDRESSING
140  DATA 216,1,228,1,240,1,254,1,8,2
150  DATA 19,2,31,2,40,2,48,2,61,2
160  DATA 70,2,82,2,94,2,106,2,116,2:
     REM                             STRUCTURE
170  DATA 130,2,143,2,155,2,163,2,174,2
180  DATA 185,2,198,2,210,2,219,2,231,2
190  DATA 245,2,253,2,9,3,17,3:
     REM                                 ----------
200  DATA 73,4,32,36,36,0: REM !
210  DATA 9,64,24,32,108,54,4,0: REM "
220  DATA 9,36,103,60,5,32,13,246,45,23,30,45,
     23,38,0: REM #
```

```
230    DATA 1,40,53,12,12,28,55,28,28,12,37,22,12,
       37,0: REM $
240    DATA 73,41,60,223,12,12,12,5,248,35,55,4,0:
       REM %
250    DATA 73,9,28,28,28,28,100,21,190,26,174,
       101,8,4,0: REM &
260    DATA 73,64,24,32,36,0: REM '
270    DATA 73,28,28,36,12,12,4,0: REM (
280    DATA 73,12,12,36,28,28,4,0: REM )
290    DATA 73,36,36,36,141,23,31,28,150,98,13,21,
       4,0: REM *
300    DATA 73,32,60,111,41,31,32,4,0: REM +
310    DATA 9,12,36,0: REM ,
320    DATA 64,24,41,45,37,0: REM -
330    DATA 73,4,0: REM .
340    DATA 1,96,12,12,12,4,0: REM /
350    DATA 9,45,12,36,36,28,63,23,54,54,12,12,12,
       4,0: REM 0
360    DATA 9,45,28,36,36,188,4,0: REM 1
370    DATA 73,9,63,63,100,12,101,228,63,23,4,0:
       REM 2
380    DATA 8,21,45,12,228,103,5,32,63,63,4,0:
       REM 3
390    DATA 73,33,44,31,63,100,12,12,54,38,0:
       REM 4
400    DATA 8,21,45,12,36,28,63,39,44,45,37,0:
       REM 5
410    DATA 9,45,12,228,63,55,38,64,3,12,12,45,
       4,0: REM 6
420    DATA 9,36,12,12,12,60,63,39,0: REM 7
430    DATA 9,45,12,228,63,23,38,64,3,100,45,21,
       38,0: REM 8
440    DATA 41,101,12,36,228,63,23,174,45,4,0:
       REM 9
450    DATA 73,64,3,4,32,0: REM :
460    DATA 9,5,32,4,32,0: REM ;
470    DATA 73,225,28,28,12,12,12,4,0: REM <
480    DATA 64,45,45,4,56,63,39,0: REM =
490    DATA 9,12,12,12,28,28,28,4,0: REM >
500    DATA 73,4,32,12,12,28,63,23,4,0: REM ?
510    DATA 9,45,37,64,3,36,28,63,23,54,54,76,229,
       36,0: REM @
520    DATA 33,36,100,12,14,14,54,63,111,17,38,0:
       REM A
530    DATA 33,36,36,44,45,21,190,31,109,50,23,63,
       4,0: REM B
```

(continued)

```
540 DATA 73,9,184,63,28,36,36,12,45,21,4,0:
    REM C
550 DATA 33,36,36,44,45,21,54,54,23,63,4,0:
    REM D
560 DATA 41,45,37,192,63,55,38,64,3,36,45,
    45,4,0: REM E
570 DATA 33,36,36,44,45,181,26,63,4,0: REM F
580 DATA 9,45,37,60,223,34,36,100,45,37,0:
    REM G
590 DATA 33,36,36,180,10,45,37,36,150,50,38,0:
    REM H
600 DATA 9,45,28,36,36,60,13,4,0: REM I
610 DATA 1,168,45,12,36,36,36,0: REM J
620 DATA 33,36,36,108,9,23,23,23,21,21,21,4,0:
    REM K
630 DATA 73,9,63,63,36,36,36,4,0: REM L
640 DATA 33,36,36,172,21,102,96,54,54,54,4,0:
    REM M
650 DATA 33,36,36,172,170,21,149,36,36,36,4,0:
    REM N
660 DATA 9,45,12,36,36,28,63,23,54,54,4,0:
    REM O
670 DATA 33,36,36,44,45,21,190,63,4,0: REM P
680 DATA 9,37,168,21,4,32,36,28,63,23,54,
    54,4,0: REM Q
690 DATA 33,36,36,44,45,21,190,63,21,21,21,4,0:
    REM R
700 DATA 8,21,45,12,60,56,231,100,45,21,4,0: REM
    S
710 DATA 73,36,36,36,63,77,37,0: REM T
720 DATA 9,45,12,36,36,252,27,54,54,38,0:
    REM U
730 DATA 73,12,12,36,36,223,51,54,174,4,0:
    REM V
740 DATA 33,36,36,108,9,54,54,54,28,28,
    180,35,0: REM W
750 DATA 33,12,12,28,28,108,9,190,22,21,38,0:
    REM X
760 DATA 73,36,228,28,108,9,246,4,0: REM Y
770 DATA 73,9,63,63,100,12,12,12,60,63,39,0: REM
    Z
780 DATA 73,9,63,63,44,60,44,60,44,28,45,
    45,4,0: REM LEFT BRACKET
790 DATA 72,73,28,28,28,28,4,0: REM BACKSLASH
800 DATA 41,45,37,39,37,39,37,39,253,63,4,0: REM
    RIGHT BRACKET
810 DATA 64,24,97,12,21,21,4,0: REM ^
820 DATA 41,45,37,0: REM UNDERLINE
```

The use of a shape table as a means of displaying text requires

1. The availability of the shape table;

2. The identification of the specific shape to be displayed; and

3. The identification of a location at which the shape is to be displayed.

Program 3.4 illustrates each of these.

Program 3.4: SHAPE TABLE TEXT FOR THE GRAPHICS PAGE

```
1    REM PROGRAM 3.4 (SHAPE TABLE TEXT FOR THE
     GRAPHICS PAGE)
2    REM DEMONSTRATES HIGH RES PRINTING WITH
     SHAPES
10   PRINT CHR$ (4);"BLOAD SHAPE ALPHABET,
     A24576"
20   POKE 232, PEEK (43634): POKE 233,
     PEEK (43635)
30   HOME : HGR : HCOLOR= 3: VTAB 21: SCALE= 1:
     ROT= 0
40 VT = 5:HT = 5:ST$ = "SHAPE TABLE TEXT FOR
   HGR"
60   GOSUB 180
70 VT = 7:HT = 5:ST$ = "PROVIDING TEXT, NUMBERS,
   AND SYMBOLS"
80   GOSUB 180
90 VT = 10:HT = 10:ST$ = "TRY IT!"
100   GOSUB 180
110 VT = 20:HT = 1:ST$ = "ENTER:"
120   GOSUB 180
130   INPUT "STRING ";ST$
140   INPUT "VTAB ";VT
150   INPUT "HTAB ";HT
160   GOSUB 180
170   END
180 HT = 7 * (HT - 1):VT = 8 * VT - 1
190   FOR I = 1 TO LEN (ST$)
200 CH = ASC ( MID$ (ST$,I,1)) - 32
210   IF CH = 0 THEN 230
220   XDRAW CH AT HT,VT
230 HT = HT + 7
240   NEXT I
250   RETURN
```

The shape table is loaded from disk in line 10. The destination of the shape table is somewhat arbitrary (don't load it on top of the program, in either graphics page, etc.). Line 20 identifies the location of the shape table, so that it may be accessed by the XDRAW command. The location is identified by reading it from 43634 and 43635, which (in a 48K system) contain the destination address of the file most recently BLOADed.

In general, location 232 and 233 contain the low and high bytes of the address of the shape table. A shape table located at address A can be made accessible by:

```
POKE 232, A-256*INT(A/256): POKE 233, INT(A/256)
```

Program line 30 sets SCALE = 1 and ROT = 0. These two parameters control the size and position of the shapes to be drawn. Each of these is discussed in the Applesoft Programming Reference Manual. Program 3.4 uses values of HT (HTAB) and VT (VTAB) to draw shapes. This allows the graphics screens to be addressed in the manner of the text page.

NOTES AND SUGGESTIONS

1. Program 3.4 positions each shape by using HT and VT, which have the effect provided on the TEXT page by HTAB and VTAB. This allows 24 lines of text, each having 40 characters. While this typically is adequate, it does constrain the location of labels unnecessarily.

If line 180 is deleted from the program, values of VT and HT may be given in the ranges $0 \leq VT \leq 191$ and $0 \leq HT \leq 279$. This allows much greater flexibility in positioning labels.

For the shape table constructed by Program 3.3, the location (HT, VT) of a character is actually the location of the bottom left dot of an 8×7 matrix which the character will occupy.

One caution: Shapes will "wrap around" the screen. The command

```
XDRAW 33 AT 276,10
```

specifies (276,10) as the bottom left corner of a 8×7 dot matrix. The right columns of this matrix will be beyond the right boundary of the screen. They will "wrap around" the screen, appearing on the left. Similarly, shapes drawn near the top of the screen may wrap around to the bottom.

2. Shapes may be scaled. Line 40 of Program 3.4 identifies SCALE = 1. Try SCALE = 2 or SCALE = 3. Alphabets with SCALE larger than 1 will require adjustments in the calculation of screen positions for adjacent characters (line 230). Shapes that are scaled will tend to disintegrate as the scale increases.

3. Shapes may be rotated. Line 40 of Program 3.4 identifies ROT = 0. If this is changed to ROT = 16, ROT = 32, or ROT = 48, the shapes drawn will be rotated in a clockwise direction by 90°, 180°, or 270° respectively.

4. Adjusting the subroutine to provide vertical labels is easy: replace line 230 with:

```
230 VT = VT + 8
```

Can you arrange for diagonal labels? For labels printed upside down and backwards?

5. Shape table text has advantages and disadvantages when compared with the bit pattern text process described above. One of the advantages is the ease with which labels may be erased without disturbing other parts of the graphic display. This allows labels to be changed interactively, and permits animation of labels or other symbols. See Chapter 8 for an example of shape animation.

6. Several of the remarks associated with the display of bit pattern text (display of calculated numbers, lower case characters, etc.) are also applicable to shape table text.

Part III

Two-Dimensional Graphics

Chapter 4
Software Tools For Computer Graphics

The large station wagon my wife drives has an automatic transmission, power brakes, power steering, and air conditioning. The car I drive has none of these. I must change gears as I drive, crank the windows down in warm weather, and use more muscle to steer and to brake.

We face similar, and perhaps more dramatic, differences if we compare full-scale graphics computers with the graphics capabilities of a microcomputer. Some of the built-in gadgetry of the large system is not available in a microcomputer; other features are available only when provided by the programmer.

It is the intent of this chapter to provide a description of some of the "tools of the trade" of a microcomputer graphics programmer. Each tool is presented in a form which explains how and why, for those who are interested. Example programs illustrate the use of the techniques discussed.

SCALING THE SCREEN

It is fairly common to find differences between the horizontal and vertical scales on a microcomputer display screen. The Apple HPLOT command is based on a grid of 280 × 192, which suggests that a horizontal unit is equivalent to 192/280 of a vertical unit. The discrepancy in scaling is further affected by the adjustment of the display screen.

There are occasions when it is important that the horizontal and vertical scales be equivalent—that a square appear to have sides of equal lengths, and that all points of a circle appear to be equidistant from the center. We can meet this need by scaling points before plotting them.

71

Since the adjustment of the display device will affect the perceived scales, it is necessary to determine the scaling factor for each computer-display screen combination. One way to identify the scaling factor is the following:

1. Plot a square on the screen.

2. Measure the displayed height (H) and width (W) of the "square."

3. Define SC = H/W.

4. For future plots, multiply the horizontal coordinate by SC before plotting.

As an example,

1.
```
10 HGR2: HCOLOR = 3
20 HPLOT 20,20 TO 180,20 TO 180,180 TO 20,180
TO 20,20
```

2. On one computer-screen combination the measured width of the "square" was 14.1 cm; the measured height was 16.3 cm.

3. SC = H/W = 16.3/14.1 ≈ 1.16.

4. To get a better square:
```
10 HGR2: HCOLOR = 3: SC = 1.16
20 HPLOT 20*SC,20 TO 180*SC,20 TO 180*SC,180
   TO 20*SC,180 TO 20*SC,20
30 END
```

Note that the value of SC is dependent on the computer-screen combination being used.

In many applications we need not be careful to have the horizontal and vertical scales equivalent. In general, the programs used in this book will not provide for equivalent scales. The equivalence is easily provided when desired.

CLIPPING AND VIEWPORTS

When specifying points or lines to be plotted, it is necessary to be careful to plot only those points, or parts of lines, that are visible on the display screen. The Apple BASIC command

```
HPLOT 90,25 TO 360,175
```

results in the message

```
?ILLEGAL QUANTITY ERROR
```

since the point 360,175 lies to the right of the screen boundary. In order to display the visible portion of this line segment, it is necessary to calculate, or have the computer calculate, the intersection of the line segment with the screen boundary.

In this case the equation of the line is
$Y = 25 + (X - 90)(175 - 25)/(360 - 90)$, or $Y = -25 + 5(X/9)$. The intersection with the right boundary occurs at $X = 279$. Since $Y = -25 + 5(279/9)$, we find that the intersection of the line segment with the screen boundary is at (279,130). We may thus use the command:

```
HPLOT 90,25 TO 279,130
```

CLIPPING

Clipping refers to the process of displaying visible points and parts of line segments while clipping and discarding points and parts of line segments that are beyond the screen boundaries. Clipping individual points is a relatively easy process. The coordinates of the point to be plotted are compared with the screen boundaries; if the point lies outside the screen boundaries, it is not plotted. In Applesoft BASIC,

```
100 IF X < 0 OR X > 279 OR Y < 0 OR Y > 191
    THEN 120
110 HPLOT X,Y
120 .
     .
     .
```

The clipping of line segments is a much more complex task. If one or both of the endpoints of a line segment lie off screen, it is necessary to determine the points of intersection of the line segment and the boundaries; then the points of intersection may be used to plot the visible portion of the line segment.

The plane of the display screen is divided into nine regions by the four lines that determine the screen boundaries (see Figure 4.1). Each of the two endpoints of a line segment must lie in one of the 9 regions. If both endpoints lie in the center (screen) region, the entire line segment is visible, and may be plotted. Otherwise the segment must be tested to determine whether any portion of it is visible.

A line clipping subroutine must systematically determine any points of intersection of the line segment and the screen boundaries. The seg-

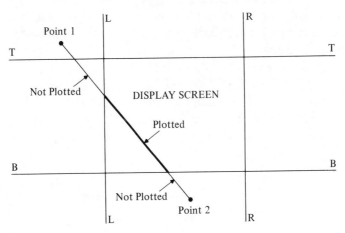

Figure 4.1

ment thus is divided into smaller portions. Any portion of the line segment which lies on the screen may be plotted; other portions are discarded.

Program 4.1 provides an example of a clipping subroutine applied
to the line segments making up a rectangle. The endpoints identified in
the DATA statements (300–330) are first classified. For endpoint
X(1),Y(1), four variables are identified. The array values L(1), R(1),
T(1), B(1) are individually set to 0 if the point X(1), Y(1) lies on the
screen side of lines L, R, T, and B, respectively. If the point lies on the
outside of the lines, the corresponding array values are set to 1. In the
same fashion values for L(2), R(2), T(2), and B(2) are identified. This
initial classification of endpoints takes place in the subroutine of lines
100 through 150.

For example, for the points shown in Figure 4.1,

$$T(1) = 1 \quad L(1) = 1 \quad B(1) = 0 \quad R(1) = 0$$
$$T(2) = 0 \quad L(2) = 0 \quad B(2) = 1 \quad R(2) = 0$$

The clipping subroutine (lines 200–250) begins by determining
whether the line segment may be discarded. If the endpoints both lie on
the outside of any boundary line, then the corresponding product
$L(1) \times L(2)$, $R(1) \times R(2)$, $T(1) \times T(2)$, or $B(1) \times B(2)$ will be 1.

Otherwise, each of the products will be 0. Thus a line segment may be discarded if the sum $L(1) \times L(2) + R(1) \times R(2) + T(1) \times T(2) + B(1) \times B(2)$ is nonzero (line 200).

Line 210 plots the line segment if both endpoints lie on the screen side of all of the boundaries. Otherwise, one of the two points (point I) is identified as lying on the outside of at least one of the boundary lines.

Lines 220 through 250 will replace point $X(I), Y(I)$ with the point of intersection of the line segment and one of the screen boundaries. The newly identified $X(I), Y(I)$ then is routed through the CLASSIFY subroutine (lines 100–150) and back to the beginning of the CLIP subroutine.

Clipping of a line segment continues until a segment is obtained which either has both endpoints on the screen (the segment is plotted by line 210), or has both endpoints on the outside of one of the screen boundaries (the segment is discarded by line 200).

The line segment PQ shown in Figure 4.2 first would be clipped to CQ, then to CE, and finally to DE, which then would be plotted.

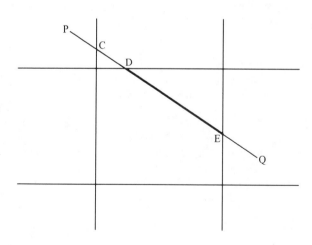

Figure 4.2

Program 4.1: CLIPPING

```
1   REM PROGRAM 4.1 (CLIPPING)
2   REM EXAMPLE OF USE OF CLIPPING SUBROUTINE
10  XR = 279:XL = 0:YT = 0:YB = 191
20  HGR2 : HCOLOR= 3:SC = 1.16
25  REM ****MAIN LOOP
30  FOR J = 1 TO 4: FOR I = 1 TO 2
40  READ X(I),Y(I): GOSUB 100
50  NEXT I
60  GOSUB 200
70  NEXT J
80  END
95  REM **** CLASSIFY SUBROUTINE
100 L(I) = 0:R(I) = 0:T(I) = 0:B(I) = 0
110  IF X(I) < XL THEN L(I) = 1
120  IF X(I) > XR THEN R(I) = 1
130  IF Y(I) < YT THEN T(I) = 1
140  IF Y(I) > YB THEN B(I) = 1
150  RETURN
190  GOSUB 100
195  REM **** CLIPPING SUBROUTINE
200  IF L(1) * L(2) + R(1) * R(2) + T(1) * T(2)
     + B(1) * B(2) < > 0 THEN RETURN
210 I = 1: IF L(I) + R(I) + T(I) + B(I) = 0
     THEN I = 2: IF L(I) + R(I) + T(I) + B(I) = 0
     THEN HPLOT X(1),Y(1) TO X(2),Y(2): RETURN
220  IF L(I) = 1 THEN Y(I) = Y(1) + (Y(2) -
     Y(1)) * (XL - X(1)) / (X(2) - X(1)):
     X(I) = XL: GOTO 190
230  IF R(I) = 1 THEN Y(I) = Y(1) + (Y(2) -
     Y(1)) * (XR - X(1)) / (X(2) - X(1)):
     X(I) = XR: GOTO 190
240  IF T(I) = 1 THEN X(I) = X(1) + (X(2) -
     X(1)) * (YT - Y(1)) / (Y(2) - Y(1)):
     Y(I) = YT: GOTO 190
250  IF B(I) = 1 THEN X(I) = X(1) + (X(2) -
     X(1)) * (YB - Y(1)) / (Y(2) - Y(1)):
     Y(I) = YB: GOTO 190
300  DATA 20,-20,300,40
310  DATA 20,-20,-10,120
320  DATA -10,120,270,180
330  DATA 300,40,270,180
```

The clipping algorithm of Program 4.1 will noticeably slow the plotting of large numbers of line segments. Because of this time consideration we will not use the algorithm if it is practical to assume that all line segments lie on the display screen. In other cases we will use faster, less accurate clipping processes in order to speed and simplify a program. (For an example, see Program 5.7.)

VIEWPORTS

The display screen is a viewport through which images can be seen. The clipping process described above allows you to discard those portions of an image that are not visible through the viewport. While we usually are interested in using all of the display screen as a viewport, there may be times when we want to use only a portion.

By resetting the variables XR, XL, YT, and YB, we may use the clipping subroutine as a viewport subroutine. For example, with $XR = 120$, $XL = 25$, $YT = 130$, and $YB = 180$, the subroutine will display only those parts of an image that are visible through a viewport in the lower left part of the display screen.

TRANSFORMATIONS

INTRODUCTION

A 20×10 rectangle may be drawn in the upper left portion of the Apple screen by program 4.2, RECTANGLE 1:

```
1    REM PROGRAM 4.2 (RECTANGLE 1)
2    REM PLOTS ONE RECTANGLE
10   HOME : HGR : HCOLOR= 3
20   HPLOT 0,0 TO 20,0 TO 20,10 TO 0,10 TO 0,0
```

or by Program 4.3, RECTANGLE 2:

```
1    REM PROGRAM 4.3 (RECTANGLE 2)
2    REM PLOTS ONE RECTANGLE
10   HOME : HGR : HCOLOR= 3
20   READ X,Y: HPLOT X,Y
30   FOR I = 1 TO 4
40   READ X,Y: HPLOT TO X,Y
50   NEXT I
60   DATA 0,0,20,0,20,10,0,10,0,0
```

While Program 4.3 is the longer it is also the more adaptable of the two. Changes in the DATA statement will result in other images of sequences of connected line segments. Of course, Program 4.2 has similar capabilities. We must look further to see the advantages of the process used in Program 4.3.

Program 4.4 generates images of eight rectangles, each derived from a common DATA statement. In contrast to Program 4.3, which reads values of X and Y, then plots a point or line segment (HPLOT TO X,Y), Program 4.4 transforms the coordinates (X,Y) to obtain the screen coordinates (SX,SY) to be plotted. The size, shape, and location of the rectangles are controlled through changes in the values of A, B, C, and D.

Two types of transformations are at work in Program 4.4, REC-TANGLES:

1. The magnitudes of coordinates are controlled by multiplication by A and C. This is referred to as *scaling* the image.

2. The location of the image is controlled by the values of B and D. This is referred to as *translating* the image.

Program 4.4: RECTANGLES

```
1    REM PROGRAM 4.4 (RECTANGLES)
2    REM PLOTS 8 RECTANGLES FROM 1 SET OF DATA
10   A = 20:B = 0:C = 10:D = 0
20    HOME : HGR : HCOLOR= 3
30    FOR J = 1 TO 8
40    READ X,Y:SX = A * X + B:SY = C * Y + D
50    HPLOT SX,SY
60    FOR I = 1 TO 4
70    READ X,Y:SX = A * X + B:SY = C * Y + D
80    HPLOT TO SX,SY
90    NEXT I
100  A = A + 15:B = B + 15:C = C + 10:D = D + 10
110   RESTORE
120   NEXT J
130   DATA 0,0,1,0,1,1,0,1,0,0
```

To become more familiar with the scaling and translation transformations, try the following:

1. Write a program that will draw eight rectangles of varying size, each with a corner in the top left corner of the screen. (Use *scaling,* not *translation.*)

2. Write a program that will draw eight rectangles, all the same size, in different regions of the screen. (Use *translation,* not *scaling.*)

Transformations are valuable in generating graphics images. While some introductory work with transformations may be pursued in the manner of Program 4.4, greater power and versatility will result from first introducing some related topics: matrices, and homogeneous coordinate representation of points.

WHAT IS A MATRIX?

A matrix is a rectangular array of numbers, such as:

$$A = \begin{pmatrix} 1 & 2 \\ 3 & 4 \end{pmatrix} \text{ or } B = \begin{pmatrix} 0 & 2 \\ 5 & -3 \end{pmatrix}$$

We can add matrices:

$$A = \begin{pmatrix} 1 & 2 \\ 3 & 4 \end{pmatrix} + \begin{pmatrix} 0 & 2 \\ 5 & -3 \end{pmatrix} = \begin{pmatrix} 1+0 & 2+2 \\ 3+5 & 4-3 \end{pmatrix} = \begin{pmatrix} 1 & 4 \\ 8 & 1 \end{pmatrix}$$

and multiply matrices:

$$\begin{pmatrix} 1 & 2 \\ 3 & 4 \end{pmatrix} \begin{pmatrix} 0 & 2 \\ 5 & -3 \end{pmatrix} = \begin{pmatrix} (1)(0)+(2)(5) & (1)(2)+(2)(-3) \\ (3)(0)+(4)(5) & (3)(2)+(4)(-3) \end{pmatrix}$$

$$= \begin{pmatrix} 10 & -4 \\ 20 & -6 \end{pmatrix}$$

A summary of matrix notation and matrix calculation is given in Appendix 4.

MATRIX REPRESENTATION OF TRANSFORMATIONS

Transformations of points in a two dimensional plane (the display screen) may be represented as products of points (1 × 2 matrices) with 2 × 2 matrices. For example, we may transform (move) a point (X,Y) to a new point (X',Y') as follows:

$$(X,Y) \begin{pmatrix} A & B \\ C & D \end{pmatrix} = (AX + CY, BX + DY) = (X', Y')$$

Thus, for each point (X,Y), we identify a transformed point

$$(X,Y)' = (X',Y') = (AX + CY, BX + DY).$$

Clearly, the effect of a transformation is determined by the choice of values for A, B, C, and D. Program 4.5 accepts values for A, B, C, and D, then shows the effect of the transformation on the points of a square. We will use the program to illustrate several transformations.

Identity

The matrix

$$\begin{pmatrix} 1 & 0 \\ 0 & 1 \end{pmatrix}$$

represents the identity transformation. Since

$$(X,Y) \begin{pmatrix} 1 & 0 \\ 0 & 1 \end{pmatrix} = (X,Y)$$

the identity transformation leaves points unchanged.

Running Program 4.5 and identifying A = 1, B = 0, C = 0, and D = 1, will result in a display of a square, modified by the identity transformation (i.e., unmodified). See Figure 4.3.

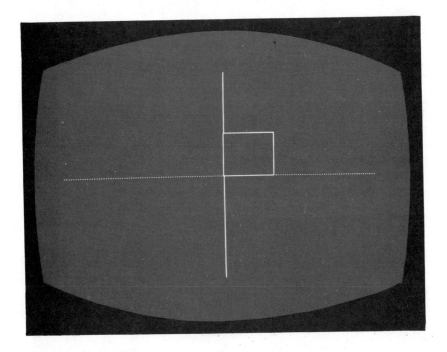

Figure 4.3

Program 4.5: MATRIX

```
1   REM PROGRAM 4.5 (MATRIX)
2   REM SHOWS EFFECT OF A 2x2 TRANSFORMATION
    MATRIX
10  CX = 140:CY = 96:SC = 1.16
20  XR = 279:XL = 0:YT = 0:YB = 191
30  TEXT : HOME
40  INPUT " A = ";A
50  INPUT " B = ";B
60  INPUT " C = ";C
70  INPUT " D = ";D
80  HGR : HCOLOR= 6
90  HPLOT 0,96 TO 279,96: HPLOT 140,0 TO 140,
    191
100  HCOLOR= 3
110  FOR S = 1 TO 4
120  FOR I = 1 TO 2
130  READ X,Y
140 TX = A * X + C * Y:TY = B * X + D * Y
150 X(I) = SC * TX + CX:Y(I) = CY - TY
160  GOSUB 300
170  NEXT I
180  GOSUB 380
190  NEXT S: RESTORE
200  VTAB 21: PRINT "A B"; TAB( 11);A;
    TAB(20);B
210  VTAB 22: PRINT TAB( 8);"="
220  VTAB 23: PRINT "C D"; TAB( 11);C;
    TAB(20);D
230  VTAB 24: PRINT "PRESS 'N' FOR NEW MATRIX;
    'ESC' TO END";
240  VTAB 10: GET A$: IF A$ = "N" THEN 30
250  IF ASC (A$) = 27 THEN TEXT : HOME : END
260  GOTO 240
270  DATA 0,0,40,0,40,0,40,40,40,40,0,40,0,40,
    0,0
280  END
290  REM **** CLASSIFY SUBROUTINE
300 L(I) = 0:R(I) = 0:T(I) = 0:B(I) = 0
310  IF X(I) < XL THEN L(I) = 1
320  IF X(I) > XR THEN R(I) = 1
330  IF Y(I) < YT THEN T(I) = 1
340  IF Y(I) > YB THEN B(I) = 1
350  RETURN
```

(continued)

```
360   GOSUB 300
370   REM **** CLIPPING SUBROUTINE
380   IF L(1) * L(2) + R(1) * R(2) + T(1) * T(2)
      + B(1) * B(2) < > 0 THEN RETURN
390 I = 1: IF L(I) + R(I) + T(I) + B(I) = 0
      THEN I = 2: IF L(I) + R(I) + T(I) + B(I) = 0
      THEN HPLOT X(1),Y(1) TO X(2),Y(2): RETURN
400   IF L(I) = 1 THEN Y(I) = Y(1) + (Y(2) -
      Y(1)) * (XL - X(1)) / (X(2) - X(1)):
      X(I) = XL: GOTO 360
410   IF R(I) = 1 THEN Y(I) = Y(1) + (Y(2) -
      Y(1)) * (XR - X(1)) / (X(2) - X(1)):
      X(I) = XR: GOTO 360
420   IF T(I) = 1 THEN X(I) = X(1) + (X(2) -
      X(1)) * (YT - Y(1)) / (Y(2) - Y(1)):
      Y(I) = YT: GOTO 360
430   IF B(I) = 1 THEN X(I) = X(1) + (X(2) -
      X(1)) * (YB - Y(1)) / (Y(2) - Y(1)):
      Y(I) = YB: GOTO 360
```

Scaling

Scaling may be controlled by a diagonal matrix. Note that:

$$(X,Y) \begin{pmatrix} A & 0 \\ 0 & D \end{pmatrix} = (AX, DY).$$

The diagonal entries of the matrix thus may be used to provide independent scaling in the direction of each of the coordinate axes. For example, we may scale (stretch) points in the X direction by a factor of 2 through multiplication by

$$\begin{pmatrix} 2 & 0 \\ 0 & 1 \end{pmatrix}$$

(See Figure 4.4).

Run Program 4.5, identifying $A = 2$, $B = 0$, $C = 0$, and $D = 1$.

To scale (shrink) points in the direction of the Y axis by a factor of 1/5, multiply by

$$\begin{pmatrix} 1 & 0 \\ 0 & .2 \end{pmatrix}$$

(figure 4.5). Overall scaling is provided by the matrix

$$\begin{pmatrix} K & 0 \\ 0 & K \end{pmatrix}$$

In Program 4.5, try a variety of values for A and D. Keep B = 0 and C = 0.

Reflection

Reflection of an object through the Y axis or X axis refers to the process of generating a mirror image of the object on the opposite side of the respective axis. A little thought will show that the matrices

$$\begin{pmatrix} -1 & 0 \\ 0 & 1 \end{pmatrix} \text{ and } \begin{pmatrix} 1 & 0 \\ 0 & -1 \end{pmatrix}$$

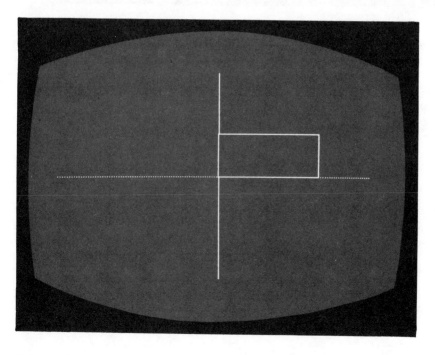

Figure 4.4

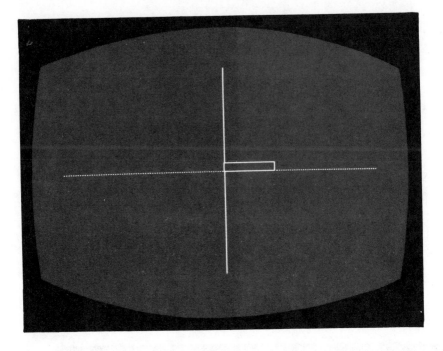

Figure 4.5

represent reflections through the Y axis and X axis respectively. Transformation through the origin (0,0) is represented by the matrix

$$\begin{pmatrix} -1 & 0 \\ 0 & -1 \end{pmatrix}$$

Note that these reflections are essentially scalings for which the scale factor is negative.

Reflection of images through other lines is possible, but the matrices, in general, are not so easy to identify.

Shear

The effect of the matrix

$$\begin{pmatrix} 1 & 1.5 \\ 0 & 1 \end{pmatrix}$$

on the points of the square of Program 4.5 is shown in Figure 4.6. Algebraically,

$$(X',Y') = (X,Y) \begin{pmatrix} 1 & 1.5 \\ 0 & 1 \end{pmatrix} = (X, 1.5X + Y).$$

The transformation is referred to as a Y shear (or shear in the direction of Y). An X shear is represented by matrices of the form:

$$\begin{pmatrix} 1 & 0 \\ C & 1 \end{pmatrix}$$

Run Program 4.5, identifying A, B, C, and D so as to define several shears.

Rotation

The points of an image may be rotated counterclockwise by multiplying the points by the matrix:

$$\begin{pmatrix} \cos\theta & \sin\theta \\ -\sin\theta & \cos\theta \end{pmatrix}$$

NOTE: The symbol θ is the Greek letter *theta*. Many math books use such letters for angles, although they could just as well use English letters (e.g., SINA). In BASIC, we'll use TH or THETA instead of θ. We'll also use parentheses, so $\sin\theta$ will be written in BASIC programs as SIN(TH).

The effect of the components of the matrices for scaling, reflection, and shear were fairly easy to identify. The components of the rotation matrix are less obvious. First note that

$$(A,\ B) = (1,\ 0) \begin{pmatrix} A & B \\ C & D \end{pmatrix}$$

and

$$(C,\ D) = (0,\ 1) \begin{pmatrix} A & B \\ C & D \end{pmatrix}$$

Thus, the first row of the matrix of a transformation shows the effect the transformation has on the point (1,0), and the second row of the matrix shows the effect the transformation has on the point (0,1).

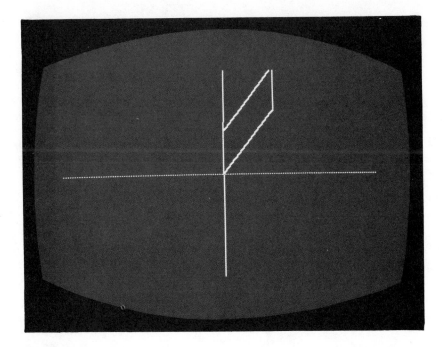

Figure 4.6

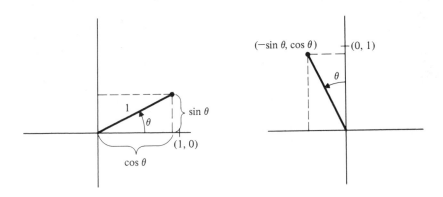

Figure 4.7

From trigonometry we observe that the rotation of (1,0) through a counterclockwise angle θ yields the point (COSθ,SINθ), while rotation of (0,1) through the same angle yields ($-$SINθ,COSθ).

NOTE: The trigonometry functions SIN and COS may be used to represent ratios of sides of a right triangle. These right triangle relationships provide the justification for the above results.

$$SIN(A) = \frac{a}{c}$$

$$COS(A) = \frac{b}{c}$$

The matrix which represents the rotation is thus

$$\begin{pmatrix} COS\theta & SIN\theta \\ -SIN\theta & COS\theta \end{pmatrix}$$

Figure 4.8 shows the result of using Program 4.5 with A = COS(.5) = .878, B = SIN(.5) = .479, C = −SIN(.5) = −.479, and D = COS(.5) = .878.

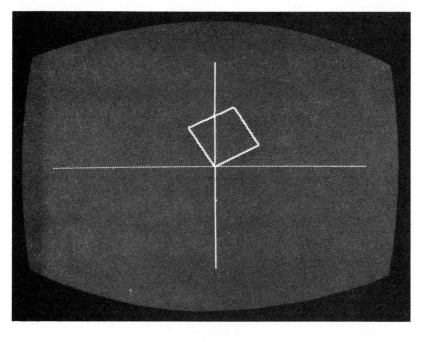

Figure 4.8

> **NOTE:** In BASIC, angles must be measured in *radians*. A radian is about 57.3 degrees. The exact relation is that 2π radians $= 360°$, so 1 radian $= 360/6.2832° = 57.2956°$. A more complete description of radian measure is given in Appendix 5.

We now may use matrices to represent the following transformations: identity, scale, reflection, shear, and rotation. Still others may be derived, either through the process used to justify the rotation matrix, or by combining the existing transformation matrices.

Example: Define transformation T to consist of rotating through a counterclockwise angle of $\theta = .4$ radians followed by scaling the X component by a factor of 2.

The rotation may be accomplished by

$$(X',Y') = (X,Y)\begin{pmatrix} \text{COS}(.4) & \text{SIN}(.4) \\ -\text{SIN}(.4) & \text{COS}(.4) \end{pmatrix}$$

and the scaling by

$$(X'',Y'') = (X',Y')\begin{pmatrix} 2 & 0 \\ 0 & 1 \end{pmatrix}$$

or, replacing (X',Y'),

$$(X'',Y'') = \left[(X,Y)\begin{pmatrix} \text{COS}(.4) & \text{SIN}(.4) \\ -\text{SIN}(.4) & \text{COS}(.4) \end{pmatrix}\right]\begin{pmatrix} 2 & 0 \\ 0 & 1 \end{pmatrix}$$

$$= (X,Y)\left[\begin{pmatrix} \text{COS}(.4) & \text{SIN}(.4) \\ -\text{SIN}(.4) & \text{COS}(.4) \end{pmatrix}\begin{pmatrix} 2 & 0 \\ 0 & 1 \end{pmatrix}\right]$$

$$= (X,Y)\begin{pmatrix} 2\text{COS}(.4) & \text{SIN}(.4) \\ -2\text{SIN}(.4) & \text{COS}(.4) \end{pmatrix}$$

The matrix of transformation T is

$$\begin{pmatrix} 2\text{COS}(.4) & \text{SIN}(.4) \\ -2\text{SIN}(.4) & \text{COS}(.4) \end{pmatrix} \approx \begin{pmatrix} 1.842 & .389 \\ -.779 & .921 \end{pmatrix}$$

> **NOTE:** In BASIC, 2COS(.4) would have to be written as
>
> ```
> 2*COS(.4)
> ```

The matrix of a series of sequentially applied transformations is the product of the matrices of the transformations. When calculating the product, one must be careful to have the matrices in the proper order. In general, matrix products are *not* commutative (i.e., the principle AB = BA does not always hold). Note that we get a transformation T^* that is very different from T if we first scale the X component by a factor of 2, then rotate through a counterclockwise angle of $\theta = .4$.

Suggestion: Show that the matrix of the transformation T^* described above is

$$\begin{pmatrix} 1.842 & .779 \\ -.389 & .921 \end{pmatrix}.$$

One serious deficiency exists in our present ability to represent transformations by matrices: each of the transformations we have considered

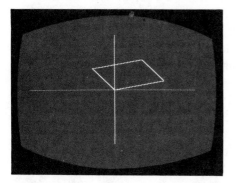

Figure 4.9a) Effect of T on the square of Program 4.5

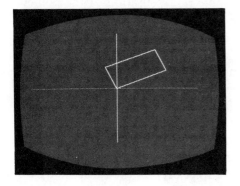

Figure 4.9b) Effect of T* on the square of Program 4.5

is centered at (0,0). Stated differently, if each of the transformations is applied to (0,0), the result is (0,0); the point (0,0) is invariant under the transformations. In the long term, this is not a healthy position. Rotation through a counterclockwise angle θ is rotation about the point (0,0). Rotation about other points is not available. Similarly, reflections may be through the X axis, the Y axis, or the origin, but not through other points or lines.

As a step in developing the ability to remove the zero-centered nature of transformations, we now will introduce homogeneous coordinates.

HOMOGENEOUS COORDINATES

The two-coordinate representation of points is a convenient and efficient reference system for points in a plane. A reference point (the origin) is established, and a pair of directed perpendicular lines intersecting at the origin is chosen as the coordinate axes. Each point in the plane is then associated with the ordered pair of its directed distances from these coordinate axes.

The homogeneous coordinate representation of points in a plane associates, with each point (A,B), an ordered triple (P,Q,R), with P, Q, and R chosen so that $A = P/R$ and $B = Q/R$.

The homogeneous coordinate representation of a point is not unique. The point (2,5), for example, may be identified as (4,10,2), $(-20, -50, -10)$, (2.1,5.25,1.05), or (2,5,1), among others. We will use the representation (2,5,1) and, in general, will refer to (A,B,1) as the normalized homogeneous coordinate representation of the point (A,B). As a result, the point with homogeneous coordinates (P,Q,R) has normalized form (P/R,Q/R,1) and Cartesian coordinates (P/R,Q/R).

When using the normalized homogeneous coordinates (A,B,1) of the point (A,B), we may consider the third coordinate to be an appendage. While unnecessary at times, homogeneous coordinates add to our ability to represent transformations as matrix products.

The most obvious effect of the introduction of homogeneous coordinates is that our previous matrix representations of transformations must be upgraded. This is easily done, since each of the earlier matrices:

$$\begin{pmatrix} A & B \\ C & D \end{pmatrix} \text{ becomes } \begin{pmatrix} A & B & 0 \\ C & D & 0 \\ 0 & 0 & 1 \end{pmatrix}$$

Translation

The problem which led to the introduction of homogeneous coordinates is easily addressed by adding *translation* to the list of transformations. By "translate through (H,K)" we intend that the points of an object be moved horizontally through H units and vertically through K units. While translations previously could not be represented by matrices, homogeneous coordinate representation of points adds the transformation matrix:

$$\begin{pmatrix} 1 & 0 & 0 \\ 0 & 1 & 0 \\ H & K & 1 \end{pmatrix}$$

Multiplying the point (X,Y,1) by this matrix yields (X + H,Y + K,1).

COMBINATIONS OF TRANSFORMATIONS

Many transformations cannot be represented by one of the matrices described above, but are combinations of several. For example, the rotation transformation matrix represents a rotation about the origin through a counterclockwise angle θ. We will now obtain the matrix of a rotation about the point (20,20) through a counterclockwise angle of 30°.

The rotation transformation matrix represents a rotation which is centered at (0,0). A rotation centered at (20,30) may be effected by

1. Translating (20,30) to the origin (translating the origin to $(-20, -30)$. The matrix of this transformation is

$$T = \begin{pmatrix} 1 & 0 & 0 \\ 0 & 1 & 0 \\ -20 & -30 & 1 \end{pmatrix}.$$

2. Rotation through 30°. The transformation matrix is

$$R = \begin{pmatrix} \text{COS } 30° & \text{SIN } 30° & 0 \\ -\text{SIN } 30° & \text{COS } 30° & 0 \\ 0 & 0 & 1 \end{pmatrix} = \begin{pmatrix} .866 & .5 & 0 \\ -.5 & .866 & 0 \\ 0 & 0 & 1 \end{pmatrix}.$$

3. Translate (0,0) to (20,30) in order to restore the system to its original position:

$$T^* = \begin{pmatrix} 1 & 0 & 0 \\ 0 & 1 & 0 \\ 20 & 30 & 1 \end{pmatrix}.$$

Thus a point (X,Y) may be rotated through 30° about the point (20,30) to a position (X′,Y′) by the sequence $(X′,Y′,1) = (X,Y,1)TRT^*$.

Rather than multiplying (X,Y,1) by the three matrices, we might first multiply the matrices together to obtain $M = TRT^*$. Then, $(X′,Y′,1) = (X,Y,1)M$. In this case,

$$M = \begin{pmatrix} .866 & .5 & 0 \\ -.5 & .866 & 0 \\ 17.68 & -5.98 & 1 \end{pmatrix}$$

and $(X′,Y′,1) = (.866X - .5Y + 17.68, .5X + .866Y - 5.98, 1)$.

Products of the transformation matrices for homogeneous coordinates will always be of the form

$$\begin{pmatrix} A & B & 0 \\ C & D & 0 \\ H & K & 1 \end{pmatrix}$$

and the effect of the transformations on a point (X,Y) may be described by

$$(X′,Y′,1) = (X,Y,1) \begin{pmatrix} A & B & 0 \\ C & D & 0 \\ H & K & 1 \end{pmatrix}$$

or $X′ = AX + CY + H$ and $Y′ = BX + DY + K$.

To illustrate the effects of such transformations, we may use Program 4.6, which is a modification of Program 4.5. Then, by providing values for A, B, C, D, H, and K, we will see the effect of a transformation on a square. Figure 4.10 shows the effect of the transformation of the example above.

Program 4.6: HOMOGENEOUS COORDINATES

```
1    REM PROGRAM 4.6 (HOMOGENEOUS COORDINATES)
2    REM ILLUSTRATES EFFECT OF 3x3 TRANSFORMATION
     MATRIX
10   CX = 140:CY = 96:SC = 1.16
20   XR = 279:XL = 0:YT = 0:YB = 191
30   TEXT : HOME
40   INPUT " A = ";A
50   INPUT " B = ";B
60   INPUT " C = ";C
70   INPUT " D = ";D
80   INPUT " H = ";H
```

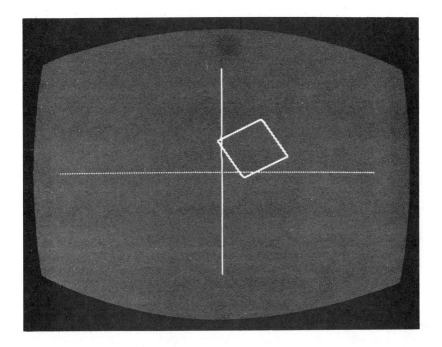

Figure 4.10

```
90    INPUT " K = ";K
100   HGR : HCOLOR= 6
110   HPLOT 0,96 TO 279,96: HPLOT 140,0
      TO 140,191
120   HCOLOR= 3
130   FOR S = 1 TO 4
140   FOR I = 1 TO 2
150   READ X,Y
160 TX = A * X + C * Y + H:
    TY = B * X + D * Y + K
170 X(I) = SC * TX + CX:Y(I) = CY - TY
180   GOSUB 320
190   NEXT I
200   GOSUB 400
210   NEXT S: RESTORE
220   VTAB 21: PRINT "A   B"; TAB( 11);A; TAB
      ( 20); B
230   VTAB 22: PRINT "C   D"; TAB( 8);"=";  TAB
      ( 11);C;  TAB( 20);D
240   VTAB 23: PRINT "H   K"; TAB( 11);H; TAB
      ( 20);K
```

(continued)

```
250    VTAB 24: PRINT "PRESS 'N' FOR NEW MATRIX;
       'ESC' TO END";
260    VTAB 10: GET A$: IF A$ = "N" THEN 30
270    IF ASC (A$) = 27 THEN TEXT : HOME : END
280    GOTO 260
290    DATA 0,0,40,0,40,0,40,40,40,40,0,40,0,40, 0,0
300    END
310    REM **** CLASSIFY SUBROUTINE
320    L(I) = 0:R(I) = 0:T(I) = 0:B(I) = 0
330    IF X(I) < XL THEN L(I) = 1
340    IF X(I) > XR THEN R(I) = 1
350    IF Y(I) < YT THEN T(I) = 1
360    IF Y(I) > YB THEN B(I) = 1
370    RETURN
380    GOSUB 320
390    REM **** CLIPPING SUBROUTINE
400    IF L(1) * L(2) + R(1) * R(2) + T(1) *
       T(2) + B(1) * B(2) < > 0 THEN RETURN
410    I = 1: IF L(I) + R(I) + T(I) + B(I) = 0
       THEN I = 2: IF L(I) + R(I) + T(I) + B(I) = 0
       THEN HPLOT X(1),Y(1) TO X(2),Y(2): RETURN
420    IF L(I) = 1 THEN Y(I) = Y(1) + (Y(2) -
       Y(1)) * (XL - X(1)) / (X(2) - X(1)):X(I) =
       XL: GOTO 380
430    IF R(I) = 1 THEN Y(I) = Y(1) + (Y(2) -
       Y(1)) * (XR - X(1)) / (X(2) - X(1)):X(I) =
       XR: GOTO 380
440    IF T(I) = 1 THEN X(I) = X(1) + (X(2) -
       X(1)) * (YT - Y(1)) / (Y(2) - Y(1)):
       Y(I) = YT: GOTO 380
450    IF B(I) = 1 THEN X(I) = X(1) + (X(2) -
       X(1)) * (YB - Y(1)) / (Y(2) - Y(1)):Y(I) =
       YB: GOTO 380
```

As a second example of the use of transformation matrices, we will work through the development of a program which draws a sequence of nested hexagons to generate the image in Figure 4.11.

We will center the hexagon at the origin (0,0) and provide one of the six vertices. Since consecutive vertices of the hexagon are separated by a central angle of 60°, the second vertex will be derived by rotating the first through 60°. The third then will be calculated by rotating the second vertex through 60°. In this manner, we will obtain vertices 4, 5, and 6.

The matrix of the rotation transformation is

$$R = \begin{pmatrix} \cos\theta & \sin\theta & 0 \\ -\sin\theta & \cos\theta & 0 \\ 0 & 0 & 1 \end{pmatrix}.$$

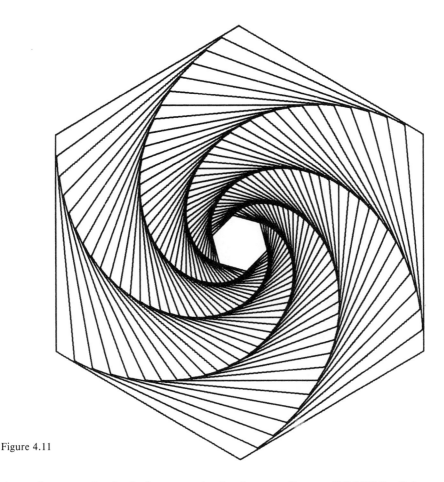

Figure 4.11

At each stage of calculation, we obtain the coordinates (XN,YN) of the next vertex from the coordinates of the current vertex by (XN,YN,1) = (X,Y,1)R, so that

```
XN = X*COS(TH) - Y*SIN(TH)
YN = X*SIN(TH) + Y*COS(TH)
```

Since the calculations of sine and cosine are time consuming, we will do this only once, identifying C = COS(60°) and S = SIN(60°). The calculation of (XN,YN) then becomes:

```
XN = X*C-Y*S
YN = X*S+Y*C
```

Locating the hexagon's center at (0,0) is convenient for use of the rotation transformation, but inconvenient for use with the Apple II display

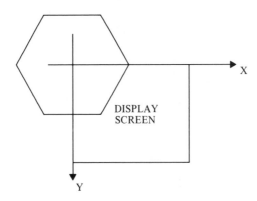

Figure 4.12

screen: most of the vertices will be off-screen, as indicated in Figure 4.12.

Before the points of the hexagon may be plotted, they must be translated to an onscreen location. Each point may be translated through (CX, CY) by multiplication by the matrix

$$\begin{pmatrix} 1 & 0 & 0 \\ 0 & 1 & 0 \\ CX & CY & 1 \end{pmatrix}.$$

At this point we may draw a single hexagon using the following program:

Program 4.7: HEXAGON

```
1    REM PROGRAM 4.7 (HEXAGON)
2    REM DRAWS A SINGLE HEXAGON
10   PI = 3.14159
20   C = COS (PI / 3):S = SIN (PI/3)
40   X = 95:Y = 0:CX = 140:CY = 96:SC = 1.16
50    HGR2 : HCOLOR= 3
70    FOR I = 0 TO 6
80   SX = X * SC + CX:SY = CY + Y
90    IF I = 0 THEN HPLOT SX,SY
100   HPLOT TO SX,SY
110  XN = X * C - Y * S:Y = X * S + Y *
     C:X = XN
120   NEXT I
```

We will add program lines to provide a sequence of hexagons nested within this first one, each slightly smaller than the previous one, and each slightly rotated.

The size of the hexagons may be controlled by multiplication by the matrix

$$\begin{pmatrix} SF & 0 & 0 \\ 0 & SF & 0 \\ 0 & 0 & 1 \end{pmatrix}$$

where SF is a scale factor of our choice. To rotate each hexagon slightly, we again will use the rotation transformation matrix with a new value for Θ.

The transition from one hexagon to the next (scaling, rotation) is effected by

$$(XN,YN,1) = (X,Y,1) \begin{pmatrix} SF & 0 & 0 \\ 0 & SF & 0 \\ 0 & 0 & 1 \end{pmatrix} \begin{pmatrix} COS\theta & SIN\theta & 0 \\ -SIN\theta & COS\theta & 0 \\ 0 & 0 & 1 \end{pmatrix}$$

or

```
XN = X*SF*COS(TH)  -  Y*SF*SIN(TH)
YN = X*SF*SIN(TH)  +  Y*SF*COS(TH)
```

Having identified one point on the next hexagon, we then use Program 4.7 to draw the hexagon.

Program 4.8: HEXAGON DESIGN

The sequence of hexagons is drawn by Program 4.8.

```
1   REM PROGRAM 4.8 (HEXAGON DESIGN)
2   REM DRAWS A SEQUENCE OF SPIRALLING HEXAGONS
10  PI = 3.14159
20  C = COS (PI / 3):S = SIN (PI / 3)
30  C1 = COS (PI / 36):S1 = SIN (PI / 36):SF =
    .95
40  X = 95:Y = 0:CX = 140:CY = 96:SC = 1.16
50   HGR2 : HCOLOR= 3
60   FOR J = 1 TO 40
70   FOR I = 0 TO 6
80  SX = X * SC + CX:SY = CY + Y
90   IF I = 0 THEN HPLOT SX,SY
```

(continued)

```
100   HPLOT TO SX,SY
110 XN = X * C - Y * S:Y = X * S + Y * C:X = XN
120   NEXT I
130 XN = SF * (X * C1 - Y * S1):Y = SF *
      (X * S1 + Y * C1):X = XN
140   NEXT J
```

NOTES AND SUGGESTIONS

1. Adapt Program 4.7 so that it will draw a pentagon or an octagon. Modify it again to ask for N, the number of sides, then draw an N-sided polygon.

2. Write a program to draw your initials on the graphics screen. Then, by using appropriate transformations, have the initials drawn:

a. at 3 locations on the screen (use translation);

b. rotated through 45° (use rotation);

c. upside down (use reflection);

d. in three sizes (use scaling).

3. Start with a program that draws a design on the screen (such as Program 4.8). Modify it to provide a viewport feature. Arrange it so that the design is drawn twice (without erasing in between):

a. with the viewport in the upper right portion of the screen, say (XR = 250, XL = 140, YT = 5, YB = 80);

b. with the viewport in the lower left portion of the screen, say (XR = 130, XL = 90, YT = 90, YB = 150).

Chapter 5
Analytic Geometry And Computer Graphics

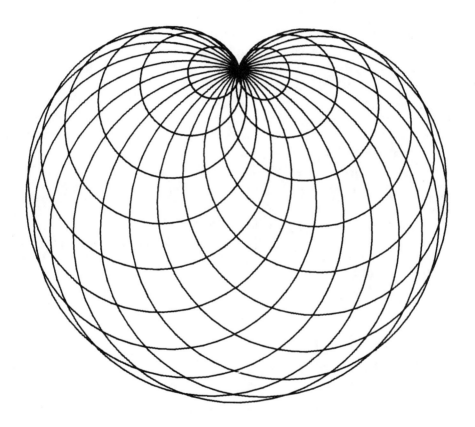

Figure 5.1

One of the topics in high school mathematics is the sketching of graphs. It is a part of analytic geometry, the study of processes for stating mathematical relationships both algebraically (or analytically) and graphically.

The pages ahead will mimic portions of a course in analytic geometry, but will leave the calculation and plotting to the computer while we focus on the design.

COORDINATE AXES

Analytic geometry is often called "coordinate geometry" because of its reliance on a coordinate axis system. Students in analytic geometry begin by drawing a pair of directed perpendicular lines intersecting in the middle of the page, as suggested in Figure 5.2.

A coordinate axis system is provided in the Apple high resolution display screen, but its location and orientation differs somewhat from that which is shown below. The Apple coordinate system is shown in Figure 5.3.

We can reorient and relocate points so that they may be identified relative to a centrally located, Y-upward, X-rightward coordinate system.

First, provide the lines for the coordinate axes:

`HPLOT 140,0 TO 140,191: HPLOT 0,96 TO 279,96`

Next, identify the center of the coordinate system:

`CX=140:  CY=96`

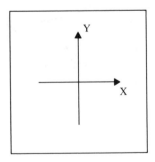

Figure 5.2

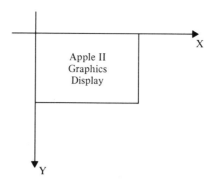

Figure 5.3

Then replace HPLOT X,Y with HPLOT X + CX,CY − Y for all future plots. The HPLOT command now will accept points (X,Y) with −140 ≤ X ≤ 139 and −96 ≤ Y ≤ 95.

Note that by replacing HPLOT X,Y with HPLOT X + CX, CY − Y, we have effected a transformation: reflection through the X axis, followed by translation through CX,CY. The matrix of the reflection is

$$\begin{pmatrix} 1 & 0 & 0 \\ 0 & -1 & 0 \\ 0 & 0 & 1 \end{pmatrix}$$

and the matrix of the translation is

$$\begin{pmatrix} 1 & 0 & 0 \\ 0 & 1 & 0 \\ CX & CY & 1 \end{pmatrix}.$$

The product of the matrices is

$$\begin{pmatrix} 1 & 0 & 0 \\ 0 & -1 & 0 \\ CX & CY & 1 \end{pmatrix}$$

and

$$(X,Y,1) \begin{pmatrix} 1 & 0 & 0 \\ 0 & -1 & 0 \\ CX & CY & 1 \end{pmatrix} = (X + CX, CY - Y, 1).$$

For specified values of X and Y, we may identify the screen coordinates (SX,SY) relative to the centered coordinate system by calculating SX = X + CX and SY = CY − Y or, if we wish to use a scaling factor SC, SX = SC ∗ X + CX and SY = CY − Y. We will use this latter form for most of the example programs in this chapter.

LINES

Aside from the point, the simplest geometric object is the line, algebraically represented by Y = MX + B. M is the slope of the line, providing a measure of its steepness; B is the value of Y at the point of intersection of the line and the Y axis. The following brief program will sketch the graph of Y = .4X + 20 on the coordinate axis system described above.

Program 5.1: LINES

```
1    REM PROGRAM 5.1 (LINES)
2    REM LINE Y = MX+B
10    HGR2 : HCOLOR= 2
20    HPLOT 140,0 TO 140,191: HPLOT 0,96 TO 279,96
30    HCOLOR= 3:CX = 140:CY = 96
40   X = -140:Y = .4 * X + 20
50   SX = X + CX:SY = CY - Y
60    HPLOT SX,SY
70   X = 139:Y = .4 * X + 20
80   SX = X + CX:SY = CY - Y
90    HPLOT TO SX,SY
```

Program 5.1 functions adequately for the line in question. However, because we have not used a scaling factor SC, the line may not appear to have the proper slope. Furthermore, a line such as Y = 2X + 20 would identify off-screen points for X = −140 and X = 139. Some form of clipping is in order. The clipping process of Chapter 4 works well in this case. With the essential portions of Program 4.1 added, the line generating program is as follows:

Program 5.2: CLIPPED LINE

```
1    REM PROGRAM 5.2 (CLIPPED LINE)
2    REM ILLUSTRATES USE OF LINE CLIPPING
     SUBROUTINE
10   XR = 279:XL = 0:YT = 0:YB = 191
```

```
20   HGR2 : HCOLOR = 2:SC = 1.16
30   HPLOT 140,0 TO 140,191: HPLOT 0,96 TO 279,96
40   HCOLOR= 3:CX = 140:CY = 96
50   I = 1:X = - 140:Y = .4 * X + 20:X(I) = SC * X
     + CX: Y(I) = CY - Y: GOSUB 100
60   I = 2:X = 139:Y = .4 * X + 20:X(I) = SC * X +
     CX: Y(I) = CY - Y: GOSUB 100
70   GOSUB 200
80   END
95   REM **** CLASSIFY SUBROUTINE
100  L(I) = 0:R(I) = 0:T(I) = 0:B(I) = 0
110   IF X(I) < XL THEN L(I) = 1
120   IF X(I) > XR THEN R(I) = 1
130   IF Y(I) < YT THEN T(I) = 1
140   IF Y(I) > YB THEN B(I) = 1
150   RETURN
190   GOSUB 100
195   REM **** CLIPPING SUBROUTINE
200   IF L(1) * L(2) + R(1) * R(2) + T(1) * T(2)
      + B(1) * B(2) < > 0 THEN RETURN
210  I = 1: IF L(I) + R(I) + T(I) + B(I) = 0 THEN
     I = 2: IF L(I) + R(I) + T(I) + B(I) = 0 THEN
     HPLOT X(1),Y(1) TO X(2),Y(2): RETURN
220   IF L(I) = 1 THEN Y(I) = Y(1) + (Y(2) -
      Y(1)) * (XL - X(1)) / (X(2) - X(1)):X(I) =
      XL: GOTO 190
230   IF R(I) = 1 THEN Y(I) = Y(1) + (Y(2) -
      Y(1)) * (XR - X(1)) / (X(2) - X(1)):X(I) =
      XR: GOTO 190
240   IF T(I) = 1 THEN X(I) = X(1) + (X(2) -
      X(1)) * (YT - Y(1)) / (Y(2) - Y(1)):Y(I) =
      YT: GOTO 190
250   IF B(I) = 1 THEN X(I) = X(1) + (X(2) -
      X(1)) * (YB - Y(1)) / (Y(2) - Y(1)):Y(I) =
      YB: GOTO 190
```

Further consideration of lines may not seem necessary. The algebraic representation of a line $Y = MX + B$, together with the command HPLOT X1,Y1 TO X2,Y2, provide means of identifying and drawing lines quickly and easily. However, there are times when it is preferable to draw a line slowly, or to have an object move along a linear path. In such cases it is necessary to have a way of identifying intermediate points of a line. Program 5.3 illustrates how this may be done.

Program 5.3: LINE

```
1    REM PROGRAM 5.3 (LINE)
2    REM DRAWS LINE SLOWLY
10   HGR2 : HCOLOR= 3
20  X1 = 10:Y1 = 150:X2 = 250:Y2 = 50
30  DX = X2 - X1:DY = Y2 - Y1
40   HPLOT X1,Y1
50   FOR T = 0 TO 1 STEP .001
60   HPLOT TO X1 + T * DX,Y1 + T * DY
70   NEXT T
```

In drawing from (X1,Y1) to (X2,Y2) it is necessary for X to change by an amount DX = X2 − X1, and for Y to change by an amount DY = Y2 − Y1. Rather than have the changes occur all at once (as in HPLOT X1,Y1 TO X2,Y2), the loop in lines 50 through 70 takes the changes in 1000 small increments. Control of the step size in this loop provides control of the rate of movement along the line.

CIRCLES

A circle is described as the set of all points (X,Y) at a fixed distance (R) from the center (H,K). Algebraically, we have $(X - H)^2 + (Y - K)^2 = R^2$. For a circle with its center at (0,0), the equation becomes

$$X^2 + Y^2 = R^2 \qquad \text{(Equation 5.1)}$$

There are several methods of using this relationship between X and Y to generate the image of a circle on the graphics screen. Three are presented below.

RECTANGULAR COORDINATE METHOD

The relation $X^2 + Y^2 = R^2$ may be decomposed into the two functions $YP = \sqrt{R^2 - X^2}$ and $YN = -\sqrt{R^2 - X^2}$. The following program will generate a sketch of the circle $X^2 + Y^2 = 8100$, using the above two functions:

Program 5.4: CIRCLE 1

```
1    REM PROGRAM 5.4 (CIRCLE 1)
2    REM RECTANGULAR COORDINATE CIRCLE
10   CX = 140:CY = 96
20   DEF FN YP(X) = SQR (8100 - X * X)
```

```
30    DEF FN YN(X) = -SQR (8100 - X * X)
40    HGR2 : HCOLOR= 3
50    X = 90:Y = 0:SX = X + CX:SY = CY - Y
60    HPLOT SX,SY
70    FOR X = 80 TO -90 STEP -10
80    Y = FN YP(X)
90    SX = X + CX:SY = CY - Y
100   HPLOT TO SX,SY
110   NEXT X
120   FOR X = - 80 TO 90 STEP 10
130   Y = FN YN(X)
140   SX = X + CX:SY = CY - Y
150   HPLOT TO SX,SY
160   NEXT X
170   END
```

Two features of the image should attract immediate attention:

1. Scaling. The circle does not appear "circular." The fault lies with the Apple high resolution screen. (See Chapter 4 for a discussion.) The cure is to multiply the X coordinate of point (X,Y) by a scaling factor before plotting.

2. Angularity. The program draws an upper semicircle (lines 50–110) and a lower semicircle (lines 120–160). The ends of each of these semicircles have an angular appearance. One cure for the problem is to choose a smaller step size for the point generating loop, thus having a larger number of points calculated. This will result in a smoother circle. Unfortunately, some time will be wasted in calculating additional points for the middle sections of the semicircles, which already have a smooth appearance.

    The fault for the angularity lies with the point generating loops, which space points at equal distances as measured by increments in the X-coordinates, rather than at equal distances around the arc of the circle. To see more clearly the lack of uniform spacing, replace lines 100 and 150 with

```
100 HPLOT SX,SY
150 HPLOT SX,SY
```

POINT GENERATION BY ANGULAR INCREMENTS

The angularity in the image generated by the above program resulted from calculating points which were not evenly spaced around the arc of the circle. We consider here a technique which provides for equally spaced points.

From trigonometry, we have, for a point (X,Y) on the circle $X^2 + Y^2 = R^2$,

$$X = RCOS(\theta)$$
$$Y = RSIN(\theta) \qquad \text{(Equations 5.2)}$$

with θ measured as indicated in Figure 5.4.

Program 5.5 makes use of these formulas to sketch a circle using equally spaced points.

Program 5.5: CIRCLE 2

```
1    REM PROGRAM 5.5 (CIRCLE 2)
2    REM DRAWS CIRCLE USING ANGULAR INCREMENTS
10   CX = 140:CY = 96:SC = 1.16:FL = 0:R = 90
20   HGR2: HCOLOR= 3
30   FOR T = 0 TO 6.4 STEP .3
40   X = R * COS (T):Y = R * SIN (T)
50   SX = SC * X + CX:SY = CY - Y
60   IF FL = 1 THEN 80
70   HPLOT SX,SY:FL = 1
80   HPLOT TO SX,SY
90   NEXT T
```

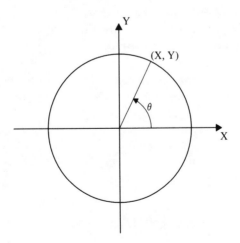

Figure 5.4

The choice of SC (line 10) is dependent on the equipment in use (see Chapter 4).

Before the command HPLOT TO may be used to draw a line segment, it is necessary that HPLOT or a previous HPLOT TO provide a point for the beginning of the line segment. In Program 5.3, an initial HPLOT was provided in line 60. Program 5.4 used a flag (variable FL) to identify whether an initial point had been provided (FL = 1) or not (FL = 0). This allows the point generating loop to handle all plotting.

RECURSIVE GENERATION OF POINTS

Program 1.7 in Chapter 1 sketched a circle. The process used is derived from the one just described, but is organized to calculate points more rapidly.

The repeated calculation of values for $COS(\theta)$ and $SIN(\theta)$ consumes a large amount of time. The process presented here requires the calculation of the sine and cosine of only one angle.

We could number the points generated for use in sketching an image. In Program 5.5, 22 points are calculated. They would be numbered as (X_1, Y_1), (X_2, Y_2), (X_3, Y_3), . . . (X_{22}, Y_{22}). Two consecutive points (X_n, Y_n) and (X_{n+1}, Y_{n+1}) are related by

$$X_n = RCOS(\theta)$$
$$Y_n = RSIN(\theta)$$
$$X_{n+1} = RCOS(\theta + D\theta)$$
$$Y_{n+1} = RSIN(\theta + D\theta),$$

where $D\theta$ is the value of the step size for the point generating loop.

From trigonometry, we get

$$X_{n+1} = RCOS(\theta + D\theta) = RCOS(\theta)COS(D\theta) - RSIN(\theta)SIN(D\theta)$$
$$= X_n COS(D\theta) - Y_n SIN(D\theta), \text{ and}$$
$$Y_{n+1} = RSIN(\theta + D\theta) = RSIN(\theta)COS(D\theta) + RCOS(\theta)SIN(D\theta)$$
$$= Y_n COS(D\theta) + X_n SIN(D\theta).$$

By calculating $COS(D\theta)$ and $SIN(D\theta)$ only once and providing initial values for X_n and Y_n, we can use the above formulas to provide successive values for X_{n+1} and Y_{n+1}. To incorporate the formulas into a program we write [using DT for $D\theta$, C for $COS(D\theta)$, and S for $SIN(D\theta)$],

```
T = X * C  -  Y * S :   Y  =  Y * C  +  X * S :   X = T
```

Note that it is necessary to use the variable T as a temporary stand-in for X until a new value for Y is calculated. Program 5.6 illustrates the process.

Program 5.6: CIRCLE 3

```
1    REM PROGRAM 5.6 (CIRCLE 3)
2    REM RECURSIVELY CALCULATES POINTS ON A CIRCLE
10   CX = 140:CY = 96:SC = 1.16:X = 90:Y = 0:FL = 0
20   DT = .1:C = COS (DT):S = SIN (DT):N = 6.4 / DT
30   HGR2 : HCOLOR= 3
40   FOR I = 1 TO N
50   T = X * C - Y * S:Y = Y * C + X * S:X = T
60   SX = SC * X + CX:SY = CY - Y
70   IF FL = 1 THEN 90
80   HPLOT SX,SY:FL = 1
90   HPLOT TO SX,SY
100  NEXT I
```

Each of the circle generating programs has centered the circle at the origin (0,0). We may generate a circle having center at point (H,K) by translation of each of the points to be plotted. Each point (X,Y) may be translated to (X + H,Y + K) by the matrix product

$$(X,Y,1) \begin{pmatrix} 1 & 0 & 0 \\ 0 & 1 & 0 \\ H & K & 1 \end{pmatrix} = (X + H, Y + K, 1).$$

We may include the translation in Program 5.6 by changing line 60 to read

```
60 SX = SC*(X+H) + CX: SY = CY - (Y+K)
```

CLIPPING

Translating the circle, or choosing larger values for the circle radius, may lead to calculation of points that are at offscreen locations. The clipping routine described at the beginning of Chapter 4 may be used in any of the circle generating programs. However, testing each line segment for intersection with each of the screen boundaries is a time consuming task when the number of points is large. We obtain effective line clipping at a smaller cost in time by discarding line segments that have at least one offscreen endpoint, as in the following modification of Program 5.6.

Program 5.7: CLIPPED CIRCLE

```
1   REM PROGRAM 5.7 (CLIPPED CIRCLE)
2   REM DRAWS A TRANSLATED CIRCLE
10  H = -40:K = 20
20  CX = 140:CY = 96:SC = 1.16:X = 90:Y = 0:FL = 0
30  DT = .1:C = COS (DT):S = SIN (DT):N = 6.4 / DT
40   HGR2 : HCOLOR= 3
50   FOR I = 1 TO N
60  T = X * C - Y * S:Y = Y * C + X * S:X = T
70  SX = SC * (X + H) + CX:SY = CY - (Y + K)
80   IF SX < 0 OR SX > 279 OR SY < 0 OR SY > 191
     THEN FL = 0: GOTO 120
90   IF FL = 1 THEN 110
100  HPLOT SX,SY:FL = 1
110  HPLOT TO SX,SY
120  NEXT I
```

Line 80 causes plotting of a segment to cease if offscreen points are encountered. Note that FL is reset to zero so that the first onscreen point will result in an HPLOT rather than an HPLOT TO.

ELLIPSES

Elementary school students are sometimes taught (in art or math class) that they can draw an ellipse by using a pencil, two thumbtacks, and a length of string. The procedure is as follows:

1. Using the thumbtacks, fasten the ends of the string to a piece of paper or cardboard (but not to the dining room table). The thumbtacks must be positioned so that some slack remains in the string.

Figure 5.5

2. Place a pencil point against the string, pulling it taut.

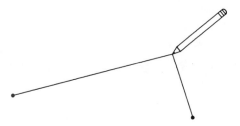

Figure 5.6

3. Keeping the pencil erect and the string taut, draw a curve on the paper through all points that the pencil can reach. The resulting curve is an ellipse.

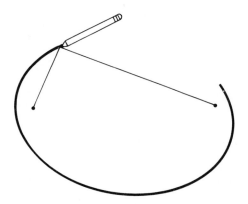

Figure 5.7

The shape of the ellipse obtained is dependent on the location of the thumbtacks and the length of the string. (The ratio of the length of the string to the distance between the thumbtacks is an item of value to students of analytic geometry.)

We describe the relationship between the thumbtacks, the length of string, and the associated ellipse by saying that

An ellipse is the set of points for which the sum of the distances from two fixed points (the thumbtacks) is a constant (the length of the string). Each of the fixed points (thumbtacks) is called a focus (plural: foci) of the ellipse.

Our interest in ellipses is related to a desire to obtain images of pleasing or useful curves. We will want to be able to identify ellipses by specifying a size, shape, and location.

In the ellipse shown in Figure 5.8, it is conventional to identify the coordinates of point C (the center) as (H,K); the distance AC (= BC) is usually designated by A; and the distance EC (= CD) is usually identified as B. (In case you are interested, the foci (thumbtacks) are located on the line segment AB at a distance $\sqrt{A^2 - B^2}$ from the center. The length of the string is 2A.) With this notation, the ellipse is represented algebraically by

$$\frac{(X - H)^2}{A^2} + \frac{(Y - K)^2}{B^2} = 1 \qquad \text{(Equation 5.3)}$$

While this equation for an ellipse is the form most commonly seen and accurately represents the points of an ellipse, other equations are available that are more effective for our purposes.

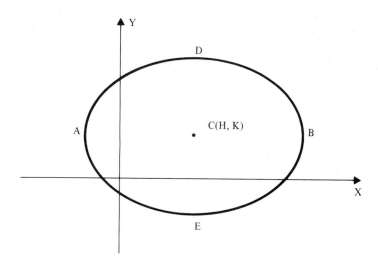

Figure 5.8

ELLIPSE WITH CENTER AT (0,0)

We may simplify the algebra, and our programming, by working with ellipses centered at the point (0,0) (The translation transformation will allow easy relocation). Equation 5.3 then becomes

$$\frac{X^2}{A^2} + \frac{Y^2}{B^2} = 1 \qquad \text{(Equation 5.4)}$$

The use of this equation for plotting purposes results in the problem associated with the use of $X^2 + Y^2 = R^2$ for the representation of a circle—the image will have angular components unless the number of points plotted is quite large.

The following are algebraically equivalent to equation 5.4:

$$X = ACOS(\theta)$$
$$Y = BSIN(\theta), \text{ for } 0 \leq \theta < 2\pi \qquad \text{(Equations 5.5)}$$

These equations are easily programmed, as Program 5.8 suggests.

Program 5.8: ELLIPSE 1

```
 1   REM PROGRAM 5.8 (ELLIPSE 1)
 2   REM DRAWS AN ELLIPSE CENTERED ON SCREEN
10 CX = 140:CY = 96:SC = 1.16:FL = 0:A = 90:
   B = 50
20   HGR2 : HCOLOR= 3
30   FOR TH = 0 TO 6.4 STEP .3
40 X = A * COS (TH):Y = B * SIN (TH)
50 SX = SC * X + CX:SY = CY - Y
60   IF SX < 0 OR SX > 279 OR SY < 0 OR SY > 191
     THEN FL = 0: GOTO 100
70   IF FL = 1 THEN 90
80   HPLOT SX,SY:FL = 1
90   HPLOT TO SX,SY
100   NEXT TH
```

TRANSLATION AND ROTATION

Changing the values of A and B in the above program will result in a variety of ellipses. The orientation and location of the image is limited, however. The center always will be at (0,0) and the axis of the ellipse (line AB of Figure 5.8) always will be parallel to either the horizontal or the vertical coordinate axis. We can add variety by rotating and translating the image.

The rotation of points through an angle of measure Θ is represented by the transformation matrix

$$\begin{pmatrix} \cos(\theta) & \sin(\theta) & 0 \\ -\sin(\theta) & \cos(\theta) & 0 \\ 0 & 0 & 1 \end{pmatrix}$$

The matrix of translation through (H,K) is

$$\begin{pmatrix} 1 & 0 & 0 \\ 0 & 1 & 0 \\ H & K & 1 \end{pmatrix}$$

The rotation of an image through an angle of measure Θ, followed by the translation of the result through (H,K), is represented by

$$\begin{pmatrix} \cos(\theta) & \sin(\theta) & 0 \\ -\sin(\theta) & \cos(\theta) & 0 \\ 0 & 0 & 1 \end{pmatrix} \begin{pmatrix} 1 & 0 & 0 \\ 0 & 1 & 0 \\ H & K & 1 \end{pmatrix} = \begin{pmatrix} \cos(\theta) & \sin(\theta) & 0 \\ -\sin(\theta) & \cos(\theta) & 0 \\ H & K & 1 \end{pmatrix}$$

The transformation of a point (X,Y) results in

$$(X,Y,1) \begin{pmatrix} \cos(\theta) & \sin(\theta) & 0 \\ -\sin(\theta) & \cos(\theta) & 0 \\ H & K & 1 \end{pmatrix} =$$

$$(X\cos(\theta) - Y\sin(\theta) + H, X\sin(\theta) + Y\cos(\theta) + K, 1).$$

Adding this transformation to Program 5.8 yields

Program 5.9: ELLIPSE 2

```
1   REM PROGRAM 5.9 (ELLIPSE 2)
2   REM ROTATION; TRANSLATION
10  CX = 140:CY = 96:SC = 1.16:FL = 0:A = 90:
    B = 50
20  H = 10:K = 30:T = .3:C1 = COS (T):
    S1 = SIN (T)
30  HGR2 : HCOLOR= 3
40  FOR TH = 0 TO 6.4 STEP .3
50  X = A * COS (TH):Y = B * SIN (TH)
```

(continued)

```
60 X1 = X * C1 - Y * S1 + H:
   Y1 = X * S1 + Y * C1 + K
70 SX = SC * X1 + CX:SY = CY - Y1
80  IF SX < 0 OR SX > 279 OR SY < 0 OR SY > 191
    THEN FL = 0: GOTO 120
90  IF FL = 1 THEN 110
100  HPLOT SX,SY:FL = 1
110  HPLOT TO SX,SY
120  NEXT TH
```

MORE TRANSFORMATIONS

We may consider an ellipse to be a deformed circle. By scaling (stretching) a circle in the direction of the X or Y axis we may change the circle to an ellipse. For example, a circle of radius 1 ($X^2 + Y^2 = 1$) may be stretched into the ellipse

$$\frac{X^2}{A^2} + \frac{Y^2}{B^2} = 1$$

by scaling the X components by A, and the Y components by B (compare equations 5.2 with equation 5.5) The matrix of such a scaling is

$$\begin{pmatrix} A & 0 & 0 \\ 0 & B & 0 \\ 0 & 0 & 1 \end{pmatrix}$$

By scaling, rotating, and translating the image of Program 5.7, we obtain the following ellipse sketching program:

Program 5.10: ELLIPSE 3

```
1   REM PROGRAM 5.10 (ELLIPSE 3)
2   REM ELLIPSE AS A TRANSFORMED CIRCLE
10  CX = 140:CY = 96:SC = 1.16:X = 1:Y = 0:FL = 0
20  A = 90:B = 50
30  DT = .1:C = COS (DT):S = SIN (DT):N = 6.4 /
    DT
40  H = 10:K = 30:T = .3:S1 = SIN (T):C1 = COS
    (T)
50  HGR2 : HCOLOR= 3
60  FOR I = 1 TO N
70  T = X * C - Y * S:Y = Y * C + X * S:X = T
80  X1 = X* A * C1 - Y * B * S1 + H:Y1 = X * A *
    S1 + Y * B * C1 + K
```

```
90 SX = SC * X1 + CX:SY = CY - Y1
100   IF SX < 0 OR SX > 279 OR SY < 0 OR SY > 191
      THEN FL = 0: GOTO 140
110   IF FL = 1 THEN 130
120   HPLOT SX,SY:FL = 1
130   HPLOT TO SX,SY
140   NEXT I
150   END
```

PARAMETRIC EQUATIONS

Equations such as

$$X = T^2 + 10$$
$$Y = T^2 - 10T$$

are called parametric equations. They make use of a parameter, T, to calculate values of X and Y. Although we have not used the word parameter before, you might recognize the technique. Program 5.5 used the parametric equations

$$X = R \cos(T)$$
$$Y = R \sin(T)$$

with R = 90 to draw a circle. Some of the ellipse programs also used parametric equations.

Applications of mathematics to science, engineering, and business frequently use parametric equations because the parameter and the values of X and Y are important to the application. We have used parametrically defined relations between X and Y primarily because they enabled us to obtain smooth curves while reducing calculation time. They also will permit us to sketch some pleasing and exotic curves.

Program 5.11 sketches the graph defined by the equations

$$X = 50 \sin(2(T - \frac{\pi}{13}))$$
$$Y = -70 \cos(T)$$

This pair of equations is a special case of the more general pair

$$X = A \sin(B(T - \frac{\pi}{C}))$$
$$Y = D \cos(T)$$

for which we have chosen A = 50, B = 2, C = 13, D = -70. Try a few other selections for A, B, C, and D.

Program 5.11: PARAMETRIC

```
1   REM PROGRAM 5.11 (PARAMETRIC)
2   REM DRAWS LISSAJOUS FIGURES
10  CX = 140:CY = 96:SC = 1.16:FL = 0
20  PI = 3.14159
30  A = 50:B = 2:C = 13:D = -70
40  HGR2 : HCOLOR= 3
50  FOR T = 0 TO 6.3 STEP .1
60  X = A * SIN (B * (T - PI / C)):Y = D * COS
    (T)
70  SX = SC * X + CX:SY = CY - Y
80  IF SX < 0 OR SX > 279 OR SY < 0 OR SY > 191
    THEN FL = 0: GOTO 110
90  IF FL = 0 THEN HPLOT SX,SY:FL = 1
100  HPLOT TO SX,SY
110  NEXT T
```

Some other parametric equations which may interest you:

$$X = 30 \; T^2$$
$$Y = 30 \; T^3, \; -2 \leq T \leq 2$$

$$X = 80 \; COS \; T$$
$$Y = 80 \; SIN \; T, \; 0 \leq T \leq 2\pi$$

$$X = 30T - 50 \; SIN \; T$$
$$Y = 30 - COS \; T, \; -4 \leq T \leq 4$$

$$X = 5(COS \; T + T \; SIN \; T)$$
$$Y = 5(SIN \; T - T \; COS \; T), \; 0 \leq T \leq 20$$

The sections ahead will provide further examples of curves defined parametrically.

PARABOLAS

The parabola is a curve which has many physical applications. For example, if a stone or baseball is tossed upward, the path it follows (if wind resistance is ignored) is a parabola. Parabolic reflectors are useful because they concentrate reflected light at a single point, the focus. Comets follow parabolic orbits as they pass the sun, which is the focus of the parabola.

The equation $Y = X^2/4P$ identifies points of the parabola shown in Figure 5.9. The origin (0,0) is the vertex of the parabola; the focus is at the point (0,P). The line containing the focus and the vertex is referred

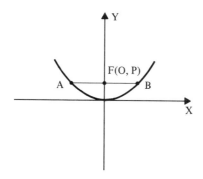

Figure 5.9

to as the axis of the parabola. The value of P determines the relative position of the focus and the vertex, and also the shape of the parabola. The line segment AB, which contains the focus and is perpendicular to the axis of the parabola, has length 4|P|. In a sense, the value 4|P| provides a measure of the "width" of the parabola.

While the equation $Y = X^2/4P$ will identify the points of a parabola, a more useful formulation is the set of parametric equations

$$X = 2PT$$
$$Y = PT^2.$$

When these equations are provided in a program, we may quickly identify parabolas of varied shapes by changing the value of P. Try several choices of P in Program 5.12.

Program 5.12: PARABOLA

```
1   REM PROGRAM 5.12 (PARABOLA)
2   REM DRAWS A PARABOLA; PARAMETRIC EQUATIONS
10  CX = 140:CY = 96:SC = 1.16:FL = 0
20  P = 10
40    HGR2 : HCOLOR= 3
50    FOR T = -5 TO 5 STEP .5
60  X = 2 * P * T:Y = P * T * T
```

(continued)

```
80 SX = SC * X + CX:SY = CY - Y
90  IF SX < 0 OR SX > 279 OR SY < 0 OR SY > 191
     THEN FL = 0: GOTO 120
100   IF FL = 0 THEN HPLOT SX,SY:FL = 1
110  HPLOT TO SX,SY
120  NEXT T
```

The process of passing to parabolas of arbitrary location and orientation by now should be obvious—we must transform the points of the parabola by rotation and translation. This is done in Program 5.13.

Program 5.13: ROTATED PARABOLA

```
1   REM PROGRAM 5.13 (ROTATED PARABOLA)
2   REM DRAWS A TRANSLATED, ROTATED PARABOLA
10  CX = 140:CY = 96:SC = 1.16:FL = 0
20  P = 10
30  H = 10:K = -80:TH = .3:S1 = SIN (TH):C1 = COS
    (TH)
40   HGR2 : HCOLOR= 3
50   FOR T = -5 TO 5 STEP .5
60  X = 2 * P * T:Y = P * T * T
70  X1 = X * C1 - Y * S1 + H:Y1 = X * S1 + Y * C1
    + K
80  SX = SC * X1 + CX:SY = CY - Y1
90   IF SX < 0 OR SX > 279 OR SY < 0 OR SY > 191
     THEN FL = 0: GOTO 120
100   IF FL = 0 THEN HPLOT SX,SY:FL = 1
110  HPLOT TO SX,SY
120  NEXT T
```

HYPERBOLAS

The circle, the ellipse, and the parabola are called conic sections because they are curves formed by the intersection of a cone and a plane. The hyperbola is another of the conic sections. We will consider the hyperbola briefly, as we leave the conic curves.

The hyperbola (Figure 5.10) is represented by the equation

$$\frac{X^2}{A^2} - \frac{Y^2}{B^2} = 1$$

The shape of the hyperbola obviously is controlled by the choice of values for A and B. The parametric equations

$$X = A \ SEC \ T$$
$$Y = B \ TAN \ T$$

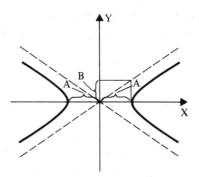

Figure 5.10

also represent the hyperbola, and are more useful in writing a program to sketch the graph.

Program 5.14: HYPERBOLA

```
1   REM PROGRAM 5.14 (HYPERBOLA)
2   REM PARAMETRIC EQUATIONS FOR A HYPERBOLA
10  CX = 140:CY = 96:SC = 1.16:FL = 0
20  A = 30:B = 35
30   HGR2 : HCOLOR= 3
40   FOR T = -1.6 TO 4.5 STEP .05
50  X = A / COS (T):Y = B * TAN (T)
60  SX = SC * X + CX:SY = CY - Y
70   IF SX < 0 OR SX > 279 OR SY < 0 OR SY > 191
     THEN FL = 0: GOTO 100
80   IF FL = 0 THEN HPLOT SX,SY:FL = 1
90   HPLOT TO SX,SY
100  NEXT T
```

POLAR COORDINATE CURVES

Program 5.5 identified the graph of a circle by use of the parametric equations

$$X = R\ COS(T)$$
$$Y = R\ SIN(T)$$

R (= 90) provided the radius of the circle.

If we cause R to vary, instead of remaining constant, we obtain some very interesting and pleasing curves. We will define R as a function of T, and thus associate the variation in R with changes in T.

Program 5.15: POLAR

```
1   REM PROGRAM 5.15 (POLAR)
2   REM DRAWS A ROSE
10  CX = 140:CY = 96:SC = 1.16:FL = 0
20   HGR2 : HCOLOR= 3
30   FOR T = 0 TO 6.3 STEP .1
40  R = 80 * COS (2 * T)
50  X = R * COS (T):Y = R * SIN (T)
60  SX = SC * X + CX:SY = CY - Y
70   IF SX < 0 OR SX > 279 OR SY < 0 OR SY > 191
     THEN FL = 0: GOTO 100
80   IF FL = 0 THEN HPLOT SX,SY:FL = 1
90   HPLOT TO SX,SY
100  NEXT T
```

The association between the shape of a curve and the relationship between R and T is, at first, somewhat obscure. Some experimentation is recommended. Try the following

```
R = 80*COS(3*T) (Try 0 ≤ T ≤ 3.2 STEP .1)
R = 80*COS(4*T) (Try 0 ≤ T ≤ 6.3 STEP .1)
R = 30*(COS(T) - 1)
R = 30*(2*COS(T) - 1)
R = 2*T (Try 0 ≤ T ≤ 70 STEP .2)
```

CURVES OF THE FORM Y = F(X)

Graphs of points (X,Y) which satisfy functions $Y = F(X)$ may be graphed using the processes discussed in previous sections. Program 5.16 illustrates one approach. Changes in the function (line 30) typically will be accompanied by changes in the domain (MINX < X < MAXX), step size (ST), and scaling factors (XS,YS). The program may be elaborated to provide axes and to allow the user to input the function, the domain, the stepsize, and scaling factors.

Program 5.16: CURVE

```
1   REM PROGRAM 5.16 (CURVE)
2   REM DRAWS A SINE CURVE
10  XS = 20:YS = 20:MINX = -6:MAXX = 6:ST = .5
```

```
20 FL = 0:CX = 140:CY = 96:SC = 1.16
30  DEF FN Y(X) = SIN (X)
40  HGR2 : HCOLOR= 3
50  FOR X = MINX TO MAXX STEP ST
60 Y = FN Y(X)
70 SX = CX + SC * XS * X:SY = CY - YS * Y
80  IF SX < 0 OR SX > 279 OR SY < 0 OR SY > 191
    THEN FL = 0: GOTO 110
90  IF FL = 0 THEN HPLOT SX,SY:FL = 1
100  HPLOT TO SX,SY
110  NEXT X
```

Part IV

Three-Dimensional Graphics

Chapter 6
Basics of Three-Dimen-
sional Graphics

The computer screen is a two-dimensional display device. However, just as an artist can create the impression of a three-dimensional scene on a canvas, so we can display three-dimensional images on our graphics computer.

WARNING—READ SLOWLY MATHEMATICS AHEAD

The process of displaying three-dimensional images requires additional mathematics. As is usual when travelling in rough terrain, we will progress more rapidly if we move slowly and carefully.

In order to be able to generate images of three-dimensional objects, it is necessary to establish a convention through which points in three-dimensional space may be identified. Two coordinate systems are described below.

COORDINATE SYSTEMS

The rectangular (or Cartesian) coordinate system requires three mutually perpendicular axes. The X and Y axes used in the two-dimensional system are augmented by a Z axis through the origin, perpendicular to the XY plane. Two possible orientations are possible for the Z axis. The orientation shown in Figure 6.1 identifies a right-hand system, so called because a right hand with first and second fingers pointing in the direction of the X and Y axes, as shown, will have the thumb pointing in the direction of the Z axis.

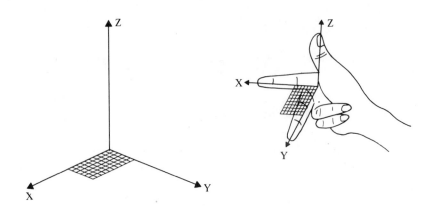

Figure 6.1

A left-hand system differs only in that the direction of the Z axis is reversed.

When viewing the two-dimensional XY plane the right-hand system will have the Z axis perpendicular to the plane, pointing toward the viewer's eye, as in Figure 6.2a. The left-hand system will have the Z axis pointing away from the viewer, as shown in Figure 6.2b.

The selection of right-hand or left-hand system is somewhat arbitrary, since the calculations of interest to us could be completed using either coordinate system. As a matter of convenience, we will establish the right-hand system as standard.

Any pair of coordinate axes identifies a plane, referred to as a coordinate plane. The three coordinate planes are identified as the XY plane, the YZ plane, and the XZ plane. Points are identified by ordered triples (A,B,C) of numbers; with A, B, and C providing the directed distance from the point to the YZ, the XZ, and the XY planes, respectively.

Figure 6.3 shows the plotting of points $(1,8,5)$, $(5,3,3)$, $(0,5,-7)$, and $(-2,5,-7)$.

The second coordinate system we will use is the spherical coordinate system (see Figure 6.4). In this system, each point P is represented by an ordered triple (ρ,Θ,ϕ) of numbers. The distance from the point to the origin is ρ. The angle between $\overrightarrow{OP}$ and the positive direction of the Z axis is ϕ. The angle between the positive direction of the X axis and the projection of $\overrightarrow{OP}$ onto the XY plane is θ, and is measured in a counterclockwise direction as viewed from a point on the positive Z axis.

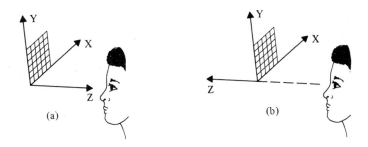

Figure 6.2

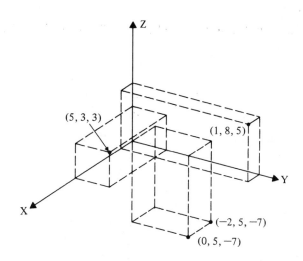

Figure 6.3

More Greek: In the tradition of mathematics books, we're using the Greek letters ρ (rho), Θ (theta), and φ (phi) for spherical coordinates. In BASIC we'll call these RHO, THETA, and PHI. Since Applesoft BASIC only recognizes the first two letters of a variable name, we could use RH, TH, and PH. Program 6.1 illustrates this usage.

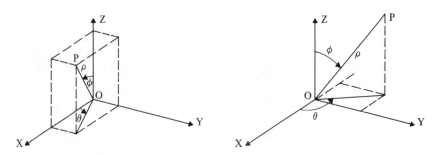

Figure 6.4

Since a point may be identified in terms of rectangular (X,Y,Z) or spherical (ρ,θ,ϕ) coordinates, it is necessary to have a means of conversion between the two systems. The following formulas are based on right triangle trigonometry:

$$x = \rho SIN\phi COS\theta$$
$$y = \rho SIN\phi SIN\theta$$
$$z = \rho COS\phi$$
$$\rho^2 = x^2 + y^2 + z^2$$

In order to obtain an image of a three-dimensional object on a two-dimensional graphics display screen, it is necessary to associate a pair of screen coordinates (SX,SY) with each triple of rectangular coordinates (X,Y,Z) or spherical coordinates (ρ,θ,ϕ). The process used to obtain the screen coordinates is illustrated in Figure 6.5.

The position of the viewer is represented by point P. The display screen is a plane onto which an object is to be projected. This projection plane is assumed to be perpendicular to the line OP, and at a fixed distance D from point P. As the points of the object are projected onto the projection plane, we obtain screen coordinates (SX,SY) for each point (X,Y,Z). See Figure 6.7.

We will adopt the practice of identifying the viewpoint (location of the viewer's eye) in terms of its spherical coordinates. This will permit easy control over the location of the viewpoint:

- ρ (rho) will represent the distance from the viewpoint to the point (0,0,0). Increasing ρ will move the viewer away from the object being viewed. This will cause the object to appear as a smaller image.

- θ (theta) and ϕ (phi) identify the direction from which the viewer will see an object.

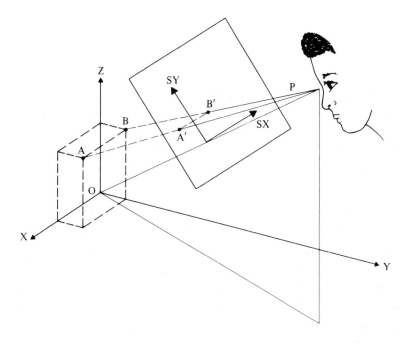

Figure 6.5

Figure 6.5 suggests that the projection plane (display screen) is located between the viewer and the object. It is not necessary that this be the case. Figure 6.6 positions the display screen on the opposite side of the object from the viewer. This results in a larger screen image. It is worth noting that

- moving the display screen closer to the viewer will result in a smaller projected image.

- moving the display screen farther from the viewer will result in a larger projected image.

Control over the viewing parameters ρ, θ, ϕ, and D provides control over the location and the direction of view and the size of the image. More on this later; first, we must acquire some tools for manipulating three-dimensional objects.

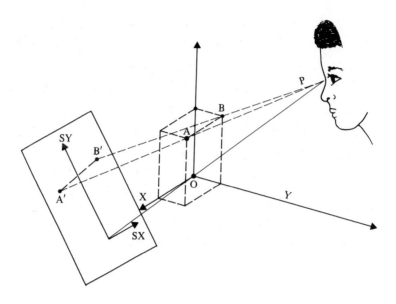

Figure 6.6

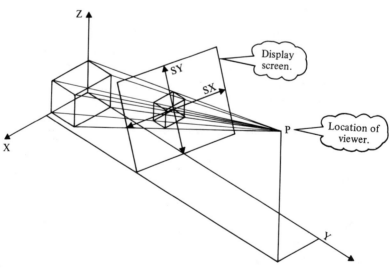

Figure 6.7

TRANSFORMATIONS

Again we will use homogeneous coordinates to represent points. A point whose rectangular coordinates are given by (X,Y,Z) will have homogeneous coordinates (X,Y,Z,1). Linear transformations then may be represented by 4×4 matrices. We will not consider all of the transformations available to us but will focus on those which are most valuable.

SCALING

Diagonal matrices represent scaling transformations. Since

$$(X,Y,Z,1) \begin{vmatrix} A & 0 & 0 & 0 \\ 0 & B & 0 & 0 \\ 0 & 0 & C & 0 \\ 0 & 0 & 0 & 1 \end{vmatrix} = (AX,BY,CZ,1)$$

we may scale each of the coordinates individually to control scale in the direction of any of the coordinate axes. Overall scaling then may be provided as follows:

$$(X,Y,Z,1) \begin{vmatrix} K & 0 & 0 & 0 \\ 0 & K & 0 & 0 \\ 0 & 0 & K & 0 \\ 0 & 0 & 0 & 1 \end{vmatrix} = (KX,KY,KZ,1)$$

Since (X,Y,Z,D), when normalized, becomes (X/D,Y/D,Z/D,1), overall scaling also may be accomplished through multiplication by the matrix

$$\begin{vmatrix} 1 & 0 & 0 & 0 \\ 0 & 1 & 0 & 0 \\ 0 & 0 & 1 & 0 \\ 0 & 0 & 0 & 1/K \end{vmatrix}$$

ROTATION

It will be sufficient for us to be able to rotate an object about each of the coordinate axes. This ability is within easy reach. In Chapter 4, when considering a rotation about the origin, we used the transformation matrix

$$R = \begin{pmatrix} \cos\theta & \sin\theta & 0 \\ -\sin\theta & \cos\theta & 0 \\ 0 & 0 & 1 \end{pmatrix}$$

Multiplication of vector (X,Y,1) by R had the effect of rotating the vector about the origin through a counterclockwise angle Θ. If we picture the Z axis pointing toward us from the XY plane, the action is described as a rotation about the Z axis. In applying the rotation to a three-dimensional vector we use the matrix

$$R_z = \begin{vmatrix} \cos\theta & \sin\theta & 0 & 0 \\ -\sin\theta & \cos\theta & 0 & 0 \\ 0 & 0 & 1 & 0 \\ 0 & 0 & 0 & 1 \end{vmatrix}$$

The transformation matrices which effect rotations about the x axis and y axis are

$$R_x = \begin{vmatrix} 1 & 0 & 0 & 0 \\ 0 & \cos\theta & \sin\theta & 0 \\ 0 & -\sin\theta & \cos\theta & 0 \\ 0 & 0 & 0 & 1 \end{vmatrix}$$

$$R_y = \begin{vmatrix} \cos\theta & 0 & -\sin\theta & 0 \\ 0 & 1 & 0 & 0 \\ \sin\theta & 0 & \cos\theta & 0 \\ 0 & 0 & 0 & 1 \end{vmatrix}$$

In each case the rotation is through a counterclockwise angle θ, as viewed from a point along the positive axis, facing the origin.

TRANSLATION

If it were not for our need for translation capability, we might not have elected to use homogeneous coordinates. It will prove convenient to represent a translation by means of a matrix transformation.

$$(X,Y,Z,1) \begin{vmatrix} 1 & 0 & 0 & 0 \\ 0 & 1 & 0 & 0 \\ 0 & 0 & 1 & 0 \\ H & K & L & 1 \end{vmatrix} = (X + H, Y + K, Z + L, 1)$$

To move a point, or collection of points, by displacing the coordinates a distance specified by the vector (H,K,L), we multiply by the above matrix. Alternately, we may consider that the effect of the translation is to move the origin to the point $(-H, -K, -L)$.

REFLECTION

The *reflection* of an object through a plane refers to generating a mirror image of all points of the object on the opposite side of the plane. Thus the reflection of points through the XY plane has the effect of changing the sign of the Z coordinates of each of the points. The transformation matrix for this reflection is

$$
M_{xy} = \begin{pmatrix} 1 & 0 & 0 & 0 \\ 0 & 1 & 0 & 0 \\ 0 & 0 & -1 & 0 \\ 0 & 0 & 0 & 1 \end{pmatrix}
$$

Transformation matrices which represent reflections through the XZ plane and the YZ plane are

$$
M_{xz} = \begin{pmatrix} 1 & 0 & 0 & 0 \\ 0 & -1 & 0 & 0 \\ 0 & 0 & 1 & 0 \\ 0 & 0 & 0 & 1 \end{pmatrix}
$$

$$
M_{yz} = \begin{pmatrix} -1 & 0 & 0 & 0 \\ 0 & 1 & 0 & 0 \\ 0 & 0 & 1 & 0 \\ 0 & 0 & 0 & 1 \end{pmatrix}
$$

SEQUENTIAL TRANSFORMATIONS

The effect of a sequence of transformations may be represented by a single matrix, the product of the matrices of the individual transformations. For example, we may create the effect of rotation through 30° about the ray $\overrightarrow{PQ}$ (P = (0,2,3), Q = (1,2,3)) by

1. Translation
$$
T = \begin{pmatrix} 1 & 0 & 0 & 0 \\ 0 & 1 & 0 & 0 \\ 0 & 0 & 1 & 0 \\ 0 & -2 & -3 & 1 \end{pmatrix} \text{ followed by}
$$

2. Rotation
$$
R = \begin{pmatrix} 1 & 0 & 0 & 0 \\ 0 & \cos 30° & \sin 30° & 0 \\ 0 & -\sin 30° & \cos 30° & 0 \\ 0 & 0 & 0 & 1 \end{pmatrix} \text{ followed by}
$$

3. Translation

$$T^* = \begin{pmatrix} 1 & 0 & 0 & 0 \\ 0 & 1 & 0 & 0 \\ 0 & 0 & 1 & 0 \\ 0 & 2 & 3 & 1 \end{pmatrix}$$

The same effect is available from the matrix

$M = TRT^* =$

$$\begin{pmatrix} 1 & 0 & 0 & 0 \\ 0 & COS30° & SIN30° & 0 \\ 0 & -SIN30° & COS30° & 0 \\ 0 & -2COS30° + 3SIN30° + 2 & -2SIN30° - 3COS30° + 3 & 1 \end{pmatrix} =$$

$$\begin{pmatrix} 1 & 0 & 0 & 0 \\ 0 & .866 & .5 & 0 \\ 0 & -.5 & .866 & 0 \\ 0 & 1.768 & -.598 & 1 \end{pmatrix}$$

The ordering of a sequence of transformations is quite important. In general, changes in the order of transformations will change the effect of the sequence. For example, a rotation followed by a translation has a different effect than the same translation followed by the rotation.

INVERSES OF MATRICES

In the last example, the matrices T and T^* had opposite effects. Multiplication by matrix T causes a translation through $(0, -2, -3)$, while T^* represents a translation through $(0,2,3)$. Successive multiplication by T and T^* would place a point in its original location, since

$$TT^* = \begin{pmatrix} 1 & 0 & 0 & 0 \\ 0 & 1 & 0 & 0 \\ 0 & 0 & 1 & 0 \\ 0 & -2 & -3 & 1 \end{pmatrix} \begin{pmatrix} 1 & 0 & 0 & 0 \\ 0 & 1 & 0 & 0 \\ 0 & 0 & 1 & 0 \\ 0 & 2 & 3 & 1 \end{pmatrix} = \begin{pmatrix} 1 & 0 & 0 & 0 \\ 0 & 1 & 0 & 0 \\ 0 & 0 & 1 & 0 \\ 0 & 0 & 0 & 1 \end{pmatrix} = I$$

Pairs of matrices whose product is I are referred to as *inverses*. The inverse of a matrix M is frequently denoted as M^{-1}. While some matrices do not have inverses, many of the ones that are useful in computer graphics do have inverses. For example, the matrix

$$R = \begin{pmatrix} 1 & 0 & 0 & 0 \\ 0 & COS30° & SIN30° & 0 \\ 0 & -SIN30° & COS30° & 0 \\ 0 & 0 & 0 & 1 \end{pmatrix} = \begin{pmatrix} 0 & 0 & 0 & 0 \\ 0 & .866 & .5 & 0 \\ 0 & -.5 & .866 & 0 \\ 0 & 0 & 0 & 1 \end{pmatrix}$$

which represents a rotation of 30° about the x axis, has an inverse R $^{-1}$ which represents a rotation of $-30°$ about the x axis:

$$R^{-1} = \begin{vmatrix} 1 & 0 & 0 & 0 \\ 0 & .866 & -.5 & 0 \\ 0 & .5 & .866 & 0 \\ 0 & 0 & 0 & 1 \end{vmatrix}$$

TRANSFORMING A COORDINATE SYSTEM

We have referred to transforming a point, or a set of points, within a coordinate system. It is also frequently useful to establish a new coordinate system through transformation of the axes. For example, we might move the origin to a new location, or rotate the axis system about one of the axes.

In such cases it is necessary to identify points in terms of the original, or standard, coordinates, and also in terms of coordinates relative to the new axis system. We will identify coordinates relative to a second axis system by affixing a prime ($'$). Thus the coordinates (2,1,3) are assumed to identify a point relative to the standard axis system, while (2,1,3)$'$ identifies a point relative to a second axis system.

As an example, a rotation about the z axis through a counterclockwise angle of 30° may be represented by the transformation matrix:

$$M = \begin{vmatrix} COS30° & SIN30° & 0 & 0 \\ -SIN30° & COS30° & 0 & 0 \\ 0 & 0 & 1 & 0 \\ 0 & 0 & 0 & 1 \end{vmatrix} = \begin{vmatrix} .866 & .5 & 0 & 0 \\ -.5 & .866 & 0 & 0 \\ 0 & 0 & 1 & 0 \\ 0 & 0 & 0 & 1 \end{vmatrix}$$

When applying this transformation matrix to points or sets of points, multiplication of the coordinate vector of a point by the matrix will yield the coordinate vector of the rotated point.

For example, the point (2,4,1) rotates to the position $(-.268, 4.464, 1)$, since

$$(2,4,1,1) \begin{vmatrix} .866 & .5 & 0 & 0 \\ -.5 & .866 & 0 & 0 \\ 0 & 0 & 1 & 0 \\ 0 & 0 & 0 & 1 \end{vmatrix} = (-.268, 4.464, 1, 1)$$

The point P$'$ results from rotation of point P through a counterclockwise angle of 30° about the Z axis. Consider the effect of rotating the coordinate system through a clockwise angle of 30° about the Z axis. The resulting coordinate system, X', Y', Z', will provide another means of referencing point P. The position of the rotated point P relative to the X,Y,Z coordinate system is the same as the position of point P relative to the rotated coordinate system X', Y', Z'.

Thus matrix M above may be used to:

1. Determine the coordinates of points following rotation of the points through a counterclockwise angle of 30°; or

2. Determine the coordinates of points following a rotation of the coordinate axes through a clockwise angle of 30°.

The example above is not an isolated case, but represents a general principle which we will find valuable: The matrix required to represent the transformation of an axis system is the inverse of that needed to transform points within an axis system.

PROJECTION

We now know how to manipulate three-dimensional figures, but we're not yet ready to show them on a computer graphics screen. The reason, of course, is that a graphics screen is a two-dimensional surface. To obtain a two-dimensional (screen) representation of a three-dimensional object we'll next develop a method for projecting each point of the object onto a plane. This process was represented in Figure 6.7. Before confronting this problem, we will consider a related one: the projection of points onto a plane parallel to the XY plane.

The projection plane is at a distance D from the XY plane, as indicated in Figure 6.8. The projection plane will be the display screen, so we will identify points on the plane by screen coordinates (SX,SY), with the SX axis and the SY axis parallel to the X and Y axes, respectively. The scale of distance measured on the projection plane will be the same as that of the coordinate axes. Thus, a point (SX,SY) on the plane is referred to as (X,Y,D), with X = SX and Y = SY.

Several types of projection are available. We will be working with perspective projections, with the center of the projection at the origin O(0,0,0). That is, a point P(X,Y,Z) will be projected to the intersection of the projection plane with the line OP.

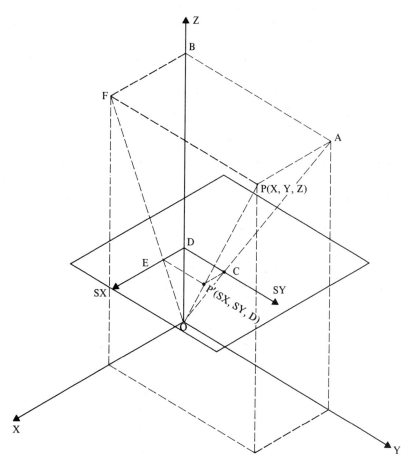

Figure 6.8

In identifying the screen coordinates (SX,SY) associated with the point P(X,Y,Z), note the right triangles OBA and ODC (Figure 6.8 and Figure 6.9). These are similar triangles with

$$\frac{DC}{OD} = \frac{BA}{OB}$$

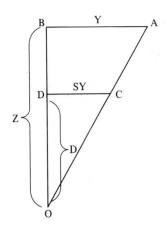 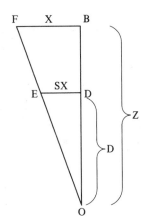

Figure 6.9

Thus

$$\frac{SY}{D} = \frac{Y}{Z}$$

so that $SY = D(Y/Z)$.

In the same fashion, from similar triangles OBF and ODE, we have

$$\frac{DE}{OD} = \frac{BF}{OB} \text{ and } \frac{SX}{D} = \frac{X}{Z}$$

Thus, $SX = D(X/Z)$.

We now have all of the elements necessary to generate screen images of three-dimensional objects and will turn to that task.

TWO-DIMENSIONAL IMAGES OF THREE-DIMENSIONAL OBJECTS

Refer to Figure 6.5. The location of the eye (point P) is identified as having rectangular coordinates (H,K,L) and spherical coordinates (ρ,θ,ϕ). We position the projection plane (display screen) at a distance D from the viewer's eye, placed so that it is perpendicular to the line connecting the viewer's eye with the origin. A second rectangular axis system is located at point P. Points then may be identified by giving eye coordinates (Xe,Ye,Ze) or standard coordinates (X,Y,Z).

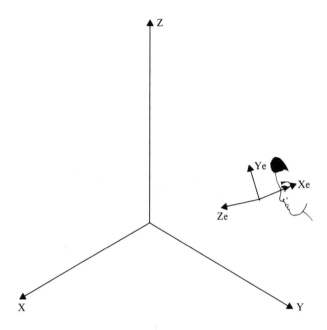

Figure 6.10

The eye coordinate system is shown in Figure 6.10. It orients the axes so that, when the viewer's line of sight is directed toward the origin of the X,Y,Z axis system, the Ze axis points in the direction of the line of sight, the Xe axis points to the right, and the Ye axis points upward. (Note that the eye coordinate system is a *left-hand* system.)

The task we face has two stages:

1. The identification of eye coordinates (Xe,Ye,Ze) associated with a point having standard coordinates (X,Y,Z);

2. The identification of screen coordinates (SX,SY) associated with a specific set of eye coordinates (Xe,Ye,Ze).

The second of these calculations is the easier. From the equations given in the previous section, we have $SX = D(Xe/Ze)$ and $SY = D(Ye/Ze)$.

We now may turn to the first task, establishing the association between the standard coordinates and the eye coordinates. This is done through a sequence of four transformations, each of which will partially transform the X,Y,Z axis system to the Xe,Ye,Ze axis system. The four transformations, along with pictorial representations of their effects, are given on pages 142, 143. There, and in our notation, the intermediate axis systems are each referred to as X',Y',Z', with the final X',Y',Z' axis system being the eye coordinate system, Xe,Ye,Ze. (Compare Figure 6.14 with Figure 6.5).

The effect of the transformations will be viewed as the establishment of a sequence of new coordinate systems, with the eye coordinate system as the final result.

For the purpose of these transformations, the point P, at the viewer's eye, is identified by rectangular coordinates (H,K,L) or by spherical coordinates (ρ,θ,ϕ), measured relative to the standard coordinate axes. Recall that $H = \rho\sin\phi\cos\theta$, $K = \rho\sin\phi\sin\theta$, and $L = \rho\cos\phi$.

In brief,

1. Step I establishes a coordinate system at the viewer's eye, retaining the orientation and directions of the original axis system. This process is represented by the transformation matrix A, as shown below.

2. Steps II and III rotate the axis system in order that the Z' axis points toward the origin of the standard axis system, with the Y' axis directed so as to intersect the positive Z axis. From the viewer's position, the Y' axis points upward and the X' axis points to the left.

3. Step IV converts to a left-hand system, inverting the X axis so that it points to the right. This provides a more conventional orientation for the viewer.

Since the transformations are best represented as matrices, we will consider each step separately, establishing the matrix of the transformation.

Step I. Establish the origin at $(H,K,L) = (\rho SIN\phi COS\theta, \rho SIN\phi SIN\theta, \rho COS\phi)$. The transformation matrix that has this effect is:

$$A = \begin{pmatrix} 1 & 0 & 0 & 0 \\ 0 & 1 & 0 & 0 \\ 0 & 0 & 1 & 0 \\ -H & -K & -L & 1 \end{pmatrix}$$

or

$$A = \begin{pmatrix} 1 & 0 & 0 & 0 \\ 0 & 1 & 0 & 0 \\ 0 & 0 & 1 & 0 \\ -\rho SIN\phi COS\theta & -\rho SIN\phi SIN\theta & -\rho COS\phi & 1 \end{pmatrix}$$

The spherical coordinate representation of H,K,L may appear to be less convenient, but will simplify calculation.

Step II. Rotate the axis system about the Z' axis through the clockwise angle $(90 - \theta)$. As a result of this rotation, the negative Y' axis should intersect the Z axis. The transformation matrix which accomplishes this is:

$$B = \begin{pmatrix} SIN\theta & COS\theta & 0 & 0 \\ -COS\theta & SIN\theta & 0 & 0 \\ 0 & 0 & 1 & 0 \\ 0 & 0 & 0 & 1 \end{pmatrix}$$

(Remember, the transformation matrix required to transform an axis system is the inverse of that needed to transform points within an axis system.)

Step III. Rotate axis system about the X' axis through the counterclockwise angle $(180 - \phi)$. As a result of this rotation, the Z' axis should be directed toward the origin of the X,Y,Z axis system. The required matrix is

$$C = \begin{pmatrix} 1 & 0 & 0 & 0 \\ 0 & -COS\phi & -SIN\phi & 0 \\ 0 & SIN\phi & -COS\phi & 0 \\ 0 & 0 & 0 & 1 \end{pmatrix}$$

Step IV. Change to a left-hand coordinate system, inverting the X' axis using matrix:

$$D = \begin{pmatrix} -1 & 0 & 0 & 0 \\ 0 & 1 & 0 & 0 \\ 0 & 0 & 1 & 0 \\ 0 & 0 & 0 & 1 \end{pmatrix}$$

If the standard coordinates (X,Y,Z) of a point are known, the eye coordinates (Xe,Ye,Ze) may be obtained as (Xe,Ye,Ze) = (X,Y,Z)ABCD. Simplicity in calculation is obtained through the use of the single matrix T = ABCD. Thus

$$(Xe,Ye,Ze,1) = (X,Y,Z,1)\begin{pmatrix} -\text{SIN}\theta & -\text{COS}\theta\text{COS}\phi & -\text{COS}\theta\text{SIN}\phi & 0 \\ \text{COS}\theta & -\text{SIN}\theta\text{COS}\phi & \text{SIN}\theta\text{SIN}\phi & 0 \\ 0 & \text{SIN}\phi & -\text{COS}\phi & 0 \\ 0 & 0 & \rho & 1 \end{pmatrix}$$

The multiplication of ABCD is outlined on page 144.

I.   TRANSLATE ORIGIN TO (H,K,L):

$$A = \begin{pmatrix} 1 & 0 & 0 & 0 \\ 0 & 1 & 0 & 0 \\ 0 & 0 & 1 & 0 \\ -\rho\text{COS}\theta\text{SIN}\phi & -\rho\text{SIN}\theta\text{SIN}\phi & -\rho\text{COS}\phi & 1 \end{pmatrix}$$

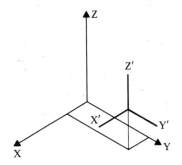

Figure 6.11

II.   ROTATE THROUGH (90° − θ) CLOCKWISE ABOUT Z'
      AXIS:

$$B = \begin{pmatrix} \text{SIN}\theta & \text{COS}\theta & 0 & 0 \\ -\text{COS}\theta & \text{SIN}\theta & 0 & 0 \\ 0 & 0 & 1 & 0 \\ 0 & 0 & 0 & 1 \end{pmatrix}$$

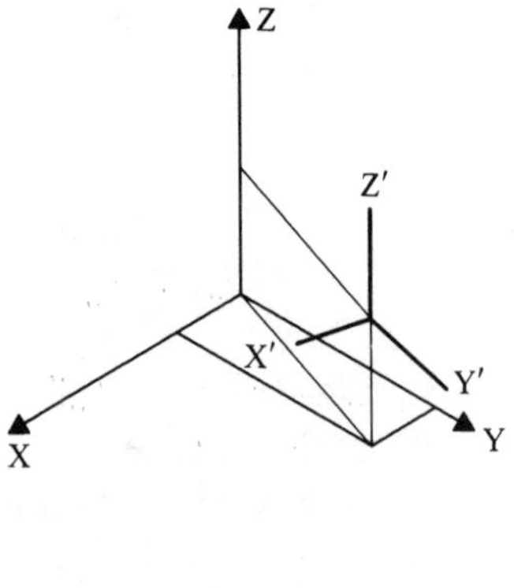

Figure 6.12

III. ROTATE THROUGH $(180° - \phi)$ COUNTERCLOCKWISE ABOUT X′ AXIS:

$$C = \begin{pmatrix} 1 & 0 & 0 & 0 \\ 0 & -\cos\phi & -\sin\phi & 0 \\ 0 & \sin\phi & -\cos\phi & 0 \\ 0 & 0 & 0 & 1 \end{pmatrix}$$

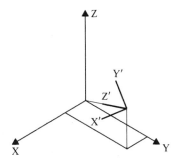

Figure 6.13

IV. CONVERT TO LEFT-HAND SYSTEM:

$$D = \begin{pmatrix} -1 & 0 & 0 & 0 \\ 0 & 1 & 0 & 0 \\ 0 & 0 & 1 & 0 \\ 0 & 0 & 0 & 1 \end{pmatrix}$$

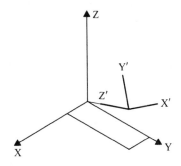

Figure 6.14

$$T = ABCD$$

$$= \begin{pmatrix} 1 & 0 & 0 & 0 \\ 0 & 1 & 0 & 0 \\ 0 & 0 & 1 & 0 \\ -\rho\cos\theta\sin\phi & -\rho\sin\theta\sin\phi & -\rho\cos\phi & 1 \end{pmatrix} \begin{pmatrix} \sin\theta & \cos\theta & 0 & 0 \\ -\cos\theta & \sin\theta & 0 & 0 \\ 0 & 0 & 1 & 0 \\ 0 & 0 & 0 & 1 \end{pmatrix} \begin{pmatrix} 1 & 0 & 0 & 0 \\ 0 & -\cos\phi & -\sin\phi & 0 \\ 0 & \sin\phi & -\cos\phi & 0 \\ 0 & 0 & 0 & 1 \end{pmatrix} \begin{pmatrix} -1 & 0 & 0 & 0 \\ 0 & 1 & 0 & 0 \\ 0 & 0 & 1 & 0 \\ 0 & 0 & 0 & 1 \end{pmatrix}$$

$$= \begin{pmatrix} \sin\theta & \cos\theta & 0 & 0 \\ -\cos\theta & \sin\theta & 0 & 0 \\ 0 & 0 & 1 & 0 \\ 0 & -\rho\sin\phi & -\rho\cos\phi & 1 \end{pmatrix} \begin{pmatrix} 1 & 0 & 0 & 0 \\ 0 & -\cos\phi & -\sin\phi & 0 \\ 0 & \sin\phi & -\cos\phi & 0 \\ 0 & 0 & 0 & 1 \end{pmatrix} \begin{pmatrix} -1 & 0 & 0 & 0 \\ 0 & 1 & 0 & 0 \\ 0 & 0 & 1 & 0 \\ 0 & 0 & 0 & 1 \end{pmatrix}$$

$$= \begin{pmatrix} \sin\theta & -\cos\theta\cos\phi & -\cos\theta\sin\phi & 0 \\ -\cos\theta & -\sin\theta\cos\phi & -\sin\theta\sin\phi & 0 \\ 0 & \sin\phi & -\cos\phi & 0 \\ 0 & 0 & \rho & 1 \end{pmatrix} \begin{pmatrix} -1 & 0 & 0 & 0 \\ 0 & 1 & 0 & 0 \\ 0 & 0 & 1 & 0 \\ 0 & 0 & 0 & 1 \end{pmatrix}$$

$$= \begin{pmatrix} -\sin\theta & -\cos\theta\cos\phi & -\cos\theta\sin\phi & 0 \\ \cos\theta & -\sin\theta\cos\phi & -\sin\theta\sin\phi & 0 \\ 0 & \sin\phi & -\cos\phi & 0 \\ 0 & 0 & \rho & 1 \end{pmatrix}$$

PROGRAMMING

While matrices provide a convenient form for establishing relationships between standard and eye coordinates of a point, languages available for microcomputers frequently do not provide for matrix arithmetic. To include the above matrix product in a BASIC program, write

```
10 S1 = SIN(THETA): C1 = COS(THETA):
   S2 = SIN(PHI): C2 = COS(PHI)
20 XE = -X*S1 + Y*C1
30 YE = -X*C1*C2 - Y*S1*C2 + Z*S2
40 ZE = -X*C1*S2 - Y*S1*S2 - Z*C2 + RHO
```

Screen coordinates then are provided by

```
50 SX = D*XE/ZE
60 SY = D*YE/ZE
```

Screen addressing techniques used by different microcomputers require changes in lines 50 and 60. In order to center the image on the Apple II screen and reorient the screen Y axis, write

```
50 SX = D*XE/ZE + 140
60 SY = 96 - D*YE/ZE
```

Program 6.1 shows one way of using the formulas above to generate an image of a three-dimensional object. Viewing parameters are defined in line 10. Note that we have chosen D larger than RHO, placing the object between the viewer and the projection plane. Line 20 calculates values that are used in the projection calculations. Line 30 identifies the center of the high resolution graphics screen. The coordinates of the visible vertices of a cube are given in lines 40 through 60. Lines 80 through 130 read the coordinates from the DATA statements and pass them to the subroutine in 150 and 160, which calculates the projected screen coordinates SX and SY. On return from the subroutine, the projected points are plotted.

Program 6.1: CUBE

```
1  REM PROGRAM 6.1  (CUBE)
2  REM DRAWS THE VISIBLE PARTS OF A CUBE
10 RHO = 10:THETA = .7:PHI = 1.3:D = 500
20 S1 = SIN (TH):C1 = COS (TH):S2 = SIN (PH):
   C2 = COS (PH)
30 CX = 140:CY = 96
```

(continued)

```
40   DATA 1,1,0, 1,1,1, 0,1,1, 0,1,0
50   DATA 1,1,0, 1,0,0, 1,0,1, 0,0,1
60   DATA 0,1,1, 1,0,1, 1,1,1
70   HGR2 : HCOLOR= 3
80   READ X,Y,Z: GOSUB 150: HPLOT SX,SY
90   FOR I = 1 TO 8: READ X,Y,Z
100    GOSUB 150: HPLOT   TO SX,SY
110    NEXT I
120    READ X,Y,Z: GOSUB 150: HPLOT SX,SY
130    READ X,Y,Z: GOSUB 150: HPLOT TO SX,SY
140    END
150  XE = - X * S1 + Y * C1:YE = - X * C1 *
     C2 - Y * S1 * C2 + Z * S2:ZE = - X * S2 *
     C1 - Y * S2 * S1 - Z * C2 + RHO
160  SX = D * XE / ZE + CX:SY = CY - D * YE / ZE:
     RETURN
```

VIEWPOINT AND PERSPECTIVE

It is worthwhile noting how each of RHO, THETA, PHI, and D affect the image generated on the display screen.

Changing the values of THETA and PHI will permit us to view an object from different angles. Changing the value of RHO (the distance from the viewer to the origin) permits us to move the viewer closer to, or farther from, the object. We thus may control the size of the image.

We have a second means of controlling the size of the screen image: changing the value of D. When a viewpoint (ρ,θ,ϕ) is specified, changes in D affect the size of the image on the projection plane—increasing D will increase the size of the image. Figure 6.15 illustrates the consequences of variations in the relative values of RHO and D.

Since RHO and D both affect the size of the image, it is important to understand the relationship between them. If the effect of each is to control size, why provide control over both? The answer to this lies in perspective: an object close to the viewer appears larger than when it is farther away because it occupies a larger proportion of field of view. Thus, for example, a perspective view of a cube will cause the edges close to the viewer to appear larger than edges farther away. To decrease the apparent effect of perspective, increase the value of RHO. This will decrease the perceived size of the image. To compensate, increase D. (What happens if the ratio RHO/D is maintained?)

Program 6.2 provides an opportunity to observe the effects of RHO, THETA, PHI, and D. The program accepts values of RHO,

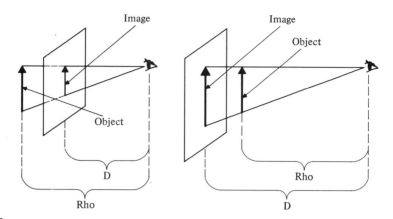

Figure 6.15

THETA, PHI, and D, then uses the values to display a view of a cube. To help maintain orientation, a diagonal line has been placed on the side of the cube that faces in the direction of the positive X axis. Try the following combinations of values, then experiment with several choices of your own. (Note that the angles THETA and PHI are again measured in radians.)

RHO	7	3	15	15	15	15
THETA	.3	.3	.3	.7	1.5	2.2
PHI	1.3	1.3	1.0	1.3	1.3	1.3
D	150	60	300	300	300	300

Program 6.2 illustrates the role of RHO, THETA, PHI, and D. It also points out another concern: it is possible to "see through" the closer faces of the cube to the farther edges. While this may be acceptable in some cases and desirable in some others, it is a problem when it leads to optical illusions. In the next chapter we will discuss two methods of eliminating "hidden" lines and surfaces from the display.

Program 6.2: VIEWPOINT

```
1    REM PROGRAM 6.2 (VIEWPOINT)
2    REM ILLUSTRATES EFFECT OF CHANGING THE
     VIEWPOINT PARAMETERS
10   TEXT : HOME : GOTO 180
```

(continued)

```
20  XE = - X * S1 + Y * C1:YE = - X * C1 *
    C2 - Y * S1 * C2 + Z * S2:ZE = - X * S2 *
    C1 - Y * S2 * S1 - Z * C2 + RHO
30  SX = D * XE / ZE + CX:SY = CY - D * YE / ZE:
    RETURN
40   HGR : ONERR GOTO 430
50  S1 = SIN (THETA):C1 = COS (THETA)
60  S2 = SIN (PHI):C2 = COS (PHI)
70   RESTORE : READ X,Y,Z: GOSUB 20: HPLOT SX,SY
80   FOR I = 1 TO 11: READ X,Y,Z: GOSUB 20:
    HPLOT TO SX,SY: NEXT I
90   FOR I = 1 TO 2: READ X,Y,Z: GOSUB 20:
    HPLOT SX, SY
100   READ X,Y,Z: GOSUB 20: HPLOT TO SX,SY:
    NEXT I
110   VTAB 21: PRINT "TO EXIT PROGRAM,
    PRESS 'ESC'"
120   VTAB 23: PRINT "TO CHANGE VALUES OF RHO,
    THETA, PHI,"
130   VTAB 24: PRINT "OR DISTANCE,
    PRESS 'RETURN'";
140   VTAB 24: HTAB 30: GET A$: VTAB 1: PRINT
150   IF ASC (A$) = 27 THEN TEXT : HOME : END
160   IF ASC (A$) < > 13 THEN 140
170   RETURN
180  RHO = 15:D = 350:THETA = .7:PHI = 1:
    CX = 140:CY = 96
190   DATA 1,1,1, 1,-1,1, -1,-1,1, -1,1,1
200   DATA 1,1,1, 1,1,-1, 1,-1,-1
210   DATA -1,-1,-1, -1,1,-1, 1,1,-1
220   DATA 1,-1,1, 1,-1,-1, -1,-1,1
230   DATA -1,-1,-1, -1,1,1,-1,1,-1
240   GOSUB 40: TEXT : HOME
250   VTAB 5: PRINT TAB( 10);"RHO = ";RHO
260   VTAB 8: PRINT TAB( 10);"THETA = ";THETA
270   VTAB 11: PRINT TAB( 10);"PHI = ";PHI
280   VTAB 14: PRINT TAB( 10);"DISTANCE = ";D
290   VTAB 20: PRINT "TO ACCEPT A VALUE,
    PRESS 'RETURN'"
300   VTAB 5: HTAB 15: INPUT R$
310   IF LEN (R$) < > 0 THEN RHO = VAL (R$)
320   VTAB 5: HTAB 15: PRINT " ";RHO;"        "
330   VTAB 8: HTAB 17: INPUT T$
340   IF LEN (T$) < > 0 THEN THETA = VAL (T$)
350   VTAB 8: HTAB 17: PRINT " ";THETA;"      "
360   VTAB 11: HTAB 15: INPUT P$
370   IF LEN (P$) < > 0 THEN PHI = VAL (P$)
```

```
380   VTAB 11:    HTAB 15: PRINT " ";PHI;"  "
390   VTAB 14: HTAB 20: INPUT D$
400   IF LEN (D$) < > 0 THEN D = VAL (D$)
410   VTAB 14: HTAB 20: PRINT " "; D;"  "
420   GOTO 240
430   TEXT : HOME : POKE 216,0
440   VTAB 10: PRINT "THE CUBE IS PARTLY
      OFFSCREEN."
450   VTAB 15: PRINT "TRY A LARGER VALUE OF
      RHO"
460   VTAB 20: PRINT "OR A SMALLER VALUE FOR
      DISTANCE"
470   FOR I = 1 TO 3000: NEXT I
480   HOME : GOTO 250
```

TRANSFORMATION OF IMAGES

Matrix transformations were introduced earlier and were used to establish a relationship between standard and eye coordinate systems of points. We will use them now to transform the points that define an object.

Program 6.3 generates images of three solids. Line 120 establishes the viewpoint. Lines 190 through 300 READ the DATA, transform it to screen coordinates, and plot the three solids. Solid number 1 is the cube of Program 6.1. Solids 2 and 3 result from transformations applied to the points before screen coordinates are calculated.

SOLID 2:

a) Scale the solid by multiplying the Z coordinates by 3. The transformation matrix is

$$A = \begin{vmatrix} 1 & 0 & 0 & 0 \\ 0 & 1 & 0 & 0 \\ 0 & 0 & 3 & 0 \\ 0 & 0 & 0 & 1 \end{vmatrix}$$

b) Rotate the solid through 30° about the Z axis. The transformation matrix is

$$B = \begin{vmatrix} COS30° & SIN30° & 0 & 0 \\ -SIN30° & COS30° & 0 & 0 \\ 0 & 0 & 1 & 0 \\ 0 & 0 & 0 & 1 \end{vmatrix} = \begin{vmatrix} .866 & .5 & 0 & 0 \\ -.5 & .866 & 0 & 0 \\ 0 & 0 & 1 & 0 \\ 0 & 0 & 0 & 1 \end{vmatrix}$$

c) Translate the solid, placing its center at $(-1,4,2)$. The transformation matrix is

$$C = \begin{pmatrix} 1 & 0 & 0 & 0 \\ 0 & 1 & 0 & 0 \\ 0 & 0 & 1 & 0 \\ -1 & 4 & 2 & 1 \end{pmatrix}$$

Applying the successive transformations to a point $P(X,Y,Z)$ results in point $P'(X1,Y1,Z1)$ with $(X1,Y1,Z1,1) = (X,Y,Z,1)ABC$

$$= (X,Y,Z,1) \begin{pmatrix} .866 & .5 & 0 & 0 \\ -.5 & .866 & 0 & 0 \\ 0 & 0 & 3 & 0 \\ -1 & 4 & 2 & 1 \end{pmatrix}$$

so that

$$X1 = .866X - .5Y - 1$$
$$Y1 = .5X + .866Y + 4$$
$$Z1 = 3Z + 2$$

In Program 6.3, lines 60 through 90 calculate the transformed coordinates, which are then passed to lines 100 through 110 to obtain screen coordinates.

SOLID 3:

a) Scale X and Y coordinates by a factor of 2
b) Rotate the solid through 60° about the X axis.
c) Rotate the solid through 15° about the Z axis.
d) Translate the solid, placing its center at $(4,2,-2)$.

For practice, write the transformation matrices of steps a, b, c, and d; multiply them to obtain the matrix

$$M = \begin{pmatrix} 1.93 & .518 & 0 & 0 \\ -.259 & .966 & 1.732 & 0 \\ .224 & -.836 & .5 & 0 \\ 4 & 2 & -2 & 1 \end{pmatrix}$$

As a result, the coordinates of the points of Solid 3 are described as

$$(X1,Y1,Z1,1) = (X,Y,Z,1)\ M$$
$$X1 = 1.93X - .259Y + .224Z + 4$$

$$Y1 = .518X + .966Y - .836Z + 2$$
$$Z1 = 1.732Y + .5Z - 2$$

Lines 20 through 50 transform the coordinates before obtaining the screen coordinates of solid 3.

Program 6.3: TRANSFORMED CUBE

```
1    REM PROGRAM 6.3 (TRANSFORMED CUBE)
2    REM DRAWS THREE IMAGES, GENERATED FROM A
     SINGLE DATA SET
10   GOTO 120
20   X1 = 1.93 * X - .259 * Y + .224 * Z + 4
30   Y1 = .518 * X + .966 * Y - .836 * Z + 2
40   Z1 = 1.732 * Y + .5 * Z - 2
50   X = X1:Y = Y1:Z = Z1: GOTO 100
60   X1 = .866 * X - .5 * Y - 1
70   Y1 = .5 * X + .866 * Y + 6
80   Z1 = 3 * Z + 2
90   X = X1:Y = Y1:Z = Z1
100  XE = - X * S1 + Y * C1:YE = - X * C1 *
     C2 - Y * S1 * C2 + Z * S2:ZE = - X * S2 *
     C1 - Y * S2 * S1 - Z * C2 + RHO
110  SX = D * XE / ZE + CX:SY = CY - D * YE /
     ZE: RETURN
120  RHO = 20:D = 250:THETA = .3:PHI = 1.3:
     CX = 140:CY = 96:S1 = SIN (THETA):S2 = SIN
     (PHI): C1 = COS (THETA) :C2 = COS (PHI)
130   DATA 1,1,1, 1,-1,1, -1,-1,1, -1,1,1
140   DATA 1,1,1, 1,1,-1, 1,-1,-1
150   DATA -1,-1,-1, -1,1,-1, 1,1,-1
160   DATA 1,-1,1, 1,-1,-1, -1,-1,1
170   DATA -1,-1,-1, -1,1,1, -1,1,-1
180   HGR2 : HCOLOR= 3
190   FOR I = 1 TO 3: READ X,Y,Z
200   ON I GOSUB 100,60,20
210   HPLOT SX,SY
220   FOR J = 1 TO 11: READ X,Y,Z
230   ON I GOSUB 100,60,20
240   HPLOT TO SX,SY
250   NEXT J
260   FOR J = 1 TO 2: READ X,Y,Z
270   ON I GOSUB 100,60,20
280   HPLOT SX,SY: READ X,Y,Z
290   ON I GOSUB 100,60,20
300   HPLOT TO SX,SY
310   NEXT J: RESTORE : NEXT I
```

NOTES AND SUGGESTIONS:

1. Modify Program 6.1 to generate images of other three-dimensional objects. Try pyramids, houses, furniture, and so forth. For each image you should make a rough sketch keeping the three-dimensional X,Y,Z coordinate system in mind. From the drawing you may make a listing of the coordinates of points to be displayed. For the present, if you wish to eliminate hidden lines and surfaces, leave the corresponding points out of your listing. With each selection of an object, it is usually necessary to experiment with choices of values for the viewing parameters RHO, THETA, PHI, and D.

2. Add a clipping routine to the programs you write. The routine described in Chapter 4 may be used. This will allow a zoom capability, without being concerned that offscreen points will result.

3. For the imaginative: You may already have tried using values of D that position the viewer between the object and the display screen (try negative values of D). If you haven't, can you predict the result before trying it on the computer? While you are at it, what will happen if the viewer is placed within the object? (Any images which are drawn with such a viewpoint must be processed by a line clipping subroutine.)

SURFACES OF THE FORM Z = F(X,Y)

Having developed the processes of generating three-dimensional images, we may apply them to a variety of surfaces. The program structure will be similar to that of Program 6.3. We must

1. Provide rectangular coordinates (X,Y,Z) of points of the surfaces;

2. Transform these to screen coordinates (SX,SY); and

3. Plot the points.

Unlike the previous programs in this chapter, we will not provide the coordinates of points as DATA in the program, but will have the points generated by a program segment. The following program will illustrate this.

Program 6.4: SURFACE

```
1    REM PROGRAM 6.4 (SURFACE)
2    REM DRAWS A SURFACE Z = F(X,Y)
10     GOTO 40
```

```
20  XE = - X * S1 + Y * C1:YE = - X * C1 * C2 - Y
    * S1 * C2 + Z * S2:ZE = - X * S2 * C1 - Y *
    S2 * S1 - Z * C2 + RHO
30  SX = D * XE / ZE + CX:SY = CY - D * YE / ZE:
    RETURN
40  RHO = 30:D = 350: THETA = .3:PHI = 1:CX =
    140:CY = 96:S1 = SIN (THETA): S2 = SIN
    (PHI):C1 = COS (THETA):C2 = COS (PHI)
50   DEF FN Z(X) = COS (.1 * (X * X + Y * Y))
60   HGR2 : HCOLOR= 3
70   FOR X = 10 TO - 10 STEP - 1
80  FL  = 0
90   FOR Y = - 10 TO 10
100  Z = FN Z(X): GOSUB 20
110   IF SX < 0 OR SX > 279 OR SY < 0 OR SY > 191
     THEN FL = 0: GOTO 140
120   IF FL = 0 THEN FL = 1: HPLOT SX,SY
130   HPLOT  TO SX,SY
140   NEXT Y,X
```

The program generates an image which represents the surface as a sequence of wire-frame curves. The curves are the intersections of the surface with vertical planes parallel to the YZ plane. We thus use two-dimensional curves to create a three-dimensional image. This is an example of a standard maxim of mathematics and computer science: When attacking a new problem, reduce it to a simpler form—one which you know how to handle.

The image obtained by the program obviously is dependent on the function selected (line 50). A pleasing image which shows the significant characteristics of the surface typically is the result of a time-consuming trial-and-error process. Minor changes in the definition of the function may affect the image significantly. You might experiment with minor variations in the above function. Try

```
Z = 3*COS(.4*(X*X+Y*Y))
```

or

```
Z = COS(.1*(X*X-Y*Y)).
```

A smoother surface will result from calculating more points on each curve (decreasing the step size of the loop beginning in line 90). Of course, this will result in an increase in execution time.

While the image is dependent on the function, it is also severely affected by the choice of the viewing parameters RHO, THETA, PHI, and D. Try RHO = 60 or PHI = 2, or experiment with other choices of your own.

As different viewing positions are selected, the image may become badly confused by overlapping curves. The program creates a "transparent" surface. We can "see through" the near parts of the surface to the farther parts that lie behind. This is sometimes desirable, but frequently is a problem, leading to confused images and optical illusions. We might obtain images that are more pleasing if the closer portions of the surface were able to "hide" the more distant portions. In general, the development of effective hidden line algorithms is one of the most challenging problems in computer graphics. The next chapter provides some approaches to the problem.

Experiment with the graphs of the following functions. It usually will be necessary to adjust the viewing parameters and the domain (limits of the FOR – NEXT loops). Selection of larger values for the STEP size will result in faster program execution, but "curves" that are more angular.

1. `Z = 3*COS(.05*(X*X - Y*Y))` Try different viewpoints.

2. `Z = 3*EXP(-.1*(X*X + Y*Y))`

3. `Z = A*SIN(X/B)*SIN(Y/C)` Try a variety of values for A, B, and C.

4. `Z = .1*(X*X - Y*Y)`

Chapter 7
Hidden Line and Hidden Surface Routines

Figure 7.1

INTRODUCTION

Faster than a speeding bullet!

More powerful than a locomotive!!

Able to leap tall buildings in a single bound!!!

Superman also had x-ray vision; he could see through objects. As ordinary people we might envy such an ability when we must make special efforts to identify a weak component in a mechanical device, or to study the inner workings of the human body, or when we are looking for lost car keys. On the other hand, uncontrolled x-ray vision would be inconvenient. An "x-ray world," in which all things are transparent or translucent, would be a very confusing place. We might then wish for the ability to look at an object, to turn it over as we study it, without being able to see through the closer surfaces of the object to the farther surfaces and vertices.

Our previous attempts to provide images of three-dimensional objects resulted in an x-ray world. Our microcomputer has Superman's vision, which we would like to have behave in a more "normal" fashion. It will require some very special efforts on our part to bring it under control. We must develop methods for identifying those surfaces and line segments which are visible, or partly visible, and those which are not. We may then display the visible portions of an object and eliminate those portions which are hidden from view.

The elimination of hidden lines and surfaces is one of the most challenging problems of computer graphics. Hidden line algorithms require large amounts of computer time and memory. These are precious commodities in a microcomputer. For this reason we will limit our discussion, presenting the theory of operation of several techniques and providing sample programs that draw images of simple three-dimensional objects. A general-purpose hidden line subroutine would be very inefficient. It is much more effective for the programmer to adapt the techniques to each specific application.

SURFACE ORIENTATION

The processes described in Chapter 6 permit the drawing of images of three-dimensional objects. If we want to avoid drawing the hidden lines and surfaces of objects it is necessary to have a method of distinguishing the visible lines from the hidden lines.

One obvious way to display only the visible portions of an object is to be careful that only the visible portions be identified to the computer. This was done in Program 6.1, which drew only the visible portions of a cube. Only the vertices of surfaces which were visible from the specified viewpoint were identified in the program. This technique requires the programmer to plan the view desired and to identify the points of the object which are visible from that view. The program is short and draws the image quickly. It is limited, however. If the image is to be drawn from a different viewpoint, it may be necessary to change the DATA statements and the program portion that draws the visible line segments.

The following method is more general. The program determines which surfaces are facing the viewpoint and identifies these as the visible surfaces.

NOTE: The following discussion assumes familiarity with vectors and the cross products and dot products of vectors. See Appendix 3 for a brief summary of these concepts.

THEORY OF OPERATION

As we look at a die, two or three of the faces are visible to us. The other faces are not visible since they are facing away from us (see Figure 7.2). It is the orientation, or "facing direction" of a surface, that we will use in our first hidden line technique.

With each face of a cube we can associate two normal (perpendicular) directions. One normal direction will point inward; the other will point outward, away from the cube. We represent these directions by normal vectors and take the outward-pointing vector as the orientation vector of the surface. The outward-pointing normals are shown in Figure 7.3.

With each surface of an object we also associate a second vector, a line-of-sight vector. This is the vector directed from one of the vertices

Figure 7.2

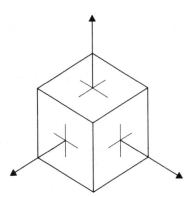

Figure 7.3

of the surface (any vertex) to the viewpoint (the location of the eye of the viewer).

For each surface we may measure the angle between the line-of-sight vector and the orientation vector. If this angle is between 0° and 90°, the surface is facing the viewer. It is visible and should be displayed. If the angle is between 90° and 180°, then the surface is facing away from the viewer. It is not visible and should not be displayed. (See Figure 7.4)

ORIENTATION VECTOR

In Figure 7.5, we have numbered the vertices of one surface of a cube. The identification of vertex number 1 is arbitrary, but it is important that the numbering of the remaining vertices of the surface continue in a counterclockwise direction, as viewed from outside the cube, facing the surface. We then identify vector $\vec{u}$, directed from vertex number 1 to vertex number 2, and vector $\vec{v}$, directed from vertex number 1 to vertex number 3. The cross product, $\vec{n} = \vec{u} \times \vec{v}$, will be normal (perpendicular) to the face of the cube and will be directed outward. (The magnitude, or length, of the orientation vector $\vec{n}$ will not be of importance to us.)

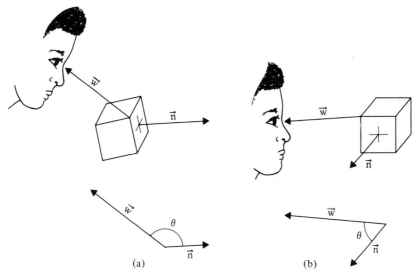

Figure 7.4

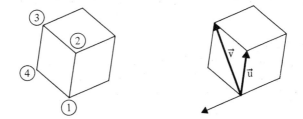

Figure 7.5

NOTE: It is important that the vertices numbered 1, 2, 3, 4 on the surface be given in counterclockwise direction as seen from outside the cube, facing the surface. If the points are assigned in a clockwise direction, the vector $\vec{n} = \vec{u} \times \vec{v}$, as described above, will be pointing inward.

VISIBILITY

The dot product of vectors $\vec{w}$ and $\vec{n}$ has the property

$$\vec{w} \cdot \vec{n} = |\vec{w}|\,|\vec{n}|\,\cos\theta$$

where θ is the angle between $\vec{w}$ and $\vec{n}$. If θ is between $0°$ and $90°$, the value of $\vec{w} \cdot \vec{n}$ will be positive. If θ is between $90°$ and $180°$, $\vec{w} \cdot \vec{n}$ will be negative.

Using $\vec{w}$ to represent the line-of-sight vector of a surface, and $\vec{n}$ to represent the orientation vector, we have a visibility test. For a visible surface, such as the surface of Figure 7.4b, the angle between $\vec{w}$ and $\vec{n}$ is between $0°$ and $90°$, and $\vec{w} \cdot \vec{n}$ is positive. For a hidden surface, as in Figure 7.4a, the angle between $\vec{w}$ and $\vec{n}$ is between $90°$ and $180°$, and $\vec{w} \cdot \vec{n}$ is negative.

Program 7.1

To illustrate the use of surface orientation in eliminating hidden lines, we will discuss a program which draws a house. (The program which draws this object is a long one, so we will present it in five parts. The complete listing of the program is given on pages 169–171.)

The house is defined by seven surfaces: two roof components, the front, the back, two ends, and the bottom. Each surface is defined by

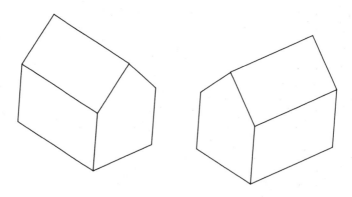

Figure 7.6

four or five edges. The two ends have five edges each; the other surfaces have four edges each. The edges, in turn, are defined by endpoints, or vertices. For the house shown (Fig. 7.6), there are 10 vertices.

The Vertex Array

We begin by identifying the ten vertices of the house. For reference purposes they are numbered as shown in Figure 7.7.

Vertex	Coordinates		
1	5	7	-5
2	5	7	5
3	5	-7	5
4	5	-7	-5
5	-5	7	-5
6	-5	-7	-5
7	-5	-7	5
8	-5	7	5
9	0	7	8
10	0	-7	8

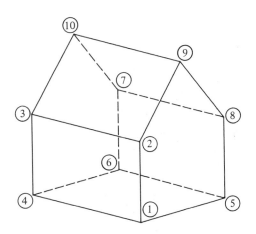

Figure 7.7

Program 7.1, Part 1

```
10   REM VIEWPOINT AND SCREEN PARAMETERS
20 RHO = 40:THETA = .7:PHI = 1:D = 250
30 CX = 140:CY = 96:S1 = SIN (TH):C1 = COS
   (TH):S2 = SIN (PH):C2 = COS (PH)
40   REM VERTICES
50   DATA 5,7,-5
60   DATA 5,7,5
70   DATA 5,-7,5
80   DATA 5,-7,-5
90   DATA -5,7,-5
100  DATA -5,-7,-5
110  DATA -5,-7,5
120  DATA -5,7,5
130  DATA 0,7,8
140  DATA 0,-7,8
150  REM FILL VERTEX ARRAYS
160  DIM V(10,3),SV(10,2)
170  FOR I = 1 TO 10
180  READ X,Y,Z
190 V(I,1) = X:V(I,2) = Y:V(I,3) = Z
200 X1 = - X * S1 + Y * C1:Y1 = - X * C1 * C2 -
    Y * S1 * C2 + Z * S2:Z1 = - X * S2 * C1 - Y
    * S2 * S1 - Z * C2 + RHO
210 SV(I,1) = D * (X1 / Z1) + CX:SV(I,2) = - D *
    (Y1 / Z1) + CY
220  NEXT I
```

Program lines 40 through 220 load the vertex coordinates into a two-dimensional vertex array. For each array entry, V(I,J), I is the identification number of the vertex (between 1 and 10), while J is the number of the coordinate identified. For example, V(8,1) will be the first (x) coordinate of the 8th vertex, V(8,2) will be the second (y) coordinate of the 8th vertex, and V(8,3) will be the third (z) coordinate of the 8th vertex. Since vertex number 8 is $(-5,7,5)$, we have

$$V(8,1) = -5$$
$$V(8,2) = 7$$
$$V(8,3) = 5$$

As the coordinates of the vertices are saved in the vertex array, the screen coordinates of each point are calculated for the screen vertex array SV(I,J). For each I, SV(I,1) and SV (I,2) are the screen coordinates SX,SY, respectively, of point number I.

The Surface Array

There are seven surfaces in the object (house) to be drawn. The surfaces
are identified by number as shown in Figure 7.8.

Each surface may be drawn by connecting the appropriate vertices:
for surface 1, connect vertex 1 to 2 to 3 to 4 to 1; for surface 2, connect
vertex 1 to 5 to 8 to 9 to 2 to 1. The other surfaces are defined in a similar manner (see Figure 7.9).

The array $S(I,J)$ identifies, for each surface I, the vertices that define
the surface. Since the boundary of surface 1 connects vertices 1,2,3,4,
and 1, these numbers are saved as $S(1,1)$, $S(1,2)$, $S(1,3)$, $S(1,4)$, and
$S(1,5)$, respectively. Similarly, $S(2,1) = 1$, $S(2,2) = 5$, $S(2,3) = 8$,
$S(2,4) = 9$, $S(2,5) = 2$, and $S(2,6) = 1$.

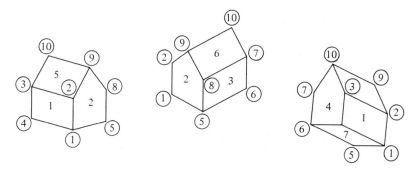

Figure 7.8

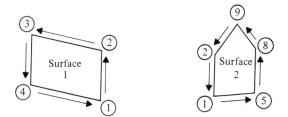

Figure 7.9

The complete array looks like this:

J

(points to be connected)

S(I,J)	1	2	3	4	5	6
1	1	2	3	4	1	0
2	1	5	8	9	2	1
3	5	6	7	8	5	0
4	4	3	10	7	6	4
5	3	2	9	10	3	0
6	7	10	9	8	7	0
7	1	4	6	5	1	0

I
(surface) corresponds to rows 1 through 7.

It is important, for each surface, that the vertices be identified in counterclockwise order as they appear from outside the object. You should verify that the points as listed in the surface array are in proper order. Refer to Figure 7.8 for outside views of each of the surfaces.

Program 7.1; Part 2

```
230 REM NUMBER OF POINTS IN EACH SURFACE
240 DATA 5,6,5,6,5,5,5
250 DIM NPS(7)
260 FOR I = 1 TO 7
270 READ NPS(I)
280 NEXT I
290 REM SURFACE ARRAY - POINTERS TO VERTICES
300 DATA 1,2,3,4,1
310 DATA 1,5,8,9,2,1
320 DATA 5,6,7,8,5
330 DATA 4,3,10,7,6,4
340 DATA 3,2,9,10,3
350 DATA 7,10,9,8,7
360 DATA 1,4,6,5,1
370 REM FILL SURFACE ARRAY
380 DIM S(7,6)
390 FOR I = 1 TO 7
400 FOR J = 1 TO NPS(I)
410 READ S(I,J)
420 NEXT J,I
```

The Normal Array

The Surface Orientation approach to hidden line elimination requires a vector normal (perpendicular) to each of the surfaces. These normals are calculated in program lines 430 through 550.

Program 7.1; Part 3

```
430    REM CALCULATE VECTOR NORMAL TO EACH SURFACE
440    DIM N(7,3)
450    FOR I = 1 TO 7
460 U1 = V(S(I,2),1) - V(S(I,1),1)
470 U2 = V(S(I,2),2) - V(S(I,1),2)
480 U3 = V(S(I,2),3) - V(S(I,1),3)
490 V1 = V(S(I,3),1) - V(S(I,1),1)
500 V2 = V(S(I,3),2) - V(S(I,1),2)
510 V3 = V(S(I,3),3) - V(S(I,1),3)
520 N(I,1) = U2 * V3 - V2 * U3
530 N(I,2) = U3 * V1 - V3 * U1
540 N(I,3) = U1 * V2 - V1 * U2
550    NEXT I
```

The order in which points are listed in the surface array is important when the normal array is developed. This array contains the coordinates of outward pointing normal vectors to the surfaces. N(1,1), N(1,2), and N(1,3) are the x, y, z components of an outward pointing normal vector to surface 1. N(2,1), N(2,2), and N(2,3) are the components of an outward pointing normal vector to surface 2. For each surface I ($1 \leq I \leq 7$), the array values N(I,1), N(I,2), and N(I,3) are the components of an outward pointing vector that is normal to the surface.

The calculation of the normal vectors makes use of the fact that the cross product of two vectors is normal to the plane containing the two vectors. To identify a vector normal to a surface, we first choose vectors $\vec{u}$ and $\vec{v}$ which are parallel to the surface. Then $\vec{u} \times \vec{v}$ will yield a normal vector.

Each surface has either five or six vertices. Program lines 460 through 510 identify $\vec{u}$ as extending from the first to the second of these vertices. Vector $\vec{v}$ extends from the first to the third vertex. Lines 520 through 540 calculate the components of the cross product of $\vec{u}$ and $\vec{v}$.

Notice how the order of vertices affects the calculation of the normal vector. If the vertices of a surface are listed in a clockwise direction, then the relative orientation of $\vec{u}$ and $\vec{v}$ will be reversed, and $\vec{u} \times \vec{v}$ will be an inward pointing normal vector, rather than an outward pointing normal vector (see Figure 7.10).

The Visibility Test

We are now ready to apply the visibility test to each surface of the object. For each surface, we choose a line-of-sight vector $\vec{w}$ extending from a point (any point) on the surface to the viewpoint (XE,YE,ZE). The

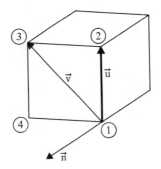 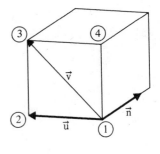

Figure 7.10

angle between $\vec{w}$ and the outward pointing normal, $\vec{n}$, provides a visibility criterion. If the angle is between 0° and 90°, the surface faces the viewer. In this case the dot product $\vec{n} \cdot \vec{w}$ will be positive. If the angle is between 90° and 180°, the surface faces away from the viewer; $\vec{n} \cdot \vec{w}$ will be negative.

Program line 650 is the visibility filter. Those surfaces which face the viewer ($\vec{n} \cdot \vec{w} > 0$) will pass through the filter, eventually to be plotted. Those surfaces which do not face the viewer ($\vec{n} \cdot \vec{w} \le 0$) will be rejected.

Program 7.1; Part 4

```
560  REM DETERMINE VISIBILITY OF EACH SURFACE
570  REM AND COLLECT VISIBLE EDGES IN EDGE ARRAY
580  XE = RH * S2 * C1:YE = RH * S2 * S1:
     ZE = RH * C2
590  DIM E(12,3):N = 1
600  FOR I = 1 TO 7
610  E2 = S(I,1)
620  WX = XE - V(E2,1)
630  WY = YE - V(E2,2)
640  WZ = ZE - V(E2,3)
650  IF N(I,1) * WX + N(I,2) * WY + N(I,3) *
     WZ < = 0 THEN 760
660  E1 = S(I,1)
670  FOR J = 2 TO NPS(I)
680  E2 = S(I,J)
690  FOR K = 1 TO N
```

```
700   IF  E(K,1)  =  E2  AND  E(K,2)  =  E1
      THEN  E(K,3)  =  2:  GOTO  740
710   NEXT  K
720 E(N,1)  =  E1:E(N,2)  =  E2:E(N,3)  =  1
730 N  =  N  +  1
740 E1  =  E2
750   NEXT  J
760   NEXT  I
```

The Edge Array

Visible surfaces are decomposed into edges that are collected in the edge array, which has been dimensioned to accept as many as 12 edges [DIM E(12,3)].

Each of the edges that are put in the array is identified by a number I (between 1 and 12). For each edge I, three numbers are saved. $E(I,1)$ and $E(I,2)$ are the identification numbers of the two endpoints of the edge. $E(I,3)$ is a tag, and identifies the number of visible surfaces for which the edge is a boundary. If the edge is a boundary of one visible edge, then the value of $E(I,3)$ is 1. If the edge is a boundary of two visible edges, then the value of $E(I,3)$ is 2.

Figure 7.11 illustrates the labelling of edges in the edge array.

Edge	Endpoints		Tag
1	1	2	2
2	2	3	2
3	3	4	1
4	4	1	1
5	1	5	1
6	5	8	1
7	8	9	1
8	9	2	2
9	9	10	1
10	10	3	1
11	0	0	0
12	0	0	0

Edges 11 and 12 are not needed for this view. The array provides more space than is necessary; no view of the object will show more than 12 edges.

Notice that the edges that are "outer" edges of the drawing (edges 3,4,5,6,7,9,10) all have a tag with a value of 1. These edges are those which are a boundary of only one visible surface. The "inner" edges of

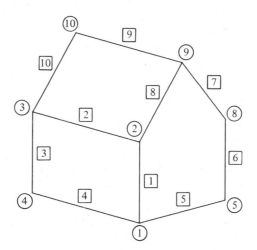

Figure 7.11

the drawing (1,2,8) are those which bound two visible surfaces. Their tags are all equal to 2. The distinction between "inner" and "outer" edges becomes important when we consider the drawing of more than one object.

Program lines 660 through 760 fill the edge array. The endpoints of each edge are read from the surface array (lines 660, 680, and 740) and stored in the edge array (line 720), and the tag is set to 1. If an edge is encountered for a second time, the tag is reset to 2 (line 700).

Plotting

It is now the time to draw the visible edges. Lines 790 through 830 identify the visible edges (those with nonzero tags), read the identification numbers of the corresponding endpoints, and plot the edges.

Program 7.1; Part 5

```
770    REM DRAW VISIBLE EDGES
780    HGR2 : HCOLOR= 3
790    FOR I = 1 TO 12
```

```
800    IF E(I,3) = 0 THEN 830
810 J = E(I,1):K = E(I,2)
820    HPLOT SV(J,1),SV(J,2) TO SV(K,1),SV(K,2)
830    NEXT I
840    END
```

Program 7.1: HIDDEN LINE ELIMINATION, SURFACE ORIENTATION
METHOD

```
1     REM PROGRAM 7.1 (HIDDEN LINE ELIMINATION)
2     REM SURFACE ORIENTATION METHOD
10    REM VIEWPOINT AND SCREEN PARAMETERS
20 RHO = 40:THETA = .7:PHI = 1:D = 250
30 CX = 140:CY = 96:S1 = SIN (TH):C1 = COS (TH):
   S2 = SIN (PH):C2=COS (PH)
40    REM VERTICES
50    DATA 5,7,-5
60    DATA 5,7,5
70    DATA 5,-7,5
80    DATA 5,-7,-5
90    DATA -5,7,-5
100   DATA -5,-7,-5
110   DATA -5,-7,5
120   DATA -5,7,5
130   DATA 0,7,8
140   DATA 0,-7,8
150   REM FILL VERTEX ARRAYS
160   DIM V(10,3),SV(10,2)
170   FOR I = 1 TO 10
180   READ X,Y,Z
190 V(I,1) = X:V(I,2) = Y:V(I,3) = Z
200 X1 = -X * S1 + Y * C1:Y1 = -X * C1 *
    C2 -Y * S1 * C2 + Z * S2:Z1 = -X * S2 *
    C1 - Y * S2 * S1 - Z * C2 + RHO
210 SV(I,1) = D * (X1 / Z1) + CX:SV(I,2) = -D *
    (Y1 / Z1) + CY
220   NEXT I
230   REM NUMBER OF POINTS IN EACH SURFACE
240   DATA 5,6,5,6,5,5,5
250   DIM NPS(7)
260   FOR I = 1 TO 7
270   READ NPS(I)
280   NEXT I
290   REM SURFACE ARRAY - POINTERS TO VERTICES
300   DATA 1,2,3,4,1
```

(continued)

```
310    DATA 1,5,8,9,2,1
320    DATA 5,6,7,8,5
330    DATA 4,3,10,7,6,4
340    DATA 3,2,9,10,3
350    DATA 7,10,9,8,7
360    DATA 1,4,6,5,1
370    REM FILL SURFACE ARRAY
380    DIM S(7,6)
390    FOR I = 1 TO 7
400    FOR J = 1 TO NPS(I)
410    READ S(I,J)
420    NEXT J,I
430    REM CALCULATE VECTOR NORMAL TO EACH SURFACE
440    DIM N(7,3)
450    FOR I = 1 TO 7
460 U1 = V(S(I,2),1) - V(S(I,1),1)
470 U2 = V(S(I,2),2) - V(S(I,1),2)
480 U3 = V(S(I,2),3) - V(S(I,1),3)
490 V1 = V(S(I,3),1) - V(S(I,1),1)
500 V2 = V(S(I,3),2) - V(S(I,1),2)
510 V3 = V(S(I,3),3) - V(S(I,1),3)
520 N(I,1) = U2 * V3 - V2 * U3
530 N(I,2) = U3 * V1 - V3 * U1
540 N(I,3) = U1 * V2 - V1 * U2
550    NEXT I
560    REM DETERMINE VISIBILITY OF EACH SURFACE
570    REM AND COLLECT VISIBLE EDGES IN EDGE ARRAY
580 XE = RH * S2 * C1:YE = RH * S2 * S1:
    ZE = RH * C2
590    DIM E(12,3):N = 1
600    FOR I = 1 TO 7
610 E2 = S(I,1)
620 WX = XE - V(E2,1)
630 WY = YE - V(E2,2)
640 WZ = ZE - V(E2,3)
650    IF N(I,1) * WX + N(I,2) * WY + N(I,3) * WZ
    < = 0 THEN 760
660 E1 = S(I,1)
670    FOR J = 2 TO NPS(I)
680 E2 = S(I,J)
690    FOR K = 1 TO N
700    IF E(K,1) = E2 AND E(K,2) = E1
    THEN E(K,3) = 2: GOTO 740
710    NEXT K
720 E(N,1) = E1:E(N,2) = E2:E(N,3) = 1
730 N = N + 1
```

```
740 E1 = E2
750   NEXT J
760   NEXT I
770   REM DRAW VISIBLE EDGES
780   HGR2 : HCOLOR= 3
790   FOR I = 1 TO 12
800   IF E(I,3) = 0 THEN 830
810 J = E(I,1):K = E(I,2)
820   HPLOT SV(J,1),SV(J,2) TO SV(K,1),SV(K,2)
830   NEXT I
840   END
```

NOTES AND SUGGESTIONS

1. If you became impatient with the above program and recognize ways that could make it more efficient, good! The program was designed to illustrate the surface orientation approach to eliminating hidden lines in a way that was easy to describe, and to introduce some techniques (such as the edge array, with tags) that will be valuable later. These goals did not lead to the most efficient program. For example, one-dimensional arrays are accessed more rapidly than are two-dimensional arrays.

2. The viewpoint parameters are specified in line 20. Try a variety of views. In general, you will want to change only THETA or PHI.

3. Choosing small values for RHO or large values for D may result in an image that will not fit on the screen. You may want to insert a clipping routine (see Chapter 4).

4. Programming other convex polygonal solids will require obvious changes in the data for the vertex array and the surface array, and related changes in the limits of the various FOR–NEXT loops. Try objects such as cubes, pyramids, and prisms.

5. Once a surface is identified as being visible (facing the viewer), components within that surface may be assumed to be visible. To each of the four walls of the house, add windows and doors, drawing these components whenever the corresponding surface is visible.

TWO OBJECTS; BLACKOUT

The methods described above permit the drawing of the visible portions of a single convex object. In the pages ahead, methods will be presented that allow the drawing of the visible portions of several objects. In addition to being concerned about the identification of those portions of an object which face toward, or away from, the viewer, it will be necessary to identify those portions which are hidden by a closer object.

When we look around us, portions of objects are hidden by closer objects because of the inability of light to pass through an opaque substance. We could consider that the hidden portions of an object have been "drawn," but were "erased" by the "drawing" of a closer object (see Figure 7.12). This approach is used in Program 7.2.

Program 7.2: HIDDEN LINE ELIMINATION, TWO OBJECTS; BLACKOUT

```
1    REM PROGRAM 7.2 (HIDDEN LINE ELIMINATION)
2    REM TWO OBJECTS; BLACKOUT
10   TEXT : HOME : GOTO 130
20   XE = -X * S1 + Y * C1:YE = -X * C1 * C2 - Y *
     S1 * C2 + Z * S2:ZE = -X * S2 * C1 - Y * S2 *
     S1 - Z * C2 + RHO
30   SX = D * XE / ZE + CX:SY = CY - D * YE / ZE:
     RETURN
40   DATA 1,1,0, 0,0,1, 0,1,0, 1,1,0, 1,0,0,
     0,0,1
50   DATA 1,1.5,1, 0,1.5,1
60   DATA 0,2.5,1, 1,2.5,1, 1,2.5,0,
     0,2.5,0,0,2.5,1, 0,1.5,1, 1,1.5,1, 1,1.5,0,
     1,2.5,0,1,2.5,1, 1,1.5,1
70   FOR I = 1 TO N: READ X,Y,Z
80   GOSUB 20
90   IF I = 1 THEN HPLOT SX,SY
100  HPLOT TO SX,SY
110  NEXT I
```

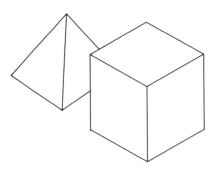

Figure 7.12

```
120    RETURN
130    RHO = 10:D = 600:THETA = 1:PHI = 1.2:
       CX = 140: CY = 96
140    S1 = SIN (THETA):C1 = COS (THETA)
150    S2 = SIN (PHI):C2 = COS (PHI)
160    HGR2 : HCOLOR= 7
170    N = 6: GOSUB 70
180    READ X,Y,Z: GOSUB 20:X1 = SX:Y1 = SY
190    READ X,Y,Z: GOSUB 20:X2 = SX:Y2 = SY
200    SL = (Y1 - Y2) / (X1 - X2)
210    HCOLOR= 4
220    FOR XP = X1 TO X2:YP = SL * (XP - X1) + Y1
230    HPLOT XP,YP TO XP,191
240    NEXT XP
250    HCOLOR= 7
260    N = 9: GOSUB 70:N = 2: GOSUB 70
```

The data in lines 40 through 60 identify the vertices of a cube and a pyramid as shown in Figure 7.12. The only vertices given are those which are part of a surface that faces the viewer. The more distant of the two objects (the pyramid) is drawn first (line 170). Before the closer object (the cube) is drawn, the hidden portions of the pyramid are removed from the screen. This is accomplished by using HCOLOR = 4 (BLACK, the background color) to draw over a portion of the screen occupied by the cube. The erasure of the hidden parts of the pyramid is handled in lines 180 through 240. Vertical black lines are drawn from the screen image of one of the cube edges to the bottom of the screen. When the erasure is complete, the cube is drawn (line 260).

This technique of hidden line elimination is fairly easy to use, and gives nice results in short execution time. It is limited, however; the viewpoint must be planned well in advance. This planning is necessary in order that only the vertices of visible surfaces are provided, and so that the region to be "blacked out" may be identified. A change in viewpoint typically will require changes in DATA statements and changes in the blackout routine.

TWO OBJECTS; BINARY SEARCH

In Figure 7.13, the cube should block vertex H of the pyramid from view. Edge VH of the pyramid should be partly hidden, with only VT visible. While the screen coordinates of vertex V are available, the coordinates of T must be calculated. Since T is the point of intersection of

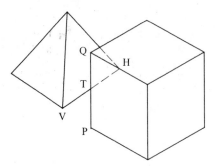

Figure 7.13

cube edge PQ and pyramid edge VH, the coordinates of T could be calculated from the equations of lines VH and PQ. The algebra involved is
straightforward, but not efficient. Instead, we will recommend a ''binary search'' to identify the coordinates of T.

Program 7.3: HIDDEN LINE ELIMINATION, TWO OBJECTS; BINARY SEARCH

```
1   REM PROGRAM 7.3 (HIDDEN LINE ELIMINATION)
2   REM TWO OBJECTS; BINARY SEARCH
10   TEXT : HOME : GOTO 140
20  XE = -X * S1 + Y * C1:YE = -X * C1 * C2 - Y *
     S1 * C2 + Z * S2:ZE = -X * S2 * C1 - Y * S2 *
     S1 - Z * C2 + RHO
30  SX = D * XE / ZE + CX:SY = CY - D * YE / ZE:
     RETURN
40   DATA 0,2.5,1, 1,2.5,1, 1,2.5,0,
     0,2.5,0,0,2.5,1, 0,1.5,1, 1,1.5,1, 1,1.5,0,
     1,2.5,0,1,2.5,1, 1,1.5,1
50   DATA 1,1,0, 0,0,1, 1,0,0, 1,1,0
60   DATA 1,1,0, 0,1,0, 1,1.5,0, 1,1.5,1
70   DATA 0,0,1, 0,1,0, 1,1.5,1, 0,1.5,1
80   FOR I = 1 TO N: READ X,Y,Z
90   GOSUB 20
100   IF I = 1 THEN HPLOT SX,SY
110   HPLOT TO SX,SY
120   NEXT I
130   RETURN
140 RHO = 10:D = 600:THETA = 1:PHI = 1.2:
     CX = 140:CY = 96
```

```
150  S1 = SIN (THETA):C1 = COS (THETA)
160  S2 = SIN (PHI):C2 = COS (PHI)
170   HGR2 : HCOLOR= 7
180  N = 9: GOSUB 80:N = 2: GOSUB 80
190  N = 4: GOSUB 80
200   FOR J = 1 TO 2
210   READ X,Y,Z: GOSUB 20:XV = SX:YV = SY
220   READ X,Y,Z: GOSUB 20:XH = SX:YH = SY
230   READ X,Y,Z: GOSUB 20:XP = SX:YP = SY
240   READ X,Y,Z: GOSUB 20:XQ = SX:YQ = SY
250  V1 = (XH - XV) / 2:V2 = (YH - YV) / 2
260  U1 = XP - XQ:U2 = YP - YQ
270  XT = XV + V1:YT = YV + V2
280   FOR I = 2 TO 7
290  VI = SGN ((U2 * (XV - XQ) - U1 *
     (YV - YQ)) * (U2 * (XT - XQ) - U1 *
     (YT - YQ)))
300  V1 = V1 / 2:V2 = V2 / 2
310  XT = XT + VI * V1:YT = YT + VI * V2
320   NEXT I
330   HPLOT XV,YV TO XT,YT
340   NEXT J
```

Lines 180 and 190 plot the visible portions of the cube and the edges of the pyramid that are completely visible. Lines 210 through 240 obtain the screen coordinates of points V, H, P, and Q. The calculation of the coordinates of point T is accomplished in lines 250 through 320. The binary search used to obtain T functions as follows:

1. Identify the vector (V1,V2), extending from point V(XV,YV) halfway to point H(XH,YH). (Line 250.)

2. Add (V1,V2) to (XV,YV) to obtain the midpoint (XT,YT) of the line segment from (XV,YV) to (XH,YH). (Line 270.)

3. Test (XT,YT) for visibility. (Line 290.)

4. Redefine (V1,V2) = (V1,V2)/2. (Line 300.)

5. If (XT,YT) is visible, then move toward (XH,YH) by redefining (XT,YT) = (XT,YT) + (V1,V2). If (XT,YT) is hidden, then move toward (XV,YV) by redefining (XT,YT) = (XT,YT) − (V1,V2). (Line 310.)

6. Return to step 3. (Line 320.)

To determine the visibility of T, we identify vector $\vec{u}$ extending from point Q to point P, the vector $(XV - XQ, YV - YQ)$ extending from point Q to point V, and the vector $(XT - XQ, YT - YQ)$ extending from point Q to point T. If T is visible, then T must lie on the same side of line PQ as point V. If that is the case, the cross product of $(XT - XQ, YT - YQ)$ and $\vec{u}$ will have the same sign as the cross product of $(XV - XQ, YV - YQ)$ and vector $\vec{u}$. If T is not visible, the cross products will have opposite signs. (May we safely assume that neither cross product is zero?) Line 290 takes care of the comparison of the cross products.

The value of (XT, YT) is accepted after the seventh value has been calculated. The length of $(V1, V2)$ is then 1/128th of the distance from (XV, YV) to (XH, YH). This provides acceptable accuracy for most images on the Apple display screen. Greater accuracy may be obtained by increasing the number of cycles through the loop.

On leaving the loop, the line segment from point V to point T is plotted. The procedure is then repeated for the second partially hidden line.

TWO OBJECTS; ARBITRARY VIEWPOINT

The previous two methods for eliminating hidden lines from images containing several convex objects place limits on the viewpoint. If it is preferred to have a more general method, we may extend the surface orientation method.

THEORY OF OPERATION

We will use the objects shown in Figure 7.14 to illustrate the calculations that are necessary.

From the angle of view provided in 7.14a, the cube lies closer to the viewer, hiding a part of the pyramid. In Figure 7.14b, the pyramid hides part of the cube. One of our concerns will be the assignment of a priority to each of the objects. When two objects are a part of a scene, the one that is not hidden by the other will be given first priority status. The object which is partly hidden will be assigned second priority status. Assignment of priority may be made on the basis of distance from the viewpoint to the center of each object, with the closer object being assigned first priority status.

A second method of assigning priority is based on a "separating plane" (a plane that separates the two objects). First priority is assigned

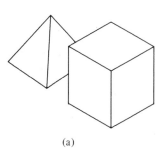
(a)

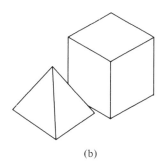
(b)

Figure 7.14

to the object that lies on the same side of the separating plane as the viewpoint. Any plane which separates the objects may be chosen as the "separating plane." (The separating plane may contain a point, an edge, or a surface of one or both of the objects.) If a change in separating planes causes a change in the priority of the objects, we need not worry. In that case, neither object will hide the other.

Once the objects have been assigned priority, the first priority object may be plotted. We will use the surface orientation process to draw only those surfaces which face the viewer.

The surface orientation process also will be applied to the second priority object in order to identify those surfaces which face the viewer. Each edge of a "visible" surface then must be considered separately to determine whether either of its endpoints are hidden by the first priority object. If neither endpoint is hidden, the edge may be plotted. If both endpoints are hidden, the edge is discarded. If exactly one endpoint is hidden, we must calculate the point of intersection of the screen image of the edge with the screen image of the boundary of the priority one object. The visible portion of the edge is then plotted.

This problem presents challenges we have not faced before. We will illustrate them with a cube and an edge of a pyramid.

In Figure 7.15a, the hidden portions of two edges of the pyramid are shown as dashed lines. Since the visible portion of each of these edges extends from the visible endpoint to the intersection with an outside boundary of the cube image, we may simplify the diagram by discarding the inner cube boundaries (Figure 7.15b).

The orientation of the outside cube edges, inherited from the definition of the surface array entries, is shown in Figure 7.15c. In that drawing, note that point H of the pyramid edge, lying inside the cube boundaries and thus hidden by the cube, is in the left half-plane of each of the

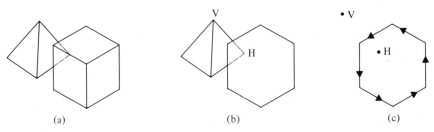

(a)	(b)	(c)

Figure 7.15

cube boundaries. Point V, which is not hidden by the cube, is in the left half-plane of several cube boundaries, and in the right half-plane of others. (See Appendix 3 for a discussion of half-planes.)

To identify the visible portions of the pyramid edge, we move along the line from H to V, testing each point for visibility. Identify T as the first point which is found to lie in the right half-plane of at least one cube boundary. Then the visible line segment from V to T may be plotted.

PROGRAM 7.4

The methods described above are illustrated in the following program. To the "house" of Program 7.1, we will add a second object: a "chimney." (Again, the program is a long one; it will be given in several parts.)

The chimney is defined by six surfaces: the top, the bottom, and four sides. Every surface is defined by four edges, each of which is identified by its endpoints (vertices of the chimney).

In defining the two objects, the vertices of the house are retained as they were defined in Program 7.1. (Figure 7.16).

Vertex	Coordinates		
1	5	7	−5
2	5	7	5
3	5	−7	5
4	5	−7	−5
5	−5	7	−5
6	−5	−7	−5
7	−5	−7	5
8	−5	7	5
9	0	7	8
10	0	−7	8

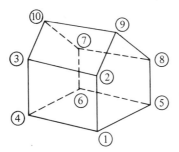

Figure 7.16

The vertices of the chimney are identified by number as shown in Figure 7.17.

Vertex	Coordinates		
11	−2	−7	−5
12	−2	−9	−5
13	−5	−9	−5
14	−5	−7	−5
15	−2	−7	9
16	−2	−9	9
17	−5	−9	9
18	−5	−7	9

The Vertex Arrays

Program lines 10 through 310 identify the viewpoint and screen parameters, and read the coordinates of the vertices into the vertex arrays. Arrays V(I,J) and SV(I,J) are dimensioned so that each accommodates the coordinates of 18 points. The vertex array V(I,J) serves the same function as before, with V(I,1), V(I,2), and V(I,3) identifying the x, y, and z coordinates of vertex I.

Program 7.4; Part 1

```
10   REM VIEWPOINT AND SCREEN PARAMETERS
20 RHO = 40:THETA = .7:PHI = 1:D = 250
30 CX = 140:CY = 96:S1 = SIN (TH):
   C1 = COS (TH):S2 = SIN (PH):C2 = COS (PH)
40   REM VERTICES OF OBJECT 1 (HOUSE)
```

(continued)

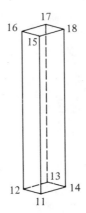

Figure 7.17

```
50    DATA 5,7,-5
60    DATA 5,7,5
70    DATA 5,-7,5
80    DATA 5,-7,-5
90    DATA -5,7,-5
100   DATA -5,-7,-5
110   DATA -5,-7,5
120   DATA -5,7,5
130   DATA 0,7,8
140   DATA 0,-7,8
150   REM VERTICES OF OBJECT 2 (CHIMNEY)
160   DATA -2,-7,-5
170   DATA -2,-9,-5
180   DATA -5,-9,-5
190   DATA -5,-7,-5
200   DATA -2,-7,9
210   DATA -2,-9,9
220   DATA -5,-9,9
230   DATA -5,-7,9
240   REM FILL VERTEX ARRAYS
250   DIM V(18,3),SV(18,3)
260   FOR I = 1 TO 18
270   READ X,Y,Z
280 V(I,1) = X:V(I,2) = Y:V(I,3) = Z
```

```
290 X1 = -X * S1 + Y * C1:Y1 = -X * C1 * C2 - Y *
    S1 * C2 + Z * S2:Z1 = -X * S2 * C1 - Y * S2 *
    S1 - Z * C2 + RHO
300 SV(I,1) = D * (X1 / Z1) + CX:
    SV(I,2) = -D * (Y1 / Z1) + CY
310 NEXT I
```

The entries SV(I,1) and SV(I,2) are calculated as the values of V(I,1),
V(I,2), and V(I,3) are identified. For each I, SV(I,1) and SV(I,2) identify the screen coordinates of the point (X,Y,Z). A third entry, SV(I,3) is
available for each vertex I. Initially, each SV(I,3) is left equal to 0.
Later, this entry will be changed in order to identify the status (visible or
hidden) of some of the vertices.

The Surface Array

The surface array is the next to be filled. The array simply is an enlargement of the one used in Progam 7.1, identifying surfaces 1 through 7 as
the surfaces of the house, and surfaces 8 through 13 as the surfaces of
the chimney. Surfaces 8 and 9 are the top and bottom of the chimney;
surfaces 10, 11, 12, and 13 are the four sides of the chimney. As before,
the array entries V(I,1) through V(I,NPS(I)) identify the vertices of surface I, listed in counterclockwise order around the surface (as seen from
outside the object).

Program 7.4; Part 2

```
320   REM NUMBER OF POINTS IN EACH SURFACE
330   DATA 5,6,5,6,5,5,5,5,5,5,5,5,5
340   DIM NPS(13)
350   FOR I = 1 TO 13
360   READ NPS(I)
370   NEXT I
380   REM SURFACE ARRAY - POINTERS TO VERTICES
390   DATA 1,2,3,4,1
400   DATA 1,5,8,9,2,1
410   DATA 5,6,7,8,5
420   DATA 4,3,10,7,6,4
430   DATA 3,2,9,10,3
440   DATA 7,10,9,8,7
450   DATA 1,4,6,5,1
460   DATA 11,12,13,14,11
```

(continued)

```
470   DATA  15,18,17,16,15
480   DATA  11,14,18,15,11
490   DATA  12,16,17,13,12
500   DATA  11,15,16,12,11
510   DATA  14,13,17,18,14
520   REM FILL SURFACE ARRAY
530   DIM  S(13,6)
540   FOR  I = 1 TO  13
550   FOR  J = 1 TO NPS(I)
560   READ  S(I,J)
570   NEXT  J,I
```

When complete, the surface array looks like this:

J

(points to be connected)

	S(I,J)	1	2	3	4	5	6
	1	1	2	3	4	1	0
	2	1	5	8	9	2	1
	3	5	6	7	8	5	0
	4	4	3	10	7	6	4
	5	3	2	9	10	3	0
	6	7	10	9	8	7	0
I	7	1	4	6	5	1	0
(surface)	8	11	12	13	14	11	0
	9	15	18	17	16	15	0
	10	11	14	18	15	11	0
	11	12	16	17	13	12	0
	12	11	15	16	12	11	0
	13	14	13	17	18	14	0

The Normal Array

The normal array is calculated as before, with $N(I,1)$, $N(I,2)$, and $N(I,3)$ identifying the three components of the outward pointing normal vector to surface I.

Program 7.4; Part 3

```
580   REM CALCULATE VECTOR NORMAL TO EACH SURFACE
590   DIM  N(13,3)
600   FOR  I = 1 TO  13
610   U1 = V(S(I,2),1) - V(S(I,1),1)
620   U2 = V(S(I,2),2) - V(S(I,1),2)
```

```
630  U3 = V(S(I,2),3)  -  V(S(I,1),3)
640  V1 = V(S(I,3),1)  -  V(S(I,1),1)
650  V2 = V(S(I,3),2)  -  V(S(I,1),2)
660  V3 = V(S(I,3),3)  -  V(S(I,1),3)
670  N(I,1) = U2 * V3  -  V2 * U3
680  N(I,2) = U3 * V1  -  V3 * U1
690  N(I,3) = U1 * V2  -  V1 * U2
700    NEXT I
```

Edge Array

In Program 7.1, the edge array provided space for the identification of the endpoints of as many as 12 visible edges of the house. The chimney adds 12 edges, no more than nine of which are visible from any given viewpoint.

Since some of the edges of the farther object may be partly hidden by the closer object, it is useful to classify each edge so that it may be referenced by object number. The edge array is dimensioned E(2,12,3). When referencing an entry in the edge array, E(I,J,K), I will have a value of 1 or 2, referring to an edge of object 1 or object 2 (house or chimney). For each I, J will have a value between 1 and 12, allowing as many as 12 visible edges for each object (at most, 12 are needed for the house; at most, 9 for the chimney). For edge J of object I, E(I,J,1) and E(I,J,2) are pointers to the vertices that are the endpoints of the edge. E(I,J,3) is a tag which identifies the number of visible surfaces for which the edge is a boundary.

Figure 7.18 shows the pattern of labelling the edges in the edge array.

I = 1; object 1 (house)				I = 2; object 2 (chimney)			
Edge	Endpoints		Tag	Edge	Endpoints		Tag
1	1	2	2	1	11	12	1
2	2	3	2	2	14	11	1
3	3	4	1	3	15	18	2
4	4	1	1	4	18	17	1
5	1	5	1	5	17	16	1
6	5	8	1	6	16	15	2
7	8	9	1	7	14	18	1
8	9	2	2	8	15	11	2
9	9	10	1	9	16	12	1
10	10	3	1	10	0	0	0
11	0	0	0	11	0	0	0
12	0	0	0	12	0	0	0

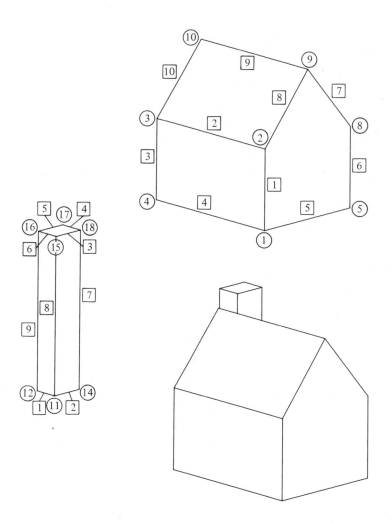

Figure 7.18

The contents of the edge array are dependent on the viewpoint selected. As the viewpoint changes, the number of edges will change, and the sequence of edges in the array and the tags will change.

Program 7.4; Part 4

```
710   REM DETERMINE VISIBILITY OF EACH SURFACE
720   REM AND COLLECT VISIBLE EDGES IN EDGE ARRAY
730 XE = RH * S2 * C1:YE = RH * S2 * S1:
    ZE = RH * C2
```

```
740    DIM  E(2,12,3)
750  O  =  1:N  =  1
760    FOR  I  =  1  TO  13
770  E2  =  S(I,1)
780  VX  =  XE  -  V(E2,1)
790  VY  =  YE  -  V(E2,2)
800  VZ  =  ZE  -  V(E2,3)
810    IF  N(I,1)  *  VX  +  N(I,2)  *  VY  +  N(I,3)  *  VZ
       <  =  0  THEN  920
820  E1  =  S(I,1)
830    FOR  J  =  2  TO  NPS(I)
840  E2  =  S(I,J)
850    FOR  K  =  1  TO  N
860    IF  E(O,K,1)  =  E2  AND  E(O,K,2)  =  E1
       THEN  E(O,K,3)  =  2:  GOTO  900
870    NEXT  K
880  E(O,N,1)  =  E1:E(O,N,2)  =  E2:E(O,N,3)  =  1
890  N  =  N  +  1
900  E1  =  E2
910    NEXT  J
920    IF  I  =  7  THEN  O  =  2:N  =  1
930    NEXT  I
```

The identification of visible edges by the program is performed in essentially the same fashion as in Program 7.1. The surfaces of object 1 (the house) are considered first (line 750). Each surface of the object is tested for visibility in line 810 and the surfaces that face away from the viewpoint are discarded. Lines 820 through 910 then consider each of the edges of a visible surface. The endpoints of each edge are identified in lines 820 and 840, and collected in the edge array by line 880. The tag $E(O,N,3)$ is set to 1 in line 880. If an edge is encountered for a second time (suggesting that it is a boundary of two visible surfaces) the tag $E(O,N,3)$ is set to 2 (line 860). When all surfaces of object 1 (the house) have been tested for visibility, the testing continues with the surfaces of object 2 (the chimney).

Object Priority

Since edges of the farther object may be partly hidden by the closer object, it is necessary to classify the objects by their relative positions. A separating plane has been used to establish the priority of the two objects. The plane $Y = -7$ is used as the separating plane, since the points of object 1 are either in the plane or on the side opposite the points of object 2.

If the viewpoint (XE,YE,ZE) lies on the same side of the separating plane as the house, then the visible edges of the house cannot be hidden by portions of the chimney. The house is given priority 1, while the chimney, the edges of which may be partly or fully hidden by the house, is given priority 2. If the viewpoint is on the same side of the separating plane as the chimney, then the chimney is given priority 1 and the house is given priority 2.

Program 7.4; Part 5

```
940   REM ESTABLISH PRIORITY OF OBJECTS
950   IF YE > = -7 THEN P(1) = 1:P(2) = 2
960   IF YE < -7 THEN P(1) = 2:P(2) = 1
```

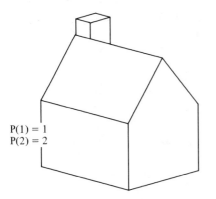
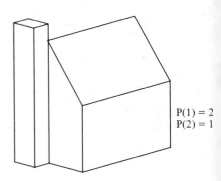

P(1) = 1
P(2) = 2

P(1) = 2
P(2) = 1

Figure 7.19

Priority One Edges

The visible edges of the object having first priority may now be drawn. Each of the edges is a boundary of a surface which has passed the surface orientation test for visibility. Since the edges are associated with the object having first priority, they could not be hidden (partly or completely) by the other object.

Program 7.4; Part 6

```
970   REM DRAW VISIBLE EDGES OF FIRST PRIORITY
      OBJECT
980   HGR2 : HCOLOR= 3
990   FOR I = 1 TO 12
1000   IF E(P(1),I,3) = 0 THEN 1030
1010 J = E(P(1),I,1):K = E(P(1),I,2)
1020   HPLOT SV(J,1),SV(J,2) TO SV(K,1),SV(K,2)
1030   NEXT I
```

Priority Two Edges

The edges associated with the second object must be scrutinized more carefully. An edge which is in the edge array may be partly or completely hidden by the priority one object.

To illustrate, consider the view of the house and chimney shown in Figure 7.20.

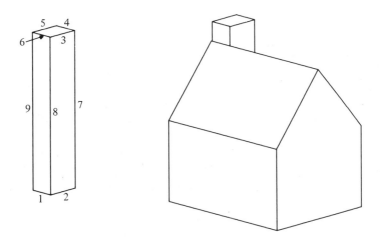

Figure 7.20

Edges 1 and 2 of the chimney are boundaries of sides of the chimney which have passed the surface orientation test for visibility. However, these edges are completely hidden by the house. They should not be plotted. Edges 3, 4, 5, and 6 are completely visible and should be plotted. On the other hand, edges 7, 8, and 9 are only partly visible. For each of these edges it will be necessary to determine at what point the edge becomes visible, then plot only the visible portion.

There are, then, three types of edges associated with the visible surfaces of the object which have second priority. Some edges are completely hidden by a closer object, some are only partly hidden, others are completely visible.

Program 7.4; Part 7

```
1040    REM TEST EACH EDGE OF SECOND PRIORITY
        OBJECT FOR VISIBILITY STATUS
1050    REM DRAW VISIBLE EDGES AND VISIBLE PARTS
        OF EDGES
```

(continued)

```
1060    FOR  E  =  1  TO  12
1070    IF  E(P(2),E,3)  =  0  THEN  1150
1080    I  =  E(P(2),E,1):J  =  E(P(2),E,2)
1090    IF  SV(I,3)  =  0  THEN  XT  =  SV(I,1):
        YT  =  SV(I,2):  GOSUB  1170:SV(I,3)  =  VI
1100    IF  SV(J,3)  =  0  THEN  XT  =  SV(J,1):
        YT  =  SV(J,2):  GOSUB  1170:SV(J,3)  =  VI
1110    IF  SV(I,3)  +  SV(J,3)  =  -2  THEN  1140
1120    IF  SV(I,3)  +  SV(J,3)  =  0  THEN  1260
1130    HPLOT  SV(I,1),SV(I,2)  TO  SV(J,1),SV(J,2)
1140    NEXT  E
1150    END
```

Program lines 1040 through 1140 oversee the disposition of the priority two edges. As each edge is considered, the screen array entries $SV(I,3)$, which have been ignored until now, will be used to indicate the visibility status of the endpoints (identified in line 1080). Line 1090 and 1100 use the subroutine beginning at line 1160 (discussed below) to determine the visibility status of each endpoint. If an endpoint I is visible, then $SV(I,3)$ is set equal to 1. If an endpoint I is hidden, then $SV(I,3)$ is set equal to -1.

An edge with vertices I and J as endpoints is identified as hidden if $SV(I,3) + SV(J,3) = -2$; such an edge may be discarded (line 1110).

If $SV(I,3) + SV(J,3) = 0$ (line 1120), then one endpoint is visible and one is hidden. The endpoints are turned over to the subroutine beginning at line 1260, which identifies and plots the visible portion of the edge.

If $SV(I,3) + SV(J,3) = 2$, then both endpoints are visible; the edge may be plotted (line 1130).

Visibility Status of Edge Endpoints

Program lines 1080 through 1100 identify the endpoints of each edge and refer each endpoint to lines 1160 through 1250 for classification as visible or hidden. Figure 7.21 will be used to illustrate the process used for endpoint classification.

In Figure 7.21a, the visible surfaces of the house have been plotted, and endpoints of one edge of the chimney are shown. Note that endpoint H, which should be hidden by the house, is inside the outer boundary of the house (Figure 7.21b), while point V is outside. Since the outside house boundaries have a counterclockwise orientation (specified in the surface array and preserved in the edge array), an "inside" point H

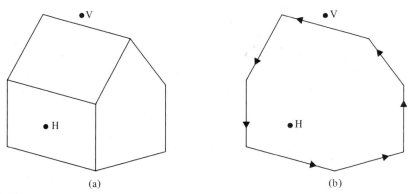

Figure 7.21

is identified as such because it lies in the left half-plane of each component of the boundary. The point V is identified as an "outside" point by noting that it is in the right half-plane of at least one boundary component.

Program 7.4; Part 8

```
1160    REM CLASSIFY ENDPOINTS OF EDGES AS VISIBLE
        OR HIDDEN
1170 VI = -1
1180    FOR L = 1 TO 12
1190    IF E(P(1),L,3) < > 1 THEN 1240
1200 P = E(P(1),L,1):Q = E(P(1),L,2)
1210 R1 = SV(Q,1) - SV(P,1):
        R2 = SV(Q,2) - SV(P,2)
1220 U1 = XT - SV(P,1):U2 = YT - SV(P,2)
1230    IF U2 * R1 - U1 * R2 > 0
        THEN VI = 1: RETURN
1240    NEXT L
1250    RETURN
```

The intent of the classification subroutine is to establish the value of the visibility variable VI as +1 for a visible endpoint (a point outside the house boundary) or −1 for a hidden endpoint (a point inside the house boundary). To this end, we assume that each point is hidden (line 1170: VI = −1) until it is proven visible.

Since a point is visible if it is in the right half-plane of at least one boundary component, the loop 1180 through 1240 compares the endpoint (XT,YT) with each visible edge of the house. In order to obtain an "inside" or "outside" classification, only those edges which are outside boundaries need be considered. Line 1190 skips over all others.

For each outside edge PQ of the house, two vectors are calculated.

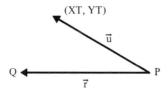

Figure 7.22

As shown in Figure 7.22, vector $\vec{r}$ extends from P to Q. Vector $\vec{u}$ extends from P to (XT,YT), the point to be classified. If (XT,YT) is in the right half-plane of line PQ (thus visible), then $\vec{u} \times \vec{r}$ is a positive multiple of (0,0,1) (See Appendix 3). In this case, program line 1230 will change the value of VI to 1, then return from the subroutine.

If the endpoint (XT,YT), is in the left half-plane of each of the outside edges of the house, then we will return from the subroutine with VI = −1.

Clipping Edges That Are Partly Hidden

If an edge has one vertex hidden and one visible, it is necessary to clip the line segment so as to display only the visible portion. Program line 1120 refers such edges to a routine beginning at line 1270. There, the point that is visible is identified as (XV,YV) and the hidden point is labelled as (XH,YH).

Program lines 1290 through 1360 use a "binary search" to locate the point (XT,YT) that divides the line segment into two parts: a visible segment from (XV,YV) to (XT,YT), and a hidden portion from (XT,YT) to (XH,YH). The binary search at first may appear to be a slow and random approach to use. In fact it is very efficient. It works like this:

1. Identify the vector (V1,V2) extending from (XV,YV) halfway to (XH,YH). (Line 1290.)

2. Add (V1,V2) to (XV,YV) to obtain the midpoint (XT,YT) of the line segment from (XV,YV) to (XH,YH). (Line 1300.)

3. Test (XT,YT) for visibility. (Line 1320.)

4. Redefine (V1,V2) = (V1,V2)/2.(Line 1330.)

5. If (XT,YT) is visible, then move towards (XH,YH) by redefining (XT,YT) = (XT,YT) + (V1,V2). (Lines 1340, 1350.) If (XT,YT) is hidden, then move towards (XV,YV) by redefining (XT,YT) = (XT,YT) − (V1,V2). (Lines 1340, 1350.)

6. Return to step 3. (Line 1360.)

The test for visibility of (XT,YT) (line 1320) uses the classification subroutine beginning at line 1170. As before, the routine returns with VI = +1 if (XT,YT) is visible or with VI = −1 if (XT,YT) is hidden. The value of VI then determines whether the next (XT,YT) is obtained by moving toward (XH,YH) if VI = +1, or by moving toward (XV,YV) if VI = −1.

The exit from the loop of steps 3 through 5 occurs when the seventh value of (XT,YT) has been calculated. The length of (V1,V2) then is 1/128th of the distance between (XV,YV) and (XH,YH). This resolution is more than adequate for most images on the Apple display screen. Of course, greater resolution may be obtained by increasing the number of cycles through the loop.

On leaving the loop, the line segment from (XV,YV) to (XT,YT) is plotted. Program control is then returned to line 1070 in order to begin consideration of another edge.

Program 7.4; Part 9

```
1260   REM PLOT VISIBLE PORTION OF EDGES WHICH
       ARE PARTLY HIDDEN
1270   IF SV(I,3) = 1 THEN XV = SV(I,1):YV =
       SV(I,2):XH = SV(J,1): YH = SV(J,2)
1280   IF SV(J,3) = 1 THEN XV = SV(J,1):YV =
       SV(J,2):XH = SV(I,1): YH = SV(I,2)
1290 V1 = (XH - XV) / 2:V2 = (YH - YV) / 2
1300 XT = XV + V1:YT = YV + V2
1310   FOR I = 2 TO 7
1320   GOSUB 1170
1330 V1 = V1 / 2:V2 = V2 / 2
1340 XT = XT + VI * V1
1350 YT = YT + VI * V2
1360   NEXT I
1370   HPLOT XV,YV TO XT,YT
1380   NEXT E
```

Program 7.4: HIDDEN LINE ELIMINATION, TWO OBJECTS; ARBITRARY VIEWPOINT

```
1   REM PROGRAM 7.4 (HIDDEN LINES)
2   REM TWO OBJECTS; ARBITRARY VIEWPOINT
10   REM VIEWPOINT AND SCREEN PARAMETERS
20  RHO = 40:THETA = .7:PHI = 1:D = 250
30  CX = 140:CY = 96:S1 = SIN (TH):C1 = COS (TH):
    S2 = SIN (PH):C2 = COS (PH)
40   REM VERTICES OF OBJECT 1 (HOUSE)
50   DATA 5,7,-5
60   DATA 5,7,5
70   DATA 5,-7,5
80   DATA 5,-7,-5
90   DATA -5,7,-5
100   DATA -5,-7,-5
110   DATA -5,-7,5
120   DATA -5,7,5
130   DATA 0,7,8
140   DATA 0,-7,8
150   REM VERTICES OF OBJECT 2 (CHIMNEY)
160   DATA -2,-7,-5
170   DATA -2,-9,-5
180   DATA -5,-9,-5
190   DATA -5,-7,-5
200   DATA -2,-7,9
210   DATA -2,-9,9
220   DATA -5,-9,9
230   DATA -5,-7,9
240   REM FILL VERTEX ARRAYS
250   DIM V(18,3),SV(18,3)
260   FOR I = 1 TO 18
270   READ X,Y,Z
280  V(I,1) = X:V(I,2) = Y:V(I,3) = Z
290  X1 = -X * S1 + Y * C1:Y1 = -X * C1 * C2 - Y *
    S1 * C2 + Z * S2:Z1 = -X * S2 * C1 - Y * S2 *
    S1 - Z * C2 + RHO
300  SV(I,1) = D * (X1 / Z1) + CX:
    SV(I,2) = -D * (Y1 / Z1) + CY
310   NEXT I
320   REM NUMBER OF POINTS IN EACH SURFACE
330   DATA 5,6,5,6,5,5,5,5,5,5,5,5,5
340   DIM NPS(13)
350   FOR I = 1 TO 13
360   READ NPS(I)
370   NEXT I
380   REM SURFACE ARRAY - POINTERS TO VERTICES
```

```
390   DATA  1,2,3,4,1
400   DATA  1,5,8,9,2,1
410   DATA  5,6,7,8,5
420   DATA  4,3,10,7,6,4
430   DATA  3,2,9,10,3
440   DATA  7,10,9,8,7
450   DATA  1,4,6,5,1
460   DATA  11,12,13,14,11
470   DATA  15,18,17,16,15
480   DATA  11,14,18,15,11
490   DATA  12,16,17,13,12
500   DATA  11,15,16,12,11
510   DATA  14,13,17,18,14
520   REM FILL SURFACE ARRAY
530   DIM S(13,6)
540   FOR I = 1 TO 13
550   FOR J = 1 TO NPS(I)
560   READ S(I,J)
570   NEXT J,I
580   REM CALCULATE VECTOR NORMAL TO EACH SURFACE
590   DIM N(13,3)
600   FOR I = 1 TO 13
610 U1 = V(S(I,2),1) - V(S(I,1),1)
620 U2 = V(S(I,2),2) - V(S(I,1),2)
630 U3 = V(S(I,2),3) - V(S(I,1),3)
640 V1 = V(S(I,3),1) - V(S(I,1),1)
650 V2 = V(S(I,3),2) - V(S(I,1),2)
660 V3 = V(S(I,3),3) - V(S(I,1),3)
670 N(I,1) = U2 * V3 - V2 * U3
680 N(I,2) = U3 * V1 - V3 * U1
690 N(I,3) = U1 * V2 - V1 * U2
700   NEXT I
710   REM DETERMINE VISIBILITY OF EACH SURFACE
720   REM AND COLLECT VISIBLE EDGES IN EDGE ARRAY
730 XE = RH * S2 * C1:YE = RH * S2 * S1:
    ZE = RH * C2
740   DIM E(2,12,3)
750 O = 1:N = 1
760   FOR I = 1 TO 13
770 E2 = S(I,1)
780 VX = XE - V(E2,1)
790 VY = YE - V(E2,2)
800 VZ = ZE - V(E2,3)
810   IF N(I,1) * VX + N(I,2) * VY + N(I,3) * VZ
    < = 0 THEN 920
820 E1 = S(I,1)
```

(continued)

```
830   FOR J = 2 TO NPS(I)
840  E2 = S(I,J)
850   FOR K = 1 TO N
860  IF E(0,K,1) = E2 AND E(0,K,2) = E1
     THEN E(0,K,3) = 2: GOTO 900
870   NEXT K
880  E(0,N,1) = E1:E(0,N,2) = E2:E(0,N,3) = 1
890  N = N + 1
900  E1 = E2
910   NEXT J
920   IF I = 7 THEN O = 2:N = 1
930   NEXT I
940   REM ESTABLISH PRIORITY OF OBJECTS
950   IF YE > = -7 THEN P(1) = 1:P(2) = 2
960   IF YE < -7 THEN P(1) = 2:P(2) = 1
970   REM DRAW VISIBLE EDGES OF FIRST PRIORITY
     OBJECT
980   HGR2 : HCOLOR= 3
990   FOR I = 1 TO 12
1000   IF E(P(1),I,3) = 0 THEN 1030
1010  J = E(P(1),I,1):K = E(P(1),I,2)
1020   HPLOT SV(J,1),SV(J,2) TO SV(K,1),SV(K,2)
1030   NEXT I
1040   REM TEST EACH EDGE OF SECOND PRIORITY
     OBJECT FOR VISIBILITY STATUS
1050   REM DRAW VISIBLE EDGES AND VISIBLE PARTS
     OF EDGES
1060   FOR E = 1 TO 12
1070   IF E(P(2),E,3) = 0 THEN 1150
1080  I = E(P(2),E,1):J = E(P(2),E,2)
1090   IF SV(I,3) = 0 THEN XT = SV(I,1):
     YT = SV(I,2): GOSUB 1170:SV(I,3) = VI
1100   IF SV(J,3) = 0 THEN XT = SV(J,1):
     YT = SV(J,2): GOSUB 1170:SV(J,3) = VI
1110   IF SV(I,3) + SV(J,3) = -2 THEN 1140
1120   IF SV(I,3) + SV(J,3) = 0 THEN 1260
1130   HPLOT SV(I,1),SV(I,2) TO SV(J,1),SV(J,2)
1140   NEXT E
1150   END
1160   REM CLASSIFY ENDPOINTS OF EDGES AS VISIBLE
     OR HIDDEN
1170  VI = -1
1180   FOR L = 1 TO 12
1190   IF E(P(1),L,3) < > 1 THEN 1240
1200  P = E(P(1),L,1):Q = E(P(1),L,2)
1210  R1 = SV(Q,1) - SV(P,1):
     R2 = SV(Q,2) - SV(P,2)
```

```
1220 U1 = XT - SV(P,1):U2 = YT - SV(P,2)
1230  IF U2 * R1 - U1 * R2 > 0
      THEN VI = 1: RETURN
1240  NEXT L
1250  RETURN
1260  REM PLOT VISIBLE PORTION OF EDGES WHICH
      ARE PARTLY HIDDEN
1270  IF SV(I,3) = 1 THEN XV = SV(I,1):
      YV = SV(I,2):XH = SV(J,1): YH = SV(J,2)
1280  IF SV(J,3) = 1 THEN XV = SV(J,1):
      YV = SV(J,2):XH = SV(I,1): YH = SV(I,2)
1290 V1 = (XH - XV) / 2:V2 = (YH - YV) / 2
1300 XT = XV + V1:YT = YV + V2
1310  FOR I = 2 TO 7
1320   GOSUB 1170
1330 V1 = V1 / 2:V2 = V2 / 2
1340 XT = XT + VI * V1
1350 YT = YT + VI * V2
1360  NEXT I
1370  HPLOT XV,YV TO XT,YT
1380  NEXT E
```

NOTES AND SUGGESTIONS

1. The techniques described are not without flaws. For example, if the endpoints of an edge of a priority two object are both outside the image of the priority one object, the edge is drawn. This may result in the drawing of edges that should be partly hidden. To illustrate, edge AB of the prism below would be drawn, even though a portion of it is hidden by the cube. From certain viewpoints, Program 7.4 can draw "hidden" parts of lines.

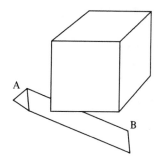

Figure 7.23

2. Modify the data and the limits in the loops of the program in order to draw other images. For example, try the pryamid and cube of Figure 7.14.

3. The techniques described here may be extended to images containing three or more objects. Of course, the program complexity will increase, and program execution will take longer.

4. Program 7.4 does not provide for line clipping should the image be too large to fit on the display screen. Modify the program so that all lines are sent to a clipping subroutine (such as the one described in Chapter 4) before being drawn.

HIDDEN LINE ELIMINATION FOR SURFACES OF THE FORM Z = F(X,Y)

Toward the end of Chapter 6, a program listing was given as an example of a means of generating images of the form $Z = F(X,Y)$. The program was brief, and drew the surface quickly. Unfortunately, no provision was made for hidden line elimination. The result was an image that sometimes was confusing. We intend to correct the situation, so that we might obtain images like the one shown on the upper right of the front cover.

Before turning to the hidden line calculations, we will review the earlier program:

Program 7.5: SURFACE

```
1   REM PROGRAM 7.5 (SURFACE)
2   REM REPEAT OF PROGRAM 6.4
10   REM INITIALIZATION
20   HGR2 : HCOLOR= 3:RHO = 30:THETA = .4:PHI =
     1.25: D = 420:CX = 140:CY = 96
30  S1 = SIN (THETA):C1 = COS (THETA)
40  S2 = SIN (PHI):C2 = COS (PHI)
50   DEF FN F(X) = COS (.1 * (X * X + Y * Y))
60   REM POINT GENERATING LOOP
70   FOR X = 10 TO -10 STEP -1
80  FL = 0
90   FOR Y = -10 TO 10 STEP .4
100 Z = FN F(X)
110   GOSUB 150
120   NEXT Y,X
130   END
140   REM PLOTTING SUBROUTINE
```

```
150 XE = -X * S1 + Y * C1
160 YE = -X * C1 * C2 - Y * S1 * C2 + Z * S2
170 ZE = -X * S2 * C1 - Y * S2 *
    S1 - Z * C2 + RHO
180 SX = D * (XE / ZE) + CX
190 SY = -D * (YE / ZE) + CY
200 IF SX < 0 OR SX > 279 OR SY < 0 OR SY > 191
    THEN FL = 0: RETURN
210 IF FL = 0 THEN HPLOT SX,SY:FL = 1
220 HPLOT TO SX,SY
230 RETURN
```

Program lines 20 through 50 identify the viewing parameters, the screen parameters, and the function to be plotted. The nested loops in lines 70 through 120 generate the coordinates of points on the surface and send the points to the plotting subroutine, which begins at line 150. There, the screen coordinates (SX,SY) are calculated (lines 150–190). If the calculated coordinates identify a point that is off-screen, it is discarded (line 200). The first point of a wire-frame curve (FL = 0), or the first onscreen point that follows an offscreen point (again, FL = 0), results in plotting via HPLOT SX,SY (line 210). Otherwise, a line segment is plotted which connects the point with the one most recently plotted (line 220). Then, control is returned to the point generating loop.

Program 7.6 is an extension of the above program to include hidden line capabilities. The initialization (lines 10–70) is similar to the beginning of Program 7.5, establishing the viewing and screen parameters and the function to be plotted. Then, in lines 60 and 70, two arrays are defined. These are for use by the hidden line routine. The intent of the arrays is as follows:

> YX(XP) [Y − maX] identifies, for each horizontal screen coordinate XP, the maximum (lowest on screen) vertical screen coordinate encountered. YN(XP) [Y − miN] identifies, for each horizontal screen coordinate XP, the minimum (highest on screen) vertical screen coordinate encountered.

Initially, the value of each YX(I) is zero and the value of each YN(I) is 191. As points (XP,YP) are plotted, the values of YX(XP) and YN(XP) are reset. As each (XP,YP) is considered for plotting, YP is compared with YX(XP) and YN(XP). If YP lies between YX(XP) and YN(XP), the point (XP,YP) is classified as hidden. Otherwise it is assumed to be visible. The function of the arrays is shown in Figure 7.24.

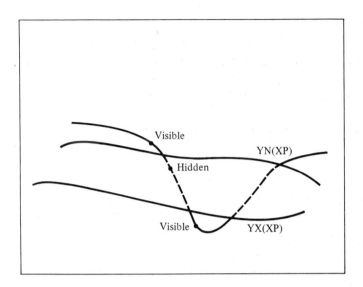

Figure 7.24

Program 7.6: HIDDEN LINES (FOR SURFACES Z = F(X,Y))

```
1   REM PROGRAM 7.6 (HIDDEN LINES)
2   REM HIDDEN LINE ELIMINATION FOR SURFACES: Z =
    F(X,Y)
10   REM INITIALIZATION
20   HGR2 : HCOLOR= 3:RHO = 30:THETA = .4:
     PHI = 1.25: D = 420:CX = 140:CY = 96
30  S1 = SIN (THETA):C1 = COS (THETA)
40  S2 = SIN (PHI):C2 = COS (PHI)
50  DEF FN Z(X) = 7 * EXP (-.1 *
    (X ^ 2 + Y ^ 2))
60   DIM YN(280),YX(280)
70   FOR I = 0 TO 279:YN(I) = 191: NEXT I
80   REM POINT GENERATING LOOP
90   FOR X = 8 TO -8 STEP -1
100 FL = 0
110  FOR  Y = -8 TO 8 STEP .5
120 Z = FN Z(X)
130  GOSUB 190
140  NEXT Y,X
150  HCOLOR= 2
160  HPLOT 0,0 TO 278,0 TO 278,191 TO 0,191 TO
     0,0
```

```
170   END
180   REM  PLOTTING  SUBROUTINE
190 XE = -X * S1 + Y * C1
200 YE = -X * C1 * C2 - Y * S1 * C2 + Z * S2
210 ZE = -X * S2 * C1 - Y * S2 * S1 - Z * C2 +
      RHO
220 SX = D * (XE / ZE) + CX
230 SY = -D * (YE / ZE) + CY
240  IF FL = 0 THEN FL = 1:F = 0: GOTO 360
250 DX = OX - SX: IF DX = 0 THEN DX = 1
260 SL = (OY - SY) / DX:YP = OY
270  FOR XP = INT (OX) + 1 TO SX
280 FG = 1
290 YP = YP + SL
300 IF XP < 0 OR XP > 279 THEN FG = 0:F = 0:
      GOTO 350
310  IF YP > 191 OR YP < 0 THEN FG = 0:F = 0
320  IF YP < = YN(XP) THEN 370
330  IF YP > = YX(XP) THEN 420
340 F = 0
350  NEXT XP
360 OX = SX:OY = SY: RETURN
370 YN(XP) = YP
380  IF FG = 0 THEN 410
390  IF F = 0 THEN HPLOT XP,YP:F = 1
400  HPLOT TO XP,YP
410  IF YP < YX(XP) THEN 350
420 YX(XP) = YP
430  IF FG = 0 THEN 460
440  IF F = 0 THEN HPLOT XP,YP:F = 1
450  HPLOT TO XP,YP
460  GOTO 350
```

This use of arrays requires that the wire-frame curves representing the surface be generated sequentially, beginning with the one closest to the viewer. The point generating loop (lines 80–140) provides that this is the case.

As each point (X,Y,Z) is generated, it is passed to the hidden line subroutine, where the corresponding screen coordinates (SX,SY) are calculated.

The point (SX,SY) could be tested for visibility (is $SY < = YN(SX)$, or is $SY > = YX(XP)$?). However, that would not be adequate. It is necessary to determine the status of each point (XP,YP) along the line segment connecting (SX,SY) with the point previously calculated (OX,OY) (old point). If (XP,YP) is hidden, it is not plotted. If (XP,YP) is visible, it is plotted and the corresponding array entry (YX(XP) or YN(XP)) is updated.

The hidden line subroutine uses three variables as flags to signal actions within the program.

1. FL: If the point (SX,SY) is the first of a wire-frame curve, then FL = 0; otherwise, FL = 1.

2. F: If F = 0, the command HPLOT XP,YP should be used to plot the next visible point (XP,YP). If F = 1, then the command HPLOT TO XP,YP should be used.

3. FG: If the current point (XP,YP) is offscreen, then FG = 0; otherwise, FG = 1.

The first point on a wire-frame curve is marked by setting FL = 0 (line 100). Within the subroutine, this is taken (line 240) as a signal to define (OX,OY) (old point) as the newly calculated (SX,SY), and the program returns to the point generating loop.

If FL = 1, the points on the line segment from (OX,OY) to (SX,SY) will be tested for visibility. Lines 250 and 260 identify the slope of the line segment. Line 270 begins a loop that steps through the integers XP (screen coordinates) between OX and SX. After YP is calculated (line 290), the point (XP,YP) is tested to see whether it lies on the screen. If it does, YP is compared with the array values YN(XP) and YX(XP) (lines 320, 330, and 410) to determine visibility of the point (XP,YP).

If YN(XP) < YP < YX(XP), then the point (XP,YP) is not visible; F is set to 0 (line 340), and the next point is considered (line 350).

If YP < = YN(XP), then YP is no larger than any previous vertical screen coordinate associated with XP. The point (XP,YP) is visible, appearing above the previously plotted portion of the surface. Array value YN(XP) is reset to YP (line 370), and the point (XP,YP) is plotted (lines 390 and 400).

If YP > = YX(XP) (line 330 and 410), then YP is as large as any previous vertical screen coordinate associated with XP. The point (XP,YP) is visible, appearing below the previously plotted portion of the surface. The array value YX(XP) is reset to YP (line 420), and the point (XP,YP) is plotted (lines 440 and 450).

When all integral values of XP along the line segment from (OX,OY) to (SX,SY) have been considered, (OX,OY) is redefined as (SX,SY), and the program returns to the point generating loop (line 360).

NOTES AND SUGGESTIONS

1. Program 7.6 assumes that each wire-frame curve is generated in a left-to-right direction on the screen. A more versatile subroutine results from adding a line such as

```
265  ST = SGN(SX  -  OX)
```

changing line 270 to read

```
270  FOR XP = INT (OX)  +  ST  TO  SX  STEP  ST
```

and changing line 290 to read

```
290  YP = YP  +  ST  *  SL
```

2. Some points (XP,YP) will identify new screen maximum values (YP> = YX(XP)) and new screen minimum values (YP< = YN(XP)). This properly will result in resetting both YX(XP) and YN(XP). However, it also will result in plotting the point or line segment twice (lines 390, 400, 440, and 450). No harm is done by replotting, although some small amount of time is wasted. Can you correct this?

3. Several hidden line techniques have been discussed in this chapter. Adapt them to generate other images, such as Saturn, with rings; a cube with a hole through it; the cube and prism of Figure 7.23.

4. To reiterate the statement made at the beginning of this chapter:

The elimination of hidden lines and surfaces is one of the most challenging problems of computer graphics.

It is a problem which has received a lot of attention; many hidden line techniques have been developed. Those given here constitute a brief introduction. The reader interested in pursuing the subject should consult texts such as Principles of Interactive Computer Graphics by Newman and Sproull or Fundamentals of Interactive Computer Graphics by Foley and Van Dam.

5. Machine level subroutines which perform some of the hidden line calculations are included on the disk (see the order card in the back of the book). The use of such subroutines greatly increases the execution speed of programs.

Part V

Animation

Chapter 8
Animated Images

ANIMATION USING HPLOT

So far we have focused our efforts on obtaining images of two- or three-dimensional objects in fixed positions. We now will point out methods of animating simple images. Of course, as in film animation, we really will be displaying a sequence of still images that only simulate motion. Several of our earlier programs provided animation. In this chapter we will elaborate on each of the methods used.

Program 1.2 provided a simulation of a bouncing ball. The ball was represented by a pair of dots which were drawn at one screen location, then erased and drawn at a new location. Since the image was a simple one (two dots) and little calculation was needed between successive HPLOTs, the ball appeared to move smoothly.

A similar ploy was used in Program 2.9. This time, since the image was slightly more complex (a square, four line segments) a noticeable flicker would have been present as the image was drawn, then erased, then redrawn. To avoid the flicker, we arranged to use both of the high resolution graphics pages. One of the pages was displayed while the other was erased and drawn on. When the new image was ready it was displayed; the other page was then erased, and drawing resumed.

The necessary ingredients of this animation program are

1. Control of the page used for drawing (POKE 230,32 for page 1, POKE 230,64 for page 2);

2. Control of the page being displayed (use of the soft switches); and

3. Fast, simple calculations between successive images.

It is the third requirement that is most demanding. For many animated images, a considerable amount of calculation time is necessary between successive displays.

> **NOTE:**   One way to speed up calculations is to write the program in machine language. This requires much greater effort on the part of the programmer, and is not a part of this book. Recently, however, Applesoft BASIC compilers have become available which provide the BASIC programmer with an easy way to obtain a machine language version of a program. If you are interested in animation, you may find a compiler to be valuable.

ROTATING SQUARE

If extensive calculations are needed to provide successive images, perhaps these calculations may be done in advance, with the results saved for access for later drawing. Program 8.1 illustrates this technique.

The vertices of a square are stored in the two arrays XO(I) and YO(I). This square is centered at (0,0) and is not intended to be drawn. Rather, it is a reference square from which others are derived by transformations. Lines 80 through 150 calculate the coordinates of ten squares. Each of the ten is obtained by rotating the reference square through an angle AN (lines 90 and 110–130) and translating it to the center of the screen. For square 1, the value of AN is 0; for square 2, the value of AN is $\pi/20$; for square 3, the value of AN is $2\pi/20$; and so on (lines 20 and 90). The calculated coordinates are stored in a pair of arrays, X(I) and Y(I). When the coordinates of the ten squares have been calculated, lines 160 through 180 copy the coordinates for the first two squares, so that squares 11 and 12 are identical to squares 1 and 2. This is done to ease the bookkeeping involved in erasing images.

Program 8.1: ROTATING SQUARE

```
 1   REM PROGRAM 8.1 (ROTATING SQUARE)
 2   REM ANIMATION VIA PRIOR CALCULATION
10   DIM X(60),Y(60)
20 PI = 3.14159:DT = PI / 20
30 C = COS (DT):S = SIN (DT)
40   DATA 80,0,0,80,-80,0,0,-80,80,0
50   FOR I = 1 TO 5
60   READ XO(I),YO(I)
70   NEXT I
80   FOR I = 0 TO 9
```

```
90 AN = I * DT
100 FOR J = 1 TO 5
110 T = COS (AN) * XO(J) - SIN (AN) *
    YO(J) + 140
120 Y(5 * I + J) = SIN (AN) * XO(J) + COS (AN) *
    YO(J) + 96
130 X(5 * I + J) = T
140  NEXT J
150  NEXT I
160  FOR I = 51 TO 60
170 X(I) = X(I - 50):Y(I) = Y(I - 50)
180  NEXT I
190  HGR : HGR2 :I = 1
200  HCOLOR= 0: POKE 230,32
210  HPLOT X(I),Y(I) TO X(I + 1),Y(I + 1)
     TO X(I + 2),Y(I + 2) TO X(I + 3),Y(I + 3)
     TO X(I + 4),Y(I + 4)
220 I = I + 10: HCOLOR= 3
230  HPLOT X(I),Y(I) TO X(I + 1),Y(I + 1)
     TO X(I + 2),Y(I + 2) TO X(I + 3),Y(I + 3)
     TO X(I + 4),Y(I + 4)
240  POKE - 16300,0: POKE 230,64:I = I - 5:
     HCOLOR= 0
250  HPLOT X(I),Y(I) TO X(I + 1),Y(I + 1)
     TO X(I + 2),Y(I + 2) TO X(I + 3),Y(I + 3)
     TO X(I + 4),Y(I + 4)
260 I = I + 10: HCOLOR= 3
270  HPLOT X(I),Y(I) TO X(I + 1),Y(I + 1)
     TO X(I + 2),Y(I + 2) TO X(I + 3),Y(I + 3)
     TO X(I + 4),Y(I + 4)
280  POKE - 16299,0:I= I - 5:IF I = 51 THEN I = 1
290  GOTO 200
```

NOTE: It may seem that after ten rotations of the original square through an angle of $\pi/20$, the resulting square would have been rotated 90° from the original and have the appearance of the original. Theoretically, it will. However, our calculations and our value of π are only approximate. To see the accumulated error of approximation, make the following adjustments:

1 Replace line 80 with

   80 FOR I = 0 to 11

2 Delete lines 160, 170 and 180

3 Run the program

The display of consecutive rotated squares is handled by lines 200 through 290. Lines 200 through 230 first erase a square on graphics page 1, then draw a new square there. With the drawing complete, line 240 displays page 1, then identifies page 2 for use in drawing. Lines 250 through 270 erase a square on graphics page 2, then draw a new square. Line 280 displays the newly drawn square. The process is then repeated (line 290). When the last square (number 12) is drawn, we return to the first, and continue drawing (line 280).

> **NOTE:** In animating these objects, we have erased images by drawing them in black, the background color. We also could have cleared the screen (CALL 62450). Usually, this is unsatisfactory. It typically takes longer, unless the image is complex. It also has the disadvantage of clearing the entire screen, including any images that are not to be animated.

THREE-DIMENSIONAL ANIMATION

The next program is quite longer than the last, but makes use of essentially the same animation processes. Program 8.2 displays a rotating pyramid. We start with a pyramid which has a base on the xy plane and a vertex on the positive z axis. This object then is rotated about the three coordinate axes.

Since the rotating pyramid will present different sides to the viewer, it is necessary to use some form of hidden line elimination to obtain satisfactory images. We saw in Chapter 7 that this was a time-consuming process, clearly not appropriate for real-time animation. For this reason, we will perform the calculation in advance so that the display of images is done with reasonable speed.

Since only one object is to be displayed, we may use the surface orientation method for identifying the visible surfaces. In using the surface orientation method, Program 8.2 includes most of Program 7.1. We will point out the differences.

Line 10 dimensions an integer array SP%(I). This array receives all screen coordinates of endpoints of visible edges of the pyramid views as they are calculated. A view of the pyramid may display as many as six edges. Each edge will be identified by two endpoints, each having two coordinates. If you have been counting, you can see that we may need as many as twenty-four numbers to identify the coordinates of the visible edges of one view of the pyramid. We will be calculating and storing thirty-six views of the rotating pyramid. This accounts for 864 array entries. We will want the first two and last two pyramid views to be identical (to allow easy erasure when the array values are recycled). For this reason, a thirty-seventh and thirty-eighth view are provided, which are duplicates of the first and second. This brings the required size of the array to 912.

In lines 40 and 50 we identify the angles through which the pyramid will be rotated, and save the SIN and COS of these angles for use in the rotation transformation.

As mentioned earlier, we will generate thirty-six pyramid views. The consecutive views are calculated and tested for visible parts in lines 260 through 740. As visible edges are found, the coordinates of their endpoints are stored in the array SP%(I) (line 610). When all visible parts of one pyramid have been calculated, the coordinates that define the pyramid are transformed by the rotation transformation (lines 640 through 720).

Line 730 prints the current value of RO (the pyramid for which calculations have been completed) on the screen, so you will know how the calculation is progressing.

When all thirty-six views are completed, line 750 copies the first two views as the thirty-seventh and thirty-eighth. This is necessary in order that the erasure of images may be easily handled.

The display of the pyramid views is handled in a manner that is very similar to that used by Program 8.1. For each of the six edges of the pyramid, four numbers (the coordinates of the endpoints) are taken from the array SP%(I) (lines 830 and 900). The edges are drawn by lines 870 through 920 and erased by lines 800 through 850. The value of ADDR, which serves as an index to the array, is adjusted after each edge is drawn (lines 840 and 910) and after each pyramid view is complete (lines 860 and 930).

NOTE: How did we know that the pyramid would return to its original position after thirty-six successive transformations? Perhaps it doesn't. In the initial stages of planning this program, all coordinates of views of the pyramid were printed and compared. It was noticed that after thirty-six rotations, the pyramid was approximately in its original position.

Program 8.2: ROTATING PYRAMID

```
1   REM PROGRAM 8.2 (ROTATING PYRAMID)
2   REM THREE DIMENSIONAL ANIMATION WITH HIDDEN
    LINES ELIMINATED
10   DIM SP%(912):ADDR = 1: DIM E(6,3)
20  RHO = 15:THETA = .5:PHI = .9:D = 400
30  CX = 140:CY = 96:S1 = SIN (TH):
    C1 = COS (TH):S2 = SIN (PH):C2 = COS (PH)
40  TN = -.1:TT = .1:CT = COS (TT):
    ST = SIN (TT):SO = SIN (TN):CO = COS (TN)
50  TP = -.1:SP = SIN (TP):CP = COS (TP)
60   DATA 0,0,3
70   DATA 1,0,0
80   DATA -.2,1,0
90   DATA -.2,-1,0
100   DIM V(4,3),SV(4,2)
110   FOR I = 1 TO 4: READ X,Y,Z
120  V(I,1) = X:V(I,2) = Y:V(I,3) = Z
130  XE  = -X * S1 + Y * C1:YE = -X * C1 *
    C2 - Y * S1 * C2 + Z * S2:ZE = -X * S2 *
    C1 - Y * S2 * S1 - Z * C2 + RHO
140   SV(I,1) = D * (XE / ZE) + CX:
    SV(I,2) = -D * (YE / ZE) + CY
150   NEXT I
160   DATA 1,4,2,1
170   DATA 1,2,3,1
180   DATA 1,3,4,1
190   DATA 2,4,3,2
200   DIM S(4,4)
210   FOR I = 1 TO 4
220   FOR J = 1 TO 4
230   READ S(I,J)
240   NEXT J,I
250   DIM N(4,3)
260   FOR RO = 1 TO 36
270   FOR I = 1 TO 6:E(I,3) = 0: NEXT I
280   FOR I = 1 TO 4
290  U1 = V(S(I,2),1) - V(S(I,1),1)
300  U2 = V(S(I,2),2) - V(S(I,1),2)
310  U3 = V(S(I,2),3) - V(S(I,1),3)
320  V1 = V(S(I,3),1) - V(S(I,1),1)
330  V2 = V(S(I,3),2) - V(S(I,1),2)
340  V3 = V(S(I,3),3) - V(S(I,1),3)
350  N(I,1) = U2 * V3 - V2 * U3
360  N(I,2) = U3 * V1 - V3 * U1
370  N(I,3) = U1 * V2 - V1 * U2
380   NEXT I
```

```
390 XE = RH * S2 * C1:YE = RH * S2 * S1:
    ZE = RH * C2
400 N = 1
410  FOR I = 1 TO 4
420 E2 = S(I,1)
430 WX = XE - V(E2,1)
440 WY = YE - V(E2,2)
450 WZ = ZE - V(E2,3)
460  IF N(I,1) * WX + N(I,2) * WY + N(I,3) * WZ
    < = 0 THEN 570
470 E1 = S(I,1)
480  FOR J = 2 TO 4
490 E2 = S(I,J)
500  FOR K = 1 TO N
510  IF E(K,1) = E2 AND E(K,2) = E1
    THEN E(K,3) = 2: GOTO 550
520  NEXT K
530 E(N,1) = E1:E(N,2) = E2:E(N,3) = 1
540 N = N + 1
550 E1 = E2
560  NEXT J
570  NEXT I
580  FOR I = 1 TO 6
590  IF E(I,3) = 0 THEN 620
600 J = E(I,1):K = E(I,2)
610 SP%(AD) = SV(J,1):SP%(AD + 1) =
    SV(J,2):SP%(ADDR + 2) = SV(K,1):
    SP%(ADDR + 3) = SV(K,2)
620 ADDR = ADDR + 4
630  NEXT I
640  FOR I = 1 TO 4
650 T1 = CP * CT * V(I,1) - (ST * CP + SO * SP) *
    V(I,2) + (SO * ST * CP - SP * CO) * V(I,3)
660 T2 = ST * V(I,1) + CO * CT * V(I,2) - SO *
    CT * V(I,3)
670 T3 = SP * CT * V(I,1) + (SO * CP - CO * ST *
    SP) * V(I,2) + (ST * SO * SP + CO * CP) *
    V(I,3)
680 V(I,1) = T1:V(I,2) = T2:V(I,3) = T3
690 X = T1:Y = T2:Z = T3
700 XE = -X * S1 + Y * C1:YE = -X * C1 *
    C2 - Y * S1 * C2 + Z * S2:ZE = -X * S2 *
    C1 - Y * S2 * S1 - Z * C2 + RHO
710 SV(I,1) = D * (XE / ZE) + CX:
    SV(I,2) = -D * (YE / ZE) + CY
```

(continued)

```
720    NEXT I
730    PRINT RO
740    NEXT RO
750    FOR I = 1 TO 48:SP%(I + 864) =
       SP%(I): NEXT I
760    HOME : INPUT "READY";A$
770    HGR : HGR2 :DP = 0
780 ADDR = 1
790    POKE 230,32 * (DP + 1)
800    HCOLOR= 4
810    FOR I = 1 TO 6
820    IF SP%(ADDR) = 0 THEN 840
830    HPLOT SP%(ADDR),SP%(ADDR + 1)
       TO SP%(ADDR + 2),SP%(ADDR+3)
840 ADDR = ADDR+4
850    NEXT I
860 ADDR = ADDR+24
870    HCOLOR = 7
880    FOR I = 1 TO 6
890    IF SP%(ADDR) = 0 THEN 910
900    HPLOT SP%(ADDR),SP%(ADDR + 1)
       TO SP%(ADDR + 2), SP%(ADDR + 3)
910 ADDR = ADDR + 4
920    NEXT I
930 ADDR = ADDR - 48
940    IF ADDR = 865 THEN ADDR = 1
950    POKE - 16300 + DP,0
960 DP = 1 - DP
970    GOTO 790
```

SHAPE TABLE ANIMATION

Animating images by using HPLOT statements typically requires preparation, so that only minimal calculation is necessary between the display of consecutive images. Preparation is also needed when simulating motion by using shape tables, since we must prepare the table of shapes to be drawn.

Program 1.9 (ARTIST'S AID) used a shape as the rotating cursor of variable length. The XDRAW and DRAW commands, together with the use of colors, permitted the cursor to "paint" a screen image.

Another example of shape animation is given in Appendix 2, as Program A2.1. Here, the shapes provide a rotating cursor and airplane images, simulating a radar screen.

In each of the examples mentioned above, movement was simulated by drawing and redrawing a shape at a sequence of locations. Program 8.3 extends this procedure, simulating motion by drawing a sequence of shapes.

Program 8.3: INCHWORM

```
1     REM PROGRAM 8.3 (INCHWORM)
2     REM SHAPE TABLE ANIMATION
10    DATA 5,0,12,0,21,0,30,0,39,0,46,0
20    DATA 45,40,32,5,168,174,21,37,0
30    DATA 45,40,32,5,40,45,21,37,0
40    DATA 45,5,40,5,40,45,21,37,0
50    DATA 45,45,45,45,45,37,0
60    DATA 9,5,32,5,40,168,21,21,173,37,0
70    FOR I = 768 TO 824
80    READ X: POKE I,X
90    NEXT I
100    POKE 232,0: POKE 233,3
110    HOME : HGR : HCOLOR= 3: SCALE= 1: ROT= 0
120    FOR X = 10 TO 100 STEP 4
130    FOR I = 1 TO 5
140    XDRAW I AT X,100
150    FOR T = 1 TO 60: NEXT T
160    XDRAW I AT X,100
170    NEXT I,X
```

The shapes drawn are those shown in Figure 8.1. They are intended to represent the positions of a crawling inchworm. The shapes were initially designed using Program A2.2 (SHAPE TABLE CONSTRUCTION). When the table was completed the contents were read and used as the DATA lines of Program 8.3. As a result, the program identifies the shape table and its location (lines 10–100). Program lines 110 through 170 use the XDRAW command to consecutively draw, then erase, the five shapes at points along a horizontal screen line.

XDRAW is used for the display of shapes, since XDRAW draws a shape using the complement of the colors found at the screen locations that the shape is to occupy. Erasure then is especially easy. Since XDRAW N AT X,Y displays shape N using the complements of colors currently at screen locations, a second XDRAW N AT X,Y command will cause a re-complementing of these colors. As a result, the screen is returned to its original status. This permits a shape to move across a background of other images without disrupting those images.

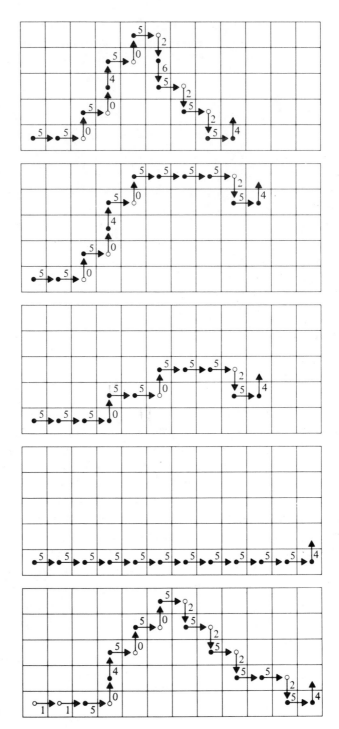

Figure 8.1

In Program 8.3, each shape is displayed by line 140 and erased by line 160. A delay loop (line 150) holds the image on the screen briefly before it is erased.

NOTES AND SUGGESTIONS

1. Simple shapes are drawn and erased quickly, but the drawing of complex shapes may be distracting to watch. In such cases, the use of both graphics pages, along with the soft switches, causes the drawing to take place on the undisplayed page.

2. Use HPLOT animation to display a rotating arrow (like the hand of a clock). Try the same with shape animation.

3. The inchworm of Program 8.3 shows the animation of a simple figure. Write a program that uses shapes to show a person walking. Use a stick figure person; design several shapes that present the person with various leg and arm positions. It may be more efficient to have the shape table (constructed by Program A2.2) BLOADed from disk rather than defined within the program.

4. In the same manner, write a program that shows a person ascending stairs.

5. To each of the programs suggested in 3 and 4, add background scenery before beginning the animation.

6. As mentioned earlier, animated images may be made to move more quickly and smoothly with machine language programs. If you have access to a BASIC compiler, you might try some of the above programs in compiled form.

7. Software is commercially available which assists in the animation of simple images. These are machine language driver programs, to which you may add data for specific images. Some simulate motion through the use of both graphics pages and the soft switches, as in HPLOT animation mentioned above. Others generate images in the manner described under Bit Pattern Text, in Chapter 3.

Part VI

Peripheral Equipment and Software

Chapter 9

System Components

There are three components of a computer graphics system:

1. Input device: a means of identifying data and passing instructions to the computer.
2. Processor: the computer.
3. Output device: the means provided for displaying the graphic image.

Up to this point we have acted as though the keyboard were the only input device available, and the display screen the only output device. Other types of input and output devices are available. Several will be discussed briefly in the pages ahead.

INPUT HARDWARE AND SOFTWARE

GAME PADDLES AND PUSHBUTTONS

The variable control dials (potentiometers) sometimes provided with microcomputers are frequently referred to as "game paddles" because of their use in video games. From a programming point of view, each paddle identifies an integer between 0 and 255. A dial that is turned to its full counterclockwise position provides a 0; a dial turned to its full clockwise position yields a reading of 255.

As many as four game paddles may be connected to the Apple II, with the values provided by the paddles available at memory locations through the PDL(I) command (I = 0, 1, 2, or 3).

Program 9.1 displays the values provided by game paddles 0 and 1.

Program 9.1: PADDLE READER

```
1    REM PROGRAM 9.1 (PADDLE READER)
2    REM DISPLAYS VALUES PROVIDED BY GAME PADDLES
10   TEXT : HOME
20   VTAB 1: PRINT PDL (0), PDL (1)
30   GOTO 20
```

Try the program. Turn both of the two game paddles and note the effect.

The numbers provided by the game paddles may be used for a variety of graphics applications. Program 9.2 uses the paddles to draw a picture. The user controls the drawing via the paddles in much the same fashion as the user of an "ETCH-A-SKETCH" toy.

Program 9.2: ELECTRONIC PEN

```
1    REM PROGRAM 9.2 (ELECTRONIC PEN)
2    REM USES PADDLES TO CONTROL DRAWING
10   HGR2 : HCOLOR= 3
20   X = 279 * PDL (0) / 255
30   Y = 191 * PDL (1) / 255
40   IF F = 0 THEN F = 1: HPLOT X,Y
50   HPLOT TO X,Y
60   GOTO 20
```

Game paddles supplied for Apple computers have pushbuttons. As many as three pushbuttons may be accomodated by the Apple, although only two are provided by the standard paddles. Each pushbutton may be used to send an ON or OFF signal. The signals are received at memory locations −16287, −16286, and −16285. Normally, the memory location corresponding to a pushbutton contains a number less than 128 (OFF). When a pushbutton is held in, the corresponding memory location is given a value 128 or larger (ON).

Program 9.3 is an enhancement of the ELECTRONIC PEN program. The additions to the program allow greater control of the drawing via the pushbuttons. Pressing pushbutton 0 causes drawing to cease. The "pen" may be moved and its location is indicated, but nothing is drawn. Pressing pushbutton 1 causes drawing to resume.

Program 9.3: IMPROVED ELECTRONIC PEN

```
1    REM PROGRAM 9.3 (IMPROVED ELECTRONIC PEN)
2    REM INCLUDES PUSHBUTTON CONTROL
10   HGR2 : HCOLOR= 3
```

```
20  X = 279 * PDL (0) / 255
30  Y = 191 * PDL (1) / 255
40   IF F = 0 THEN F = 1: HPLOT X,Y
50   HPLOT  TO X,Y
60   IF PEEK ( - 16287) > 127 THEN 80
70   GOTO 20
80  X = 279 * PDL (0) / 255
90  Y = 191 * PDL (1) / 255
100   HCOLOR= 3: HPLOT X,Y
110   FOR I = 1 TO 10: NEXT I
120   IF PEEK ( - 16286) > 127
      THEN F = 0: GOTO 20
130   HCOLOR= 0: HPLOT X,Y
140   GOTO 80
```

LIGHT PENS

A light pen is a pencil-like device with which the user may reference the display screen. A cable attaches the light pen to the computer. When the tip of the pen is pressed against the display screen, the location of the light pen is transmitted to the computer. The information is used to draw lines on the graphics screen as was done with the game paddles. The light pen also may be used to point to an image on the screen. In this way it can identify a component of a graphic image that is to be modified or studied in greater detail, or make a selection from a menu displayed on the screen.

GRAPHICS TABLETS

A graphics tablet functions somewhat like a light pen. Indeed, it uses a pen-like device that is connected by wire to the computer. However, instead of referencing the display screen, the pen is pressed against a "tablet." The tablet is a thin rectangular board, also connected by wires to the computer. When the pen is pressed against the tablet, its position on the tablet is communicated to the computer.

While the graphics tablet performs some of the functions of the light pen, it can be less convenient. It is a separate device. While it identifies locations of selected graphic elements on the screen, the pen cannot read screen locations directly; it must reference the tablet.

The advantage of the tablet is in its separate nature. It lies flat, and is much easier to use for drawing purposes. If a map is laid on the tablet, the pen can trace rivers, highways, or topographic features. As the tracing progresses, a copy may be produced on the screen and the information stored in the computer memory for later use.

The tablet typically has much finer resolution than the light pen. While a light pen may provide the 280×192 resolution available to the Apple display screen, the graphics tablet may far exceed this. The increased precision is valuable when an image is to be subject to enlargement, or when components are to be used for calculation. Further, while the display screen may not be able to make use of greater resolution, other output devices are available.

Figure 9.1 shows a graphics tablet that is available for microcomputer use. An example of an image created by use of a graphics tablet is given in Figure 9.4.

Some very powerful software is available for use with light pens and graphics tablets. With the proper support software, the pen may be used to draw and erase easily. Portions of the display may be enlarged, reduced, or rotated. A graphic element may be colored in easily; an estimate of perimeter or area may be calculated as the pen traces around an object.

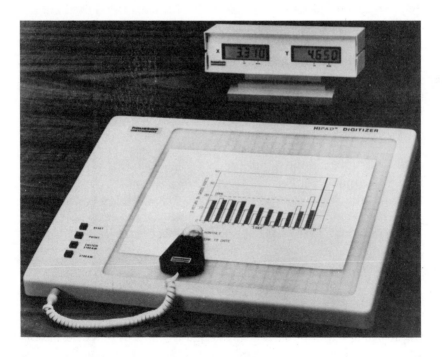

Figure 9.1   Graphics Tablet
Photo courtesy of Houston Instruments

OUTPUT HARDWARE AND SOFTWARE

PLOTTERS

Each of the graphics devices described above is for input. A plotter is an output device, rendering a graphic image on paper using pen and ink. The location of the pen is controlled by the computer in somewhat the same fashion as BASIC commands HPLOT and HPLOT TO control the plotting of points on the display screen. Of course, when the plotter is used as a supplement or replacement for the display screen, the information sent to the plotter must be formatted in a manner acceptable to the plotter.

In its most elementary form, the information sent to the plotter identifies the pen status (UP or DOWN) and position (coordinates of the desired pen location). A sequence of instructions such as

UP
100,120
DOWN
UP

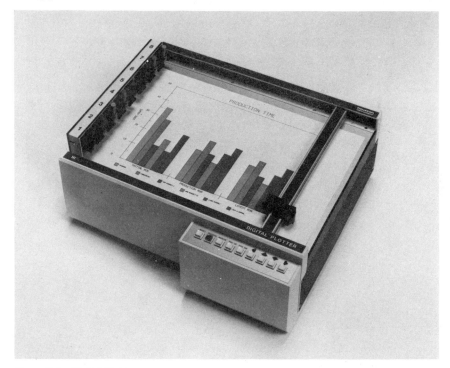

Figure 9.2   Digital Plotter
Photo courtesy of Houston Instruments

will result in raising the pen, moving to location (100,120), pressing the pen to the paper, then raising it again. Thus a single dot would be plotted.

To draw a line from location (100,120) to (200,10), a sequence such as the following would be used:

UP	(raise pen)
100,120	(move pen to (100,120))
DOWN	(lower pen)
200,10	(move pen to (200,10))
UP	(raise pen)

Capabilities of plotters vary. Many have built-in character sets, allowing easy inclusion of labels in an image. Various line modes (solid, dash, dot, dot-dash, etc.) also may be available. Programmable pauses permit pen changes for color plots, but more sophisticated plotters may be instructed to make pen changes automatically.

Examples of plotter output appear in this book as Figures 4.11, 5.1, and 7.1.

Figure 9.3　Dot Matrix Printer
Photo courtesy of Integral Data Systems

GRAPHICS PRINTERS

Several printers are available which may be used to obtain graphic output. The print head of the dot matrix printer has an array of pins. Software that uses the printer for graphics output sends to the printer a byte-by-byte map of the bit patterns on one of the graphics pages. If a bit of a byte is turned on, the corresponding pin of the print head is extended. Typically, the bit patterns of a vertical block of bytes are read and transmitted to the printer at one time. Thermal printers function in a similar manner, but transmit the bit pattern to paper by heat rather than ink.

An example of dot matrix printer graphics is shown in Figure 9.4. The image is one which was developed through the use of a graphics tablet.

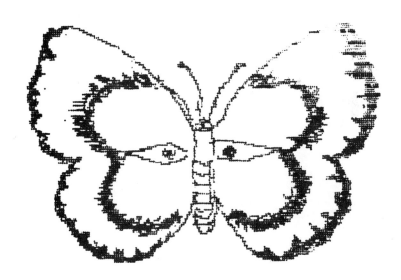

Figure 9.4

Appendix 1

Binary, Decimal, and Hexadecimal Number Systems

It is said to be an accident of nature that we use a base 10 number system. If our ancestors had 6 fingers on each hand we might be using base 12. If they had 1 finger on each hand perhaps we would calculate in base 2. We might then have less trouble communicating with a computer. The conversion between base 2 and base 10 is one of the inconveniences we must live with in order to get the most out of a computer.

The structure of number systems is the same, regardless of the base used. The number 243.72 (base 10) represents

$$2(10)^2 + 4(10)^1 + 3(10)^0 + 7(10)^{-1} + 2(10)^{-2}$$

If we write a number $a_1a_2a_3.a_4a_5$ (base b), it is assumed that the number represents

$$a_1(b)^2 + a_2(b)^1 + a_3(b)^0 + a_4(b)^{-1} + a_5(b)^{-2}$$

Thus, 423.51 (base 7) represents

$$4(7)^2 + 2(7)^1 + 3(7)^0 + 5(7)^{-1} + 1(7)^{-2}$$

and 13.423 (base 5) represents

$$1(5)^1 + 3(5)^0 + 4(5)^{-1} + 2(5)^{-2} + 3(5)^{-3} \text{ (8.904 (base 10))}$$

It is necessary to be familiar with three number systems in order to communicate properly with the Apple II. We assume you are familiar with base 10 (decimal). The other two systems we will use are base 2 (binary) and base 16 (hexadecimal). Base 2 is the native language of digital computers; base 16 happens to be convenient for conversation between people and computers. Base 16 is convenient because it is, in a way, a shorthand base 2 notation. This will be apparent later.

BINARY

When working in base 10 we have the ten symbols 0, 1, 2, 3, 4, 5, 6, 7, 8, and 9 with which to represent numbers. In base 2 we have only two symbols: 0, and 1. Any number may be represented in base 2 as a pattern of 0s and 1s. For example, the binary 1011011 represents (starting from the left):

$$1(2)^6 + 0(2)^5 + 1(2)^4 + 1(2)^3 + 0(2)^2 + 1(2)^1 + 1(2)^0 =$$
$$64 + 0(32) + 16 + 8 + 0(4) + 2 + 1 = 91$$

Thus the binary number 1011011 represents the number that we would write as decimal 91.

Similarly, the binary 110111 represents the decimal 55, since

$$1(2)^5 + 1(2)^4 + 0(2)^3 + 1(2)^2 + 1(2)^1 + 1(2)^0 = 55$$

Conversion of a number from decimal to binary representation is accomplished through subtraction of powers of 2, starting with the largest possible power. To write the number 237 in binary form, we note that $128 = 2^7$ is the largest power of 2 which can be subtracted from 237 ($237 = 128 + 109$). We then turn to 109. The largest power of 2 which can be subtracted from 109 is $2^6 = 64$ ($109 = 64 + 45$). Thus $237 = 128 + 64 + 45$. Since $45 = 32 + 13$, and $13 = 8 + 4 + 1$, we may write:

$$237 = 128 + 64 + 32 + 8 + 4 + 1$$
$$= 1(2)^7 + 1(2)^6 + 1(2)^5 + 0(2)^4 + 1(2)^3 + 1(2)^2 + 0(2)^1 + 1(2)^0$$
$$= 11101101 \text{ (base 2)}$$

EXERCISES
1. Convert each of the following from decimal to binary form
   a)   145   b)   252
   c)   201   d)   75
2. Convert each of the following from binary to decimal form
   a)   11011100   b)   10110111
   c)   10010001   d)   11001101

The Apple II is a digital computer, performing its arithmetic in base 2. Further, it is an *eight bit* computer, which means that the largest number of 0s and 1s it can handle at one time is eight. Because of this, the memory available for the computer to use is configured in blocks of eight. Each eight-bit unit is referred to as a *byte*. A half-byte is called a *nybble*. The number 10111110 (decimal 190) is one byte. The lower, or *least significant,* nybble is 1110, and the higher, or *most significant,* nybble is 1011.

You may have figured out that the largest number that can be represented as an eight-bit binary is decimal 255 (11111111). That doesn't prevent the computer from considering larger numbers (or fractions). It simply breaks the number up into components and stores the parts in several bytes.

HEXADECIMAL

The hexadecimal (or hex) notation for a number is the base 16 representation of the number. In this numeration system, the number 235 refers to $2(16)^2 + 3(16)^1 + 5(16)^0 = 565$. In order to avoid confusing the hex number 235 with the decimal number 235, it is common practice to add a "$" prefix to the hex notation. Thus $235 = 565$.

In base 10, ten symbols are available to represent numbers. Base 2 provides only the symbols 0 and 1. For work with hexadecimal notation, we need 16 symbols. It is conventional to use the symbols 0 through 9 for their normal duty, and the symbols A, B, C, D, E, and F to represent the decimal numbers 10, 11, 12, 13, 14, and 15.

If we were counting in hex, our count would go like this: $1, $2, $3, $4, $5, $6, $7, $8, $9, $A, $B, $C, $D, $E, $F, $10, $11, $12, $13, $14, $15, $16, $17, $18, $19, $1A, $1B, $1C, $1D, $1E, $1F, $20, $21. . . .

NOTE: It is considered poor form to refer to $24 as "hex twenty-four," since "twenty-four" implies decimal. Proper reading of $24 is "hex-two-four."

To convert $2A3E to decimal, we write

$$\$2A3E = 2(16)^3 + 10(16)^2 + 3(16)^1 + 14(16)^0$$
$$= 2(4096) + 10(256) + 3(16) + 14(1)$$
$$= 8192 + 2560 + 48 + 14$$
$$= 10814$$

Similarly,

$$\$E38F = 14(16)^3 + 3(16)^2 + 8(16)^1 + 15(16)^0$$
$$= 57344 + 768 + 128 + 15$$
$$= 58255$$

Table A1.1 may be used to save calculation time. Using the table, we read

$$\$1111 \text{ as } 4096 + 256 + 16 + 1 = 4369$$
$$\$2202 \text{ as } 8192 + 512 + 0 + 2 = 8706$$
$$\$253B \text{ as } 8192 + 1280 + 48 + 11 = 9531$$
$$\$EB29 \text{ as } 57344 + 2816 + 32 + 9 = 60201$$

Table A1.1

	16^3	16^2	16^1	16^0	
$1	4096	256	16	1	$1
$2	8192	512	32	2	$2
$3	12288	768	48	3	$3
$4	16384	1024	64	4	$4
$5	20480	1280	80	5	$5
$6	24576	1536	96	6	$6
$7	28672	1792	112	7	$7
$8	32768	2048	128	8	$8
$9	36864	2304	144	9	$9
$A	40960	2560	160	10	$A
$B	45056	2816	176	11	$B
$C	49152	3072	192	12	$C
$D	53248	3328	208	13	$D
$E	57344	3584	224	14	$E
$F	61440	3840	240	15	$F

To convert the decimal 29143 to hex notation, we first identify the largest multiple of the largest power of 16 that may be subtracted from 29143. That number is $7(16)^3 = 28672$. Subtracting yields $29143 - 28672 = 471$. Next, identify the largest multiple of the largest power of 16 that may be subtracted from 471. That number is $1(16)^2 = 256$. Subtracting yields $471 - 256 = 215$. Continuing, the largest multiple of $(16)^1$ that may be subtracted from 215 is $13(16) = 208$, and $215 - 208 = 7$. Thus,

$$
\begin{aligned}
29143 &= 28672 + 471 \\
&= 7(16)^3 + 256 + 215 \\
&= 7(16)^3 + 1(16)^2 + 208 + 7 \\
&= 7(16)^3 + 1(16)^2 + 13(16)^1 + 7 \\
&= \$71D7
\end{aligned}
$$

Similarly,

$$43618 = 40960 + 2658$$
$$= 10(4096) + 2560 + 98$$
$$= 10(16)^3 + 10(256)^2 + 96 + 2$$
$$= 10(16)^3 + 10(16)^2 + 6(16)^1 + 2(16)$$
$$= \$AA62$$

If you find the conversion between decimal and hex to be tedious, unpleasant, and frustrating, you may appreciate the following programs. The first provides for conversion from decimal to hexadecimal, while the second provides for conversion from hex to decimal. You may easily merge them into a single program if you like. Similar programs may be designed for conversions involving binary numbers.

Program A1.1: BASE CONVERTER (HEX TO DECIMAL)

```
1    REM PROGRAM A1.1 (BASE CONVERTER)
2    REM HEX TO DECIMAL
10   INPUT "NUMBER (HEX) ";A$
20   L = LEN (A$):N = 0
30   FOR I = 0 TO L - 1:
     T = ASC ( MID$ (A$,L - I,1))
40   IF T = 36 THEN GOTO 80
50   T = T - 48: IF T > 9 THEN T = T - 7
60   N = N + T * 16 ^ I
70   NEXT I
80   PRINT N
```

Program A1.2: BASE CONVERTER (DECIMAL TO HEX)

```
1    REM PROGRAM A1.2 (BASE CONVERTER)
2    REM DECIMAL TO HEX
10   H$ = "0123456789ABCDEF"
20   BASE = 16:I = 1
30   INPUT "NUMBER (DECIMAL) ";N:N = INT (N)
40   Q = INT (N / BASE)
50   A(I) = N - BASE * Q:I = I + 1
60   IF Q > BASE THEN N = Q: GOTO 40
70   A(I) = Q
80   PRINT "$";
90   FOR J = I TO 1 STEP - 1
100  PRINT MID$ (H$,A(J) + 1,1);
110  NEXT J
```

RELATIONSHIP OF HEX TO BINARY

Each of the decimal numbers from 0 to 15 may be represented by a four-bit binary (0000 through 1111), or by a one-digit hex ($0 through $F). The decimal numbers from 0 through 255 have one-byte (eight-bit) binary representation (00000000 through 11111111) and two-digit hex representation ($00 through $FF).

The decimal 181 is represented by binary 10110101, and by hex $B5. Note here that the lower nybble 0101 has hex value $5, while the upper nybble has hex value $B. This association is not an accidental occurrance, and is consistent. To convert between binary and hex representations of a number, we may associate hex digits with binary nybbles.

EXAMPLE: Write $6C in binary form.
Since $6 = 0110 (binary) and $C = 1100 (binary),
then $6C = 01101100 (binary)
EXAMPLE: Write 10111101 in hex notation.
The upper nybble, 1011, has hex equivalent $B;
the lower nybble, 1101, has hex equivalent $D.
Thus 10111101 (binary) = $BD.

EXERCISES
Convert the following binary representations to hex.
A)   10111001   C)   10001111
B)   10111100   D)   11011011
Convert the following to binary form.
A) $3F   C) $2D
B) $CA   D) $E6

Appendix 2
Shape Tables

The Applesoft commands HPLOT and HPLOT TO provide one means of generating graphic images. A second method is available, one which is especially useful for displaying frequently used graphic components. When these components, or *shapes,* are assembled into a *shape table,* the commands DRAW and XDRAW may be used to add the shapes to a graphic image. There are several reasons for using shape tables.

1) Once the shape table is made available to a program, a single command will display a shape, no matter how complex the shape.

2) A shape easily may be displayed, then erased, without disturbing the background image. This capability is valuable in animating an image.

3) Scaling and rotation of shapes is possible.

There are, of course, some inconveniences associated with the use of shapes. For example, shapes that are scaled or rotated are somewhat distorted. However, the most pronounced difficulty is in the design and construction of the shape table. When this is undertaken by hand, it is an onerous task, and is susceptible to many errors and frustrations. Fortunately, it can be handled by the computer, when an appropriate program is available. Such programs have appeared in computer magazines and several are commercially available. One is given in this Appendix as Program A2.2.

The next several pages discuss the process of assembling a shape table, and the basis of Program A2.2. The program may be used without an understanding of this discussion. If this is your intent, you only need note the instructions given under Using Shapes.

SHAPES AND SHAPE TABLES

A shape is a coded sequence of numbers representing line segments that define the form of a graphic element. It could be considered to be a set of instructions about where to draw the dots and line segments that define the object.

In order to be accessed for drawing purposes, a shape must be part of a shape table. The first part of a shape table consists of an addressing structure. The first byte of the table identifies N, the number of shapes contained in the table, which may be as large as 255. The second byte of the table is unused. The 2N bytes that follow are used to identify the displacement from the first byte of the table to the first byte of each of the shapes in the table. The displacements are stored as two bytes, low order byte first.

Each shape consists of a sequence of codes representing vectors that trace the shape. Each vector is an instruction to move a distance of one unit up, right, down, or left. Further, the vectors are of two types: plot-then-move vectors, and don't-plot-just-move vectors. The eight vectors available for use in defining shapes are shown, together with their codes, in Table A2.1:

Table A2.1

Don't-plot-just-move vectors		Plot-then-move vectors	
Vector	Code	Vector	Code
Up	0	Up	4
Right	1	Right	5
Down	2	Down	6
Left	3	Left	7

To illustrate the effects of these codes, select an initial point and draw the following vectors: 6, 6, 2, 6, 6, 1, 1, 6, 3, 6, 3, 7, 0, 4, 3, and 5. The resulting shape is shown as Figure A2.1.

While we may draw a shape when given a sequence of coded vectors, the form in which the vectors are presented by the shape table is very important to the shape drawing commands. It might seem reasonable to store the vector codes sequentially in memory, using one byte of memory per vector. However, there are hazards in that practice. Further, memory is not efficiently used—the vector code numbers each use at most three of the eight bits available in each byte.

The shape drawing commands can read as many as three vectors from a single byte of the shape table. However, it is not always possible to be this efficient. There are two factors which may prevent the inclusion of three vectors in a byte:

1. The vector codes are three bits long. If the leading bit of the third vector code is not zero, nine bits are necessary, not the eight available in a byte;

2. The shape drawing commands ignore leading zeros that appear in any byte of the table, and interpret a zero byte as an end-of-shape code. For this reason, zero vectors (don't-plot-just-move-up) must be stored carefully.

The vectors that define the shape of Figure A2.1 will be used to illustrate the preparation of the vector table for the shape.

The sequence 6, 6, 2, which begins the shape of Figure A2.1, has binary form 110, 110, 10. Listing the three in order from right to left, we have 10, 110, 110. With the commas removed, we have an eight bit number 10110110. Similarly, the next sequence of three (6, 6, 1) may be written as 01, 110, 110; or 01110110. The sequence 1, 6, 3 becomes 11110001. In this way, the first nine vectors of the shape are coded as the three bytes 10110110, 01110110, and 11110001.

The next three vectors (6, 3, 7), in binary form, are 110, 011, 111. Listed in order from right to left, the code becomes 111011110. This code will not fit in an eight-bit byte. The first two vectors may be entered in the byte as 00011110 (leading zeros are ignored), while the third is deferred to the next byte.

The next three vectors to be considered are 7, 0, 4. Again, the three will not fit in a single byte. Further, since the shape-drawing commands will ignore leading zeros, the first two vectors cannot be entered as one byte. Instead, the 7 will be entered into one byte while the other two vectors are deferred to the next byte.

The three vectors 0, 4, 3 may be put into one byte as 11100000. The final vector, 5, is left for a byte by itself. A zero byte marks the end of the shape.

The shape of Figure A2.1, as described by the vector codes 6, 6, 2, 6, 6, 1, 1, 6, 3, 6, 3, 7, 0, 4, 3, and 5, may be stored in 8 bytes as follows:

Binary	Decimal
10110110 =	182
2 6 6	
01110110 =	118
1 6 6	
11110001 =	241
3 6 1	
00011110 =	30
3 6	
00000111 =	7
7	
11100000 =	224
3 4 0	
00000101 =	5
5	
00000000 =	0
end-of-shape code	

A short shape table, containing only this shape, may be constructed as follows:

```
BYTE number  1 :   1      (number of shapes)
BYTE number  2 :   0      (unused)
BYTE number  3 :   4      (displacement to first
BYTE number  4 :   0       byte of shape number 1)
BYTE number  5 : 182
BYTE number  6 : 118
BYTE number  7 : 241
BYTE number  8 :  30      (codes for shape number 1)
BYTE number  9 :   7
BYTE number 10 : 224
BYTE number 11 :   5
BYTE number 12 :   0      (end of shape code)
```

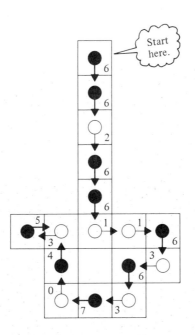

Figure A2.1

NOTES ON THE PROGRAM A2.2

Much of this program is taken up with the user interface. That part of the program will not be discussed here.

The program allows the creation of a new shape table or the loading of an existing table from disk (lines 40–90). In either case, the shape table is located just above the second high resolution graphics page. If a new table is indicated, the space for the addressing structure is allocated (line 230), and the displacement from the beginning of the table to the beginning of the first shape is stored (lines 200–220). After communication with the user permits the shape creating grid to be drawn, the program turns to the task of assembling shapes.

The design of a shape consists of two stages: (1) identifying the vectors that define the shape, and (2) assembling the vector codes to obtain the bytes of the shape table. These stages were evident in the design of the shape of Figure A2.1, and form the basis of Program A2.2. The heart of the program, less some of the user interface commands, is listed below.

```
410    GET  V$:  PRINT
420    IF,  V$  =  "Q"  THEN  POKE  ADDR,P:
       POKE  ADDR  +  1,255:  GOTO  520
440    IF  V$  =  "P"  THEN  P  =  4:  GOTO  410
450    IF  V$  =  "U"  THEN  V  =  P
460    IF  V$  =  "R"  THEN  V  =  P  +  1
470    IF  V$  =  "D"  THEN  V  =  P  +  2
480    IF  V$  =  "L"  THEN  V  =  P  +  3
500    POKE  ADDR,V:  ADDR  =  ADDR  +  1
510  P  =  0:  GOTO  410
520  ADDR  =  PEEK  (TA  +  SN  *  2  +  2)  +  256  *
       PEEK  (TA  +  SN  *  2  +  3)  +  TA:BYTE  =  ADDR
530  C1  =  PEEK  (BYTE):  IF  C1  =  255
       THEN  POKE  ADDR,0:  ADDR  =  ADDR  +  1:  GOTO  660
540  C2  =  PEEK  (BYTE  +  1):  IF  C2  =  255
       THEN  POKE  ADDR,C1:  POKE  ADDR  +  1,0:
       ADDR  =  ADDR  +  2:  GOTO  660
550  C3  =  PEEK  (BYTE  +  2):  IF  C3  =  255
       THEN  POKE  ADDR,C1  +  8  *  C2:  POKE  ADDR  +  1,0:
       ADDR  =  ADDR  +  2:  GOTO  660
560  CODE  =  C1  +  8  *  C2  +  64  *  C3
570    IF  CODE  =  0  THEN  POKE  ADDR,64:
       POKE  ADDR  +  1,24:  ADDR  =  ADDR  +  1:
       BYTE  =  BYTE  +  2:  GOTO  650
580    IF  CODE  <  8  THEN  POKE  ADDR,CODE:  GOTO  650
590    IF  CODE  <  64  THEN  POKE  ADDR,CODE:
       BYTE  =  BYTE  +  1:  GOTO  650
600    IF  CODE  <  256  THEN  POKE  ADDR,CODE:BYTE  =
       BYTE  +  2:  GOTO  650
610  CODE  =  CODE  -  64  *  C3
620    IF  CODE  =  0  THEN  POKE  ADDR,64:
       POKE  ADDR  +  1,3:ADDR  =  ADDR  +  1:
       BYTE  =  BYTE  +  1:  GOTO  650
630    IF  CODE  <  8  THEN  POKE  ADDR,CODE:  GOTO  650
640    POKE  ADDR,CODE:BYTE  =  BYTE  +  1
650  ADDR  =  ADDR  +  1:BYTE  =  BYTE  +  1:  GOTO  530
```

As vectors are received from the keyboard, the vector codes are stored in a temporary table by line 500. A "Q," indicating the end of a shape, results in the final vector being stored, along with a temporary end-of-shape code (255).

Line 520 resets ADDR to the beginning of the temporary table and BYTE to the address of the beginning of the shape (both are the same here).

Lines 530 through 550 read three consecutive vectors from the temporary table. If any of the three is 255 (end-of-shape code), the shape is closed out. Otherwise, line 560 calculates the CODE that represents the three vectors.

If the value of CODE is 0 (line 570), then each of the three vectors is a DON'T-PLOT-JUST-MOVE-UP vector. Since a zero byte would be interpreted as an end-of-shape code by the shape drawing commands, the sequence of vectors 0,0,0 is revised as 0,0,1,0,3. The addition of move-right (1) and move-left (3) vectors serves to break up the upward movement. The five vectors 0,0,1,0,3 translate into two bytes: 64 (0,0,1), and 24 (0,3).

If the value of CODE is between 1 and 7 (line 580), it must represent a nonzero vector code followed by two zero vector codes. Since leading zeros are ignored by the shape drawing commands, the leading zeros are deferred for use in the next byte.

If the value of CODE is between 8 and 63 (line 590), it must represent a sequence of vectors in which the second is nonzero, but the third is zero. Again, the third must be deferred to the next byte.

If CODE is between 64 and 255, the three vectors read from the temporary table may be put into a single byte (line 600).

If CODE is 256 or larger, then the binary representation of CODE requires 9 bits. The third vector must be deferred to the following byte (line 610), and the first two vectors must be analyzed for zero vectors (lines 620 and 630).

When the shape assembly is completed, the program displays the result (line 670), then asks the user if he or she wishes to include the shape in the table. If the shape is to be included in the table, the shape number, SN, is incremented, and the displacement to the next shape is stored (line 680).

USING SHAPES

Before the shapes in a table may be drawn, the shape table must be designed, or loaded from disk, and placed in a safe area of memory that will not be used for other purposes. A limited amount of memory is available beginning at location 768 ($300), and may be used for storing a short shape table. Large tables may be stored at the upper end of memory (just below DOS) and protected by setting HIMEM to a value below the beginning of the table. Another area that usually is safe lies just above the second page of high resolution graphics. Program A2.2 stores a shape table there.

While the location of a shape table in memory is somewhat arbitrary, the address of the beginning of the table must be made known to the shape drawing commands. When either DRAW or XDRAW is used, the address of the shape table is found in locations 232 (low part of the address) and 233 (high part of the address). It is the programmer's responsibility to see that these locations contain the proper addresses.

In general, for a shape table stored at location A, location 232 should contain the value `A-256*(INT(A/256))`, while location 233 should contain `INT(A/256)`. These values may be set when the table is loaded from disk. Several tables may be used within a program if the contents of locations 232 and 233 are redefined at appropriate times.

Values of ROT, SCALE, and HCOLOR should be defined before using either DRAW or XDRAW. (See the Applesoft Basic Programming Reference Manual for a description of these commands.) You will find that some distortion occurs when shapes are rotated or scaled. Also, since most shapes contain vertical line segments, you will find that colors are not easily used. White is the preferred color for shapes.

The following short program illustrates a use of shape tables to simulate a radar screen. The shape table is identified in lines 20 and 30. It consists of two shapes: a single plot-then-move-up vector, and a collection of vectors that define an airplane. The shapes are illustrated in Fig-

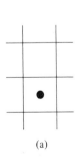

(a)

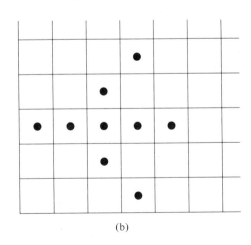

(b)

Figure A2.2

ure A2.2. When shape number 1 is scaled (SCALE = 75), it appears as a line and is used as the scanning line for the radar screen. As the scanning line sweeps around the screen, the positions of the two airplanes change slightly. This display may be incorporated into a larger game program to simulate an aircraft battle or an airport.

Program A2.1: RADAR

```
1    REM PROGRAM A2.1 (RADAR)
2    REM ILLUSTRATES THE USE OF SHAPES
10    FOR I = 768 TO 782: READ X: POKE I,X: NEXT I
20    POKE 233,3: POKE 232,0
30    HGR2 : ROT= 0: SCALE= 2
40   DT = .1:C = COS (DT):S = SIN (DT):N = 6.4 / DT
50   CX = 140:CY = 96:SC = 1.16:X = 50:Y = 0:FL = 0
60    GOSUB 190
70   X = 30:Y = 0:FL = 0: GOSUB 190
80   A = 175:B = 61:C = 191:D = 113
90    XDRAW 2 AT A,B: XDRAW 2 AT C,D
100    SCALE= 75: FOR I = 0 TO 63
110    ROT= I: XDRAW 1 AT 140,96
120    FOR J = 1 TO 15: NEXT J
130    IF I = 8 THEN SCALE= 2: ROT= 1:
       XDRAW 2 AT A,B:A = A - 3:B = B + 3:
       XDRAW 2 AT A,B: SCALE= 75
140    IF I = 19 THEN SCALE= 2: ROT= 1:
       XDRAW 2 AT C,D:C = C - 3:D = D - 1:
       XDRAW 2 AT C,D: SCALE= 75
150    IF A < 140 THEN TEXT : HOME : END
160    ROT= I: XDRAW 1 AT 140,96
170    NEXT I: GOTO 100
180    DATA 2,0,6,0,8,0,4,0,109,229,240,54,14,4,0
190    FOR J = 1 TO N
200   T = X * C - Y * S:Y = Y * C + X * S:X = T
210   SX = SC * X + CX:SY = CY - Y
220    IF FL = 1 THEN 240
230    HPLOT SX,SY:FL = 1
240    HPLOT  TO SX,SY
250    NEXT J: RETURN
```

PROGRAM A2.2 (SHAPE CONSTRUCTION)

This program will assemble shapes into a shape table and store the table on disk (if desired) as a binary file. The program provides a chance to store and recall tables from disk. Thus, a shape table may be developed over several sessions.

The program allows the user to define a shape as a pattern of dots on a grid, which is displayed on the screen. The size of the grid (up to 15 × 15) may be specified by the user. Control over the size of the grid is useful when designing shapes that are to be of a uniform size (such as alphabet characters).

The square of the grid that is used as the starting point for the shape also is under user control. This point of the shape is placed at the screen location that is referenced by the shape drawing commands. When designing a collection of shapes, it usually is useful to have a uniform position to use as the starting point.

The keys U, D, L, and R are used to move the cursor a distance of one unit up, down, left, or right (attempts to move off the grid are thwarted). The P key will plot a dot at the current cursor location. Press Q when the shape is completed, or when you would like to try again. When Q is pressed, the computer takes a short time to assemble the shape you have drawn, then displays the result at the right of the grid.

> **NOTE:**   If you prefer to use I, J, K, and M for moving the cursor (as in text screen editing), make those substitutions in lines 450 through 480.

As each shape is completed, you have the option of including it in the shape table or rejecting it. You then have the option of developing another shape, changing the grid size, changing the starting point, saving the current shape table to disk, or leaving the program.

Program A2.2: SHAPE CONSTRUCTION

```
1    REM PROGRAM A2.2 (SHAPE CONSTRUCTION)
2    REM ASSISTS IN CONSTRUCTING SHAPE TABLES
10   HCOLOR= 3: SCALE= 1: ROT= 0:TA = 24576
20   POKE 768,1: POKE 769,0: POKE 770,4: POKE
     771,0
30   POKE 772,58: POKE 773,36: POKE 774,45: POKE
     775,54: POKE 776,7: POKE 778,0
40   TEXT : HOME : PRINT "CHOOSE:": PRINT
50   PRINT "L --> LOAD A SHAPE TABLE FROM DISK":
     PRINT
60   PRINT "N --> START A NEW SHAPE TABLE":
     PRINT
70   PRINT "YOUR CHOICE "; CHR$ (95);: HTAB 12:
     INPUT A$
```

```
80    IF A$ = "N" THEN 180
90   IF A$ < > "L" THEN 40
100   PRINT : INPUT "NAME OF THE TABLE ":N$
110   PRINT CHR$ (4);"BLOAD ";N$;",A$6000"
120  N = ( PEEK (TA + 2) + 256 *
     PEEK (TA + 3) - 2) / 2
130  SN = PEEK (TA): PRINT : IF SN = N THEN PRINT
     "TABLE FULL": END
140   PRINT "THIS TABLE CAN HOLD ";N;" SHAPES":
     PRINT
150   PRINT "IT PRESENTLY HAS ";SN;" SHAPE(S) IN
     IT": PRINT
160   FOR I = 1 TO 2500: NEXT I
170   GOTO 240
180   TEXT : HOME : INPUT "NUMBER OF SHAPES IN
     THIS TABLE: ";N
190   POKE TA,0: POKE TA + 1,0
200  DA= 2 * N + 2
210   POKE TA + 2,DA - 256 * INT (DA / 256)
220   POKE TA + 3,INT (DA / 256)
230   FOR I = TA + 4 TO TA + 2 * N + 3: POKE I,0:
     NEXT I
240   PRINT : PRINT "CHOOSE SIZE OF SHAPE DESIGN
     GRID"
250   INPUT "NUMBER OF COLUMNS (1 - 15) ";C:C =
     10 * C
260   INPUT "NUMBER OF ROWS (1 - 15) ";R:R = 150
     - 10 * R
270   HGR
280   FOR I = R TO 150 STEP 10: HPLOT 0,I TO C,I:
     NEXT I
290   FOR I = 0 TO C STEP 10: HPLOT I,R TO I,150:
     NEXT I
300   IF A = 1 THEN 330
310   HOME : VTAB 21: PRINT "STARTING POSITION?
     LOWER LEFT IS (1,1)"
320   INPUT "COLUMN ";X1: INPUT "ROW ";Y1
330  X = 10 * X1 - 5:Y = 155 - 10 * Y1
340  ADDR = PEEK (TA + SN * 2 + 2) + 256 * PEEK
     (TA + SN * 2 + 3) + TA
350   POKE 232,0: POKE 233,3
360   XDRAW 1 AT X,Y:P = 0:V = - 1
370   HOME: VTAB 21: PRINT "TABLE CAPACITY: ";N;"
     SHAPES-THIS IS # ";SN + 1
380   VTAB 22: PRINT TAB( 10);"DIRECTION
     (U/D/L/R) "
```

(continued)

```
390    VTAB 23: PRINT "CHOOSE: PLOT (P)"
400    VTAB 24: PRINT TAB( 10);"QUIT THIS SHAPE
       (Q)";
410    VTAB 23: HTAB 35: GET V$: PRINT
420    IF V$ = "Q" THEN POKE ADDR,P: POKE ADDR +
       1,255: GOTO 520
430    XDRAW 1 AT X,Y
440    IF V$ = "P" THEN P = 4:
       FOR I = X - 3 TO X + 3: HPLOT I,Y - 3 TO
       I,Y + 3: NEXT I: XDRAW 1 AT X,Y: GOTO 410
450    IF V$ = "U" THEN V = P:Y = Y - 10: IF Y < R
       THEN Y = Y + 10: PRINT CHR$ (7);:V = - 1
460    IF V$ = "R" THEN V = P + 1:X = X + 10: IF X
       > C THEN X = X - 10: PRINT CHR$ (7);:V = -
       1
470    IF V$ = "D" THEN V = P + 2:Y = Y + 10: IF Y
       > 150 THEN Y = Y - 10: PRINT CHR$ (7);:V =
       - 1
480    IF V$ = "L" THEN V = P + 3:X = X - 10: IF X
       < 0 THEN X = X + 10: PRINT CHR $ (7);:V = -
       1
490    IF V = - 1 THEN XDRAW 1 AT X,Y: GOTO 410
500    POKE ADDR,V:ADDR = ADDR + 1
510    XDRAW 1 AT X,Y:P = 0:V = - 1: GOTO 410
520 ADDR = PEEK (TA + SN * 2 + 2) + 256 * PEEK
    (TA + SN * 2 + 3) + TA:BYTE = ADDR
530 C1 = PEEK (BYTE): IF C1 = 255 THEN POKE
    ADDR,0:ADDR = ADDR + 1: GOTO 660
540 C2 = PEEK (BYTE + 1): IF C2 = 255 THEN POKE
    ADDR,C1: POKE ADDR + 1,0 :ADDR = ADDR + 2:
    GOTO 660
550 C3 = PEEK (BYTE + 2): IF C3 = 255 THEN POKE
    ADDR,C1 + 8 * C2: POKE ADDR + 1,0:ADDR =
    ADDR + 2: GOTO 660
560 CODE = C1 + 8 * C2 + 64 * C3
570    IF CODE = 0 THEN POKE ADDR,64: POKE ADDR +
       1,24:ADDR = ADDR + 1:BYTE = BYTE + 2: GOTO
       650
580    IF CODE < 8 THEN POKE ADDR,CODE: GOTO 650
590    IF CODE < 64 THEN POKE ADDR,CODE:BYTE =
       BYTE + 1: GOTO 650
600    IF CODE < 256 THEN POKE ADDR,CODE:BYTE =
       BYTE + 2: GOTO 650
610 CODE = CODE - 64 * C3
620    IF CODE = 0 THEN POKE ADDR,64: POKE ADDR +
       1,3:ADDR = ADDR + 1:BYTE = BYTE + 1: GOTO
       650
```

```
630   IF CODE < 8 THEN POKE ADDR,CODE: GOTO 650
640   POKE ADDR,CODE:BYTE = BYTE + 1
650  ADDR = ADDR + 1:BYTE = BYTE + 1: GOTO 530
660   POKE TA,SN + 1: POKE 233,96: DRAW SN + 1 AT
      200,100
670   HOME : VTAB 22: PRINT "SAVE THIS AS SHAPE
      NUMBER ";SN + 1;"(Y/N)";: INPUT A$
680   IF A$ = "Y" THEN SN = SN + 1: IF SN < N
      THEN DA = ADDR - TA: POKE TA + 2 * SN +
      2,DA - 256 * INT (DA / 256): POKE TA + 2 *
      SN + 3, INT (DA / 256)
690   IF A$ < > "N" AND A$ < > "Y" THEN 670
700   POKE TA,SN
710   TEXT : HOME : VTAB 17: PRINT "CHOOSE:"
720   PRINT TAB( 5);"(1) DRAW ANOTHER SHAPE"
730   PRINT TAB( 5);"(2) CHANGE DOT MATRIX"
740   PRINT TAB( 5);"(3) CHANGE STARTING POINT"
750   PRINT TAB( 5);"(4) SAVE SHAPE TABLE TO
      DISK"
760   PRINT TAB( 5);"(5) LEAVE THE PROGRAM"
770   INPUT A$:A = VAL (A$)
780   IF A < 1 OR A > 5 THEN 710
790   IF SN = N AND A < 4 THEN PRINT "TABLE
      FULL": FOR I = 1 TO 1000: NEXT I: GOTO 710
800   ON A GOTO 270,240,270,820
810   TEXT : HOME : END
820   INPUT "NAME ";N$
830   PRINT CHR$ (4);"BSAVE ";
      N$;",A24576,L";ADDR - 24576
840   GOTO 710
```

Appendix 3

Vectors

For our purposes, a vector may be considered to be a directed line segment. For points P and Q, the vector extending from P to Q may be represented by $\overrightarrow{PQ}$ or by a single character $\vec{v}$. If coordinates are provided for P and Q, say P(a,b) and Q(c,d), then the vector $\vec{v}$ may be identified by its components. The x-component of the vector is $v_x = c - a$, and $v_y = d - b$ is the y-component.

For P($-3,1$) and Q(4,6), as shown in Figure A3.1, vector $\vec{v} = \overrightarrow{PQ}$ has components $v_x = 7$ and $v_y = 5$. It is customary to write $\vec{v} = (7,5)$.

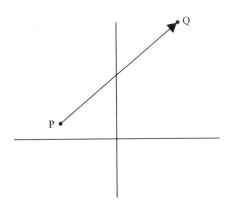

Figure A3.1

Although the notation (3,7) is used to specify the point P(3,7), and also to identify the vector extending from Q(0,0) to P, the ambiguity should not be a problem for us.

Vector addition (see Figure A3.2) is easily defined in terms of components. For $\vec{u}$ = (a,b) and $\vec{v}$ = (c,d), we define $\vec{u} + \vec{v}$ = (a + c,b + d).

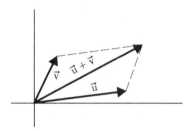

Figure A3.2

Vector subtraction (see Figure A3.3) follows from the definition of addition: for $\vec{u}$ = (a,b) and $\vec{v}$ = (c,d), $\vec{u} - \vec{v}$ = (a − c,b − d).

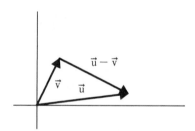

Figure A3.3

SCALAR MULTIPLES OF VECTORS

The multiplication of a vector by a number (scalar) is referred to as scalar multiplication. For $\vec{u}$ = (a,b) the product $t\vec{u}$ is defined as $t\vec{u}$ = t(a,b) = (ta,tb). Multiplication of a vector by a positive scalar has the effect of multiplying the length of the vector by the scalar, without affecting the direction of the vector. Multiplication of a vector by a negative scalar multiplies the length of the vector by the absolute value of the scalar, while reversing the direction of the vector. See Figure A3.4.

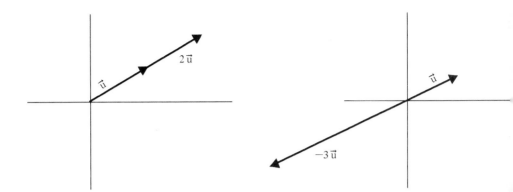

Figure A3.4

VECTOR REPRESENTATION OF LINES

If $\vec{v}$ and $\vec{w}$ are vectors extending from O(0,0) to points P and Q, then $\vec{u} = \vec{w} - \vec{v}$ is a vector extending from P to Q. If $\vec{x}$ is another vector which extends from O(0,0) to a point on the line containing P and Q, then $\vec{x} - \vec{v}$ will be a multiple of $\vec{u}$: $\vec{x} - \vec{v} = t\vec{u}$, or $\vec{x} = \vec{v} + t\vec{u}$ (see figure A3.5 and figure A3.6).

To illustrate, let $\vec{v} = (10,3)$ and $\vec{w} = (1,7)$ (see Figure A3.6). Then, $\vec{u} = \vec{w} - \vec{v} = (1,7) - (10,3) = (-9,4)$. For any choice of $\vec{x} = (x,y)$ lying on the line PQ, then $\vec{x} = \vec{v} + t\vec{u}$, or $(x,y) = (10,3) + t(-9,4)$. Each

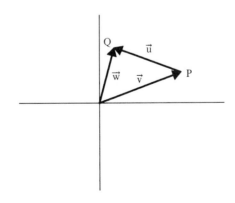

Figure A3.5

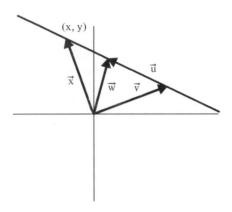

Figure A3.6

choice of a value for t will result in a specific pair of values (x,y) that identifies a point on the line PQ (see Figure A3.7). For example,

t	x	y
1	1	7
2	-8	11
3	-17	15
0	10	3
-1	19	-1
-2	28	-5

Notice that the line has positive and negative directions, inherited from the positive and negative directions of the vector $\vec{u}$.

VECTORS IN THREE-DIMENSIONAL SPACE

The previous discussion of vectors, based in two-dimensional space, is easily extended to higher dimensions. Most of our need for vectors will be for three-dimensional calculations. For vectors $\vec{v} = (2,1,7)$ and $\vec{w} = (3,2,-5)$ we calculate

$$\vec{v} + \vec{w} = (2,1,7) + (3,2,-5) = (5,3,2)$$
$$\vec{v} - \vec{w} = (2,1,7) - (3,2,-5) = (-1,-1,12)$$
$$4\vec{v} = 4(2,1,7) = (8,4,28).$$

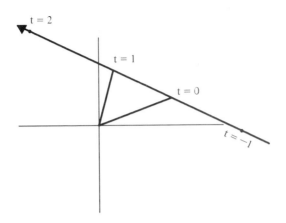

Figure A3.7

The line passing through the points $(2,1,7)$ and $(3,2,-5)$ may be represented as $\vec{x} = \vec{v} + t\vec{u}$, where $\vec{u} = \vec{w} - \vec{v} = (3,2,-5) - (2,1,7) = (1,1,-12)$. Thus, the vector form of the equation of the line is $(x,y,z) = (2,1,7) + t(1,1,-12)$.

DOT PRODUCTS OF VECTORS

We define the dot product of vectors $\vec{u} = (a,b,c)$ and $\vec{v} = (d,e,f)$ to be $\vec{u} \cdot \vec{v} = (a,b,c) \cdot (d,e,f) = ad + be + cf$. For example, if $\vec{u} = (9,1,2)$ and $\vec{v} = (3,-5,7)$, then $\vec{u} \cdot \vec{v} = (9,1,2) \cdot (3,-5,7) = 27 - 5 + 14 = 36$.

For two-dimensional vectors, the definition of the dot product is similar: $(a,b) \cdot (c,d) = ac + bd$. For example, $(3,5) \cdot (7,-3) = 21 - 15 = 6$.

While these definitions provide an easy means of calculating the dot product of two vectors, no hint is given of the significance of the dot product. It may be shown that $\vec{u} \cdot \vec{v} = |\vec{u}||\vec{v}| \cos\theta$. Here, $|\vec{u}|$ refers to the magnitude, or length, of $\vec{u}$. The length of $\vec{v}$ is $|\vec{v}|$, and θ is the angle between $\vec{u}$ and $\vec{v}$. Many useful applications may be derived from this interpretation of the dot product, but we shall require only one: If the angle between $\vec{u}$ and $\vec{v}$ is between $0°$ and $90°$, the dot product of $\vec{u}$ and $\vec{v}$ is positive. If the angle is between $90°$ and $180°$, the dot product is negative.

The value of θ may be calculated from the dot product:

Since $\vec{u} \cdot \vec{v} = |\vec{u}||\vec{v}| \cos\theta$,

then $\cos\theta = \dfrac{\vec{u} \cdot \vec{v}}{|\vec{u}||\vec{v}|}$

and $\theta = \text{arc cos} \left(\dfrac{\vec{u} \cdot \vec{v}}{|\vec{u}||\vec{v}|} \right)$

Since $|\vec{u}|$ and $|\vec{v}|$ are always positive, the sign of $\vec{u} \cdot \vec{v} = |\vec{u}||\vec{v}| \cos \theta$ is the sign of $\cos \theta$. The truth of the above statement thus rests on the characteristics of the cosine. If θ is between $0°$ and $90°$, then $\cos\theta$ is positive. If θ is between $90°$ and $180°$, $\cos\theta$ is negative.

To illustrate, if $\vec{u} = (1,3)$, $\vec{v} = (3, -5)$, and $\vec{w} = (-1, -6)$ (see Figure A3.8), then $\vec{u} \cdot \vec{v} = (1,3) \cdot (3, -5) = 3 - 15 = -12$ is negative, since the angle between $\vec{u}$ and $\vec{v}$ is between $90°$ and $180°$; and $\vec{u} \cdot \vec{w} = (1,3) \cdot (-1, -6) = -1 - 18 = -19$. Again, the angle is between $90°$ and $180°$. But $\vec{v} \cdot \vec{w} = (3, -5) \cdot (-1, -6) = -3 + 30 = 27$ is positive; the angle is between $0°$ and $90°$.

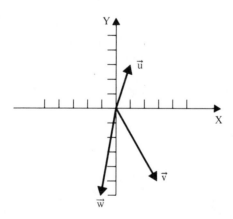

Figure A3.8

CROSS PRODUCTS OF VECTORS

The definition of the cross product is more cumbersome than that of the dot product. For $\vec{u} = (a,b,c)$ and $\vec{v} = (d,e,f)$, we have $\vec{u} \times \vec{v} =$ (bf − ce,cd − af,ae − bd). Note that while $\vec{u} \cdot \vec{v}$ is a number, $\vec{u} \times \vec{v}$ is a vector. Further, while $\vec{u} \cdot \vec{v}$ may be calculated for two- or three-dimensional vectors, $\vec{u} \times \vec{v}$ is defined only for three-dimensional vectors.

$$\text{For } \vec{u} = (1,9,8) \text{ and } \vec{v} = (3,0,7)$$
$$\vec{u} \times \vec{v} = (1,9,8) \times (3,0,7)$$
$$= (63 − 0,24 − 7,0 − 27)$$
$$= (63,17,−27)$$

What is the significance of the cross product? Only one application is of interest to us: In a right hand coordinate system, the cross product of vectors $\vec{u}$ and $\vec{v}$ will yield a vector $\vec{w}$ which is normal (perpendicular) to the plane of $\vec{u}$ and $\vec{v}$. The orientation of $\vec{w} = \vec{u} \times \vec{v}$ is such that, if the index and second finger of the *right* hand are pointing in the direction of $\vec{u}$ and $\vec{v}$, respectively, then $\vec{w}$ has the direction of the thumb.

Note that $\vec{v} \times \vec{u}$ and $\vec{u} \times \vec{v}$ have opposite directions. For vectors $\vec{u} = (1,3,0)$ and $\vec{v} = (−3,7,0)$, lying in the xy plane, $\vec{u} \times \vec{v}$ is a positive multiple of (0,0,1), while $\vec{v} \times \vec{u}$ is a negative multiple of (0,0,1). In a left hand coordinate system (such as the Apple display screen), when the index finger and second fingers of the *left* hand point in the direction of $\vec{u}$ and $\vec{v}$, respectively, $\vec{u} \times \vec{v}$ will be normal to the plane of $\vec{u}$ and $\vec{v}$, having the direction of the thumb.

HALF-PLANES

The line $(x,y) = (a,b) + t(c,d)$ divides the xy plane into two *half-planes.* When facing in the direction of the vector $\vec{v} = (c,d)$, the half-plane on the left is referred to as the *left half-plane,* while the half-plane on the right is called the *right half-plane.* Note that the designation of left and right half-planes rests on the orientation of the vector $\vec{v} = (c,d)$.

For example, the line $(x,y) = (2,5) + t(−1,3)$ divides the plane as shown in Figure A3.9b. The line $(x,y) = (2,5) + t(1,−3)$ (same line, opposite orientation) divides the plane as shown in Figure A3.9a.

Our concern with half-planes occurs in Chapter 7, when we must determine which half-plane contains a given point. For the half-planes determined by the line $\vec{x} = \vec{u} + t\vec{v}$, the left and right half-planes are as

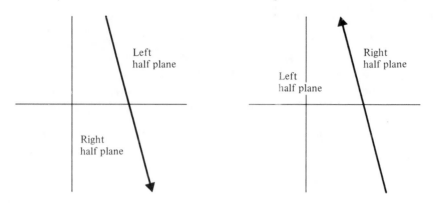

Figure A3.9

indicated in Figure A3.10. To determine which half-plane contains point P(a,b), we will define vector $\vec{r} = (a,b)$ and vector $\vec{w} = \vec{r} - \vec{u}$. If P is in the left half-plane, then $\vec{v} \times \vec{w}$ will be a positive multiple of (0,0,1). If P is in the right half-plane, then $\vec{v} \times \vec{w}$ will be a negative multiple of (0,0,1).

To illustrate, consider line $(x,y) = (2,5) + t(1, -3)$ and point P(4,8). Then

$$\vec{u} = (2,5,0), \vec{v} = (1, -3,0), \vec{r} = (4,8,0)$$
$$\vec{w} = \vec{r} - \vec{u} = (4,8,0) - (2,5,0) = (2,3,0)$$

and

$$\vec{v} \times \vec{w} = (1, -3,0) \times (2,3,0)$$
$$= (0,0,3 + 6)$$
$$= (0,0,9) = 9(0,0,1)$$

which is a positive multiple of (0,0,1). We can see from Figure A3.10 that P is indeed in the left half-plane.

> **NOTE:**   The test above for location of a point in either the left or right half-plane is valid for points located in a right-hand coordinate system, which is a conventional context for calculation. However, the Apple display screen has a left-hand coordinate system. When working with points and half-planes on the Apple display screen, the rule above must be modified: With $\vec{u}$, $\vec{v}$, $\vec{r}$, $\vec{w}$, and P as defined above, we will find that P is in the left half-plane if $\vec{v} \times \vec{w}$ is a negative multiple of (0,0,1); but P is in the right half-plane if $\vec{v} \times \vec{w}$ is a positive multiple of (0,0,1).

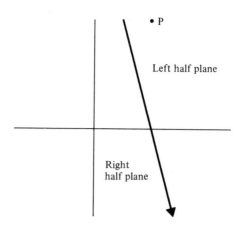

Figure A3.10

Appendix 4
Matrices

A matrix is a rectangular array of numbers, such as

$$\begin{pmatrix} 3 & -9 \\ 4 & 2 \end{pmatrix} \quad \text{or} \quad \begin{pmatrix} 5 & 8 \\ 2 & 1 \\ 3 & 4 \end{pmatrix}$$

Matrices have a wide range of applications, and a large number of matrix formulas and techniques have been developed. Our interest in the use of matrices for representing transformations will require only a very basic knowledge of matrices and matrix products.

The labelling and referencing of the elements of a matrix is illustrated by

$$A = \begin{pmatrix} a_{11} & a_{12} & a_{13} & a_{14} \\ a_{21} & a_{22} & a_{23} & a_{24} \\ a_{31} & a_{32} & a_{33} & a_{34} \end{pmatrix}$$

The subscripts of an element identify the row and column position of that element. Thus a_{24} is in the 2nd row, 4th column, and a_{31} is in the 3rd row, 1st column. A matrix such as A, which has 3 rows and 4 columns, is referred to as a 3×4 matrix.

PRODUCTS OF MATRICES

The following example illustrates matrix multiplication:

$$\begin{array}{ccccc} A & \times & B & = & C \end{array}$$

$$\begin{pmatrix} a_{11} & a_{12} \\ a_{21} & a_{22} \end{pmatrix} \begin{pmatrix} b_{11} & b_{12} \\ b_{21} & b_{22} \end{pmatrix} = \begin{pmatrix} a_{11}b_{11} + a_{12}b_{21} & a_{11}b_{12} + a_{12}b_{22} \\ a_{21}b_{11} + a_{22}b_{21} & a_{21}b_{12} + a_{22}b_{22} \end{pmatrix}$$

Note that in obtaining the matrix product $AB = C$, each entry c_{ij} of the product is the sum of the products of the entries of the ith row of A with the corresponding entries of the jth column of B. Thus, c_{21} is the sum of the products of the 2nd row entries of $A(a_{21}, a_{22})$ with the corresponding entries of the first column of B (b_{11}, b_{21}).

Because of this definition of matrix product, AB is defined only if each row of A has as many entries as a column of B. Thus, if A is an $m \times n$ matrix and B is a $p \times q$ matrix, the product AB is possible only if $n = p$. We then may expect the product to have as many rows as A and as many columns as B: AB will be an $m \times q$ matrix. For example:

$$\begin{pmatrix} 1 & 4 & 2 \\ 3 & 0 & -1 \\ 1 & 5 & 2 \end{pmatrix} \begin{pmatrix} 4 & 9 & 8 \\ 3 & -4 & -7 \\ -5 & 0 & 6 \end{pmatrix} = \begin{pmatrix} 6 & -7 & -8 \\ 17 & 27 & 18 \\ 9 & -11 & -15 \end{pmatrix}$$

$$(2, 1, 3) \begin{pmatrix} 4 & 2 & -5 \\ 8 & 9 & 3 \\ 1 & -4 & 7 \end{pmatrix} = (19, 1, 14)$$

We note without proof that matrix multiplication in general is not commutative ($AB \neq BA$) but is associative ($A(BC) = (AB)C$).

The coordinates of a point may be considered to form a 1×2 matrix. The product

$$(x, y) \begin{pmatrix} 4 & 2 \\ 8 & 9 \end{pmatrix}$$

shows that the matrix

$$\begin{pmatrix} 4 & 2 \\ 8 & 9 \end{pmatrix}$$

provides a means of associating each point (x, y) with a second point $(4x + 8y, 2x + 9y)$. For example:

$$(1, -1) \begin{pmatrix} 4 & 2 \\ 8 & 9 \end{pmatrix} = (-4, -7) \text{ and } (-2, 1) \begin{pmatrix} 4 & 2 \\ 8 & 9 \end{pmatrix} = (0, 5)$$

In a similar manner, any matrix

$$\begin{pmatrix} a & b \\ c & d \end{pmatrix}$$

may be considered to provide a means of associating the point (x,y) with the point $(ax + cy, bx + dy)$. We speak of transforming the point (x,y) to the point $(ax + cy, bx + dy)$, and refer to

$$\begin{pmatrix} a & b \\ c & d \end{pmatrix}$$

as being the matrix of the transformation.

Appendix 5
Radian Measure of Angles

There are several units available for measuring angles. While degree measurement is commonly used, it is not the preferred system for work in science or engineering; nor is it used by computers. Measurement of angles in radians is more conventional.

Figure A5.1 shows a unit circle (radius 1), and an angle $\angle APB$ with its vertex at the center of the circle. The radian measure of angle $\angle APB$ is the length of the arc **AB**.

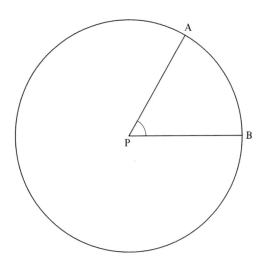

Figure A5.1

Thus, radian measure is defined in terms of arc length measured on a circle of radius 1.

The association between degrees and radians is established by noting that the circumference of a unit circle is given by $C = 2\pi r = 2\pi(1) = 2\pi$. Thus, an angle of 360° has a radian equivalent of 2π. As a result, an angle of 1° has a radian measure of $2\pi/360$.

The following rule converts degrees to radians:

RADIANS = DEGREES × $\pi/180$.

To convert from radians to degrees:

DEGREES = RADIANS × $180/\pi$

Table A5.1 shows the degree-radian equivalence of some commonly-used angles.

Table A5.1

Degrees	Radians
0°	0
30°	$\pi/6 \approx .5236$
45°	$\pi/4 \approx .7854$
60°	$\pi/3 \approx 1.0472$
90°	$\pi/2 \approx 1.5708$
180°	$\pi \approx 3.1416$
270°	$3\pi/2 \approx 4.7124$
360°	$2\pi \approx 6.2832$

To use radian measure within a program it usually is convenient to provide the value of π. This may be done by defining the variable, as

```
PI = 3.141592654
```

or, since $\tan(45°) = \tan(\pi/4) = 1$,

```
PI = 4 * ATN(1)
```

Appendix 6
Cover Program Listings

In the following pages we provide listings of the programs which draw the images used on the cover of this book. In addition we list the program which draws the image of Figure 5.1. Each of the programs is accompanied by a brief description which references pertinent chapters. The documentation for the programs is brief, and assumes familiarity with the concepts and programs discussed in the related chapters.

FRONT COVER: UPPER LEFT

Although this program is long, it is quite simple in structure. The length is due to the large number of points which must be individually identified.

In planning the program, approximate measurements (in inches) were taken from an Apple II, using the lower left rear corner as the reference point. Some of the numbers were later "fudged" slightly to improve the appearance of the image. Some of the measurements are provided in DATA statements, identifying the x,y,z coordinates of points to be plotted. The coordinates of others are identified as needed.

The program uses the projection subroutine of lines 20–60 to obtain screen coordinates of points to be plotted. The subroutine was introduced in Chapter 6, and used in the programs of Chapters 6 and 7.

The hidden line elimination is handled in lines 1490–1600, using the "blackout" method described in Chapter 7.

The variable T is used for two purposes. First, it identifies the top-of-screen Y coordinate which is used by the blackout routine (T = 0 for the first image; T = 40 for the second image). Secondly, T is used to branch around parts of the program when the second image is being drawn. As a result, the second, smaller image looses some of the detail provided in the first. The third image looses a lot of detail, since it provides only a pair of rectangles (lines 1940, 1950).

Program A6.1

```
1    REM PROGRAM A6.1   (APPLE II)
2    REM   DRAWS UPPER LEFT IMAGE ON FRONT COVER
10   GOTO 130
20 XE =  - X * S1 + Y * C1
30 YE =  - X * C1 * C2 - Y * S1 * C2 + Z * S2
40 ZE =  - X * S2 * C1 - Y * S2 * S1 - Z * C2
     + RHO
50 SX = D * XE / ZE + CX
60 SY = CY - D * YE / ZE: RETURN
70   GOSUB 20
80   HPLOT SX,SY
90   RETURN
100   GOSUB 20
110   HPLOT  TO SX,SY
120   RETURN
130 RHO = 100:D = 1100:CX = 116:CY = 105
140 THETA = .45:S1 =  SIN (TH):C1 =  COS (TH)
150 PHI = 1.25:S2 =  SIN (PH):C2 =  COS (PH)
160   HGR2 : HCOLOR= 3
170   DATA 17.75,   15.25,   2
180   DATA 17.75,   15.25,   1.25
190   DATA 15,      15.25,   0
200   DATA 0,   15.25,   0
210   DATA 0,   15.25,   4
220   DATA  8.75,   15.25,   4
230   DATA 17.75,   15.25,   2
240   DATA 17.75,   0,   2
250   DATA 17.75,   0,   1.25
260   DATA 17.75,   15.25,   1.25
270   DATA 17.75, 0, 2
280   DATA 8.75, 0, 4
290   DATA 0, 0, 4
300   DATA 0, 15.25, 4
310   READ X,Y,Z: GOSUB 70
320   FOR I = 1 TO 9
330   READ X,Y,Z: GOSUB 100
340   NEXT I
350   READ X,Y,Z: GOSUB 70
360   FOR I = 1 TO 3
```

```
370   READ X,Y,Z: GOSUB 100
380   NEXT I
390   IF T < > 0 THEN 470
400 X = .875
410   FOR I = 1 TO 18 STEP 2
420 Y = 14.625:Z = 4: GOSUB 70
430 Y = 15.25: GOSUB 100
440 Z = 2.5: GOSUB 100
450 X = X + .75
460   NEXT I
470   REM LID
480   DATA 1,1, 1,14.3, 7.75,14.3, 7.75,1, 1,1
490 Z = 4: READ X,Y: GOSUB 70
500   FOR I = 1 TO 4
510   READ X,Y: GOSUB 100
520   NEXT I
530 Y = 0:X = 11:Z = 3.5: GOSUB 70
540 Y = 15.25: GOSUB 100
550 X = 12.25:Z = 3.22: GOSUB 70
560 Y = 0: GOSUB 100
570   REM KEYBOARD
580 X = 13.25:Z = 3.125:Y = 3: GOSUB 70
590 Y = 12.5: GOSUB 100
600   IF T < > 0 THEN 670
610 X = 13.75: GOSUB 100
620 Y = 3: GOSUB 100
630   FOR Y = 3 TO 11.77 STEP .73
640 X = 13.25: GOSUB 70
650 X = 13.75: GOSUB 100
660   NEXT Y
670 X = 14:Z = 2.88:Y = 2.625: GOSUB 70
680 Y = 12.5: GOSUB 100
690   IF T < > 0 THEN 760
700 X = 14.5: GOSUB 100
710 Y = 2.625: GOSUB 100
720   FOR Y = 2.625 TO 11.425 STEP .73
730 X = 14: GOSUB 70
740 X = 14.5: GOSUB 100
750   NEXT Y
760 X = 14.75:Z = 2.635:Y = 2.7
770   GOSUB 70
780 Y = 12.2: GOSUB 100
790   IF T < > 0 THEN 860
800 X = 15.25: GOSUB 100
810 Y = 2.7: GOSUB 100
820   FOR Y = 2.7 TO 12.2 STEP .73
```

(continued)

```
830 X = 14.75: GOSUB 70
840 X = 15.25: GOSUB 100
850  NEXT Y
860 X = 15.5:Z = 2.39:Y = 2.7: GOSUB 70
870 Y = 12.2: GOSUB 100
880  IF T <  > 0 THEN 970
890 X = 16: GOSUB 100
900 Y = 2.7: GOSUB 100
910 Y = 2.7:X = 15.5: GOSUB 70
920 X = 16: GOSUB 100
930  FOR Y = 3.7 TO 11.2 STEP .73
940 X = 15.5: GOSUB 70
950 X = 16: GOSUB 100
960  NEXT Y
970 X = 16.25:Z = 2.145:Y = 4.7: GOSUB 70
980 Y = 10.45: GOSUB 100
990  IF T <  > 0 THEN 1070
1000 X = 16.75: GOSUB 100
1010 Y = 4.7: GOSUB 100
1020 X = 16.25: GOSUB 100
1030  FOR Y = 2.7 TO 3.45 STEP .1
1040 X = 16.25: GOSUB 70
1050 X = 16.75: GOSUB 100
1060  NEXT Y
1070  DEF  FN Z(X) = 5.94 - .2 * X
1080  IF T <  > 0 THEN 1480
1090  REM A
1100 Y = 7:X = 9.95:Z =  FN Z(X): GOSUB 70
1110 X = 9.75:Z =  FN Z(X): GOSUB 100
1120 Y = 6.7: GOSUB 100
1130 X = 9.95:Z =  FN Z(X): GOSUB 100
1140  REM PP
1150  FOR LY = 7.2 TO 7.7 STEP .5
1160 X = 10.05:Y = LY:Z =  FN Z(X): GOSUB 70
1170 X = 9.75:Z =  FN Z(X): GOSUB 100
1180 Y = LY + .3: GOSUB 100
1190 X = 9.95:Z =  FN Z(X): GOSUB 100
1200 Y = LY: GOSUB 100
1210  NEXT LY
1220  REM ㄴ
1230 Y = 8.2: GOSUB 70
1240 X = 9.65:Z =  FN Z(X): GOSUB 100
1250  REM  E
1260 Y = 8.8:X = 9.95:Z =  FN Z(X): GOSUB 70
1270 Y = 8.45: GOSUB 100
1280 X = 9.75:Z =  FN Z(X): GOSUB 100
1290 Y = 8.8: GOSUB 100
```

```
1300  X = 9.95:Y = 8.45:Z =   FN Z(X):  GOSUB 100
1310   REM    ]
1320  Y = 9:  GOSUB 70
1330  X = 9.65:Z =   FN Z(X):  GOSUB 100
1340  Y = 9.25:  GOSUB 70
1350  X = 9.95:Z =   FN Z(X):  GOSUB 100
1360   REM BOX
1370  Y = 5.5:X = 10.4:Z =   FN Z(X):  GOSUB 70
1380  Y = 9.5:  GOSUB 100
1390  X = 9.4:Z =   FN Z(X):  GOSUB 100
1400  Y = 5.5:  GOSUB 100
1410  X = 10.4:Z =   FN Z(X):  GOSUB 100
1420   REM   APPLE
1430   HCOLOR= 5
1440   FOR X = 9.8 TO 10.1 STEP .1:Z =   FN Z(X)
1450  Y = 6:  GOSUB 70
1460  Y = 6.3:  GOSUB 100
1470   NEXT X
1480   REM   BLACKOUT
1490  X = 8.75:Y = 3.4:Z = 4:  GOSUB 20:P1 = SX:P2
      = SY
1500  Y = 12.4:  GOSUB 20:Q1 = SX:Q2 = SY
1510  X = 0:  GOSUB 20:R1 = SX:R2 = SY
1520  SL = (Q2 - P2) / (Q1 - P1)
1530   HCOLOR= 4
1540   FOR X = P1 TO Q1
1550  Y = SL * (X - P1) + P2
1560   HPLOT X,T TO X,Y
1570   NEXT X
1580  SL = (R2 - Q2) / (R1 - Q1)
1590   FOR X = Q1 TO R1:Y = SL * (X - Q1) + Q2
1600   HPLOT X,T TO X,Y:  NEXT X
1610   REM MONITOR
1620   HCOLOR= 3
1630  X = 8.75:Y = 3.4:Z = 4:  GOSUB 70
1640  Y = 12.4:  GOSUB 100
1650  Z = 10:  GOSUB 100
1660  Y = 3.4:  GOSUB 100
1670  Z = 4:  GOSUB 100
1680   IF T <  > 0 THEN 1780
1690   REM DIALS
1700  X = 8.75:Y = 11:Z = 6.5:  GOSUB 20
1710   FOR TH = 0 TO 6.3 STEP .4
1720   HPLOT SX,SY TO SX + 4 *   COS (TH),SY + 4
      *  SIN (TH)
1730   NEXT TH
```

(continued)

```
1740 Z = 8: GOSUB 20
1750  FOR TH = 0 TO 6.3 STEP .4
1760  HPLOT SX,SY TO SX + 4 *  COS (TH),SY + 4
      *  SIN (TH)
1770  NEXT TH
1780 Y = 3.9:Z = 4.5: GOSUB 20:P1 = SX:P2 = SY
1790 Y = 9.9: GOSUB 20:Q1 = SX:Q2 = SY
1800 Z = 9.5: GOSUB 20:R1 = SX:R2 = SY
1810 Y = 3.9: GOSUB 20:T1 = SX:T2 = SY
1820  HPLOT P1,P2 TO Q1,Q2 TO R1,R2 TO T1,T2 TO
      P1,P2
1830 Z = 4:Y = 12.4: GOSUB 70
1840 X = 0: GOSUB 100
1850 Z = 10: GOSUB 100
1860 Y = 3.4: GOSUB 100
1870 X = 8.75: GOSUB 100
1880 Y = 12.4: GOSUB 70
1890 X = 0: GOSUB 100
1900  IF T < > 0 THEN 1940
1910  REM  RETURN FOR SECOND IMAGE
1920 T = 40: RESTORE :RHO = 435:CX = 140:CY =
      64: GOTO 310
1930  REM  FAKE THIRD IMAGE
1940  HPLOT 143,55 TO 149,57 TO 149,59 TO 143,58
      TO 143,55
1950  HPLOT 144,56 TO 144,52 TO 148,53
      TO 148,57
]
```

FRONT COVER: UPPER RIGHT

Program A6.2 is almost the same as Program 7.6. The differences lie in the function being used (line 50) and the limits used in the FOR . . . NEXT loops (lines 90, 110) which generate points of the surface. As a result of plotting the surface over such a wide range of values of x and y, and the associated projection and hidden line calculations, the program requires approximately forty minutes to complete the image.

Program A6.2

```
1  REM PROGRAM A6.2  (COSINE SURFACE)
2  REM DRAWS UPPER RIGHT IMAGE ON FRONT COVER
10  HGR2 : HCOLOR= 5:CX = 140:CY = 96
20 RHO = 80:D = 750
30 THETA = .4:S1 =  SIN (TH):C1 =  COS (TH)
```

```
40 PHI = 1.25:S2 =  SIN (PH):C2 =   COS (PH)
50  DEF   FN Z(X) =   COS (.06 * (X * X + Y * Y))
60  DIM YN(280),YX(280)
70  FOR I = 0 TO 279:YN(I) = 191: NEXT I
80  REM   POINT GENERATING LOOP
90  FOR X = 22 TO  -55 STEP  -1
100 FL = 0
110  FOR Y =  - 40 TO 19
120 Z =  FN Z(X)
130  GOSUB 190
140  NEXT Y,X
150  HCOLOR= 2
160  HPLOT 0,0 TO 278,0 TO 278,191 TO 0,191 TO
     0,0
170  END
180  REM   PLOTTING SUBROUTINE
190 XE =  - X * S1 + Y * C1
200 YE =  - X * C1 * C2 - Y * S1 * C2 + Z * S2
210 ZE =  - X * S2 * C1 - Y * S2 * S1 - Z * C2 +
     RHO
220 SX = D * (XE / ZE) + CX
230 SY =  - D * (YE / ZE) + CY
240  IF FL = 0 THEN FL = 1:F = 0: GOTO 360
250 DX = OX - SX: IF DX = 0 THEN DX = 1
260 SL = (OY - SY) / DX:YP = OY
270  FOR XP =  INT (OX) + 1 TO SX
280 FG = 1
290 YP = YP + SL
300  IF XP < 0 OR XP > 279 THEN FG = 0:F = 0:
     GOTO 350
310  IF YP > 191 OR YP < 0 THEN FG = 0:F = 0
320  IF YP <  = YN(XP) THEN 370
330  IF YP >  = YX(XP) THEN 420
340 F = 0
350  NEXT XP
360 OX = SX:OY = SY: RETURN
370 YN(XP) = YP
380  IF FG = 0 THEN 410
390  IF F = 0 THEN  HPLOT XP,YP:F = 1
400  HPLOT  TO XP,YP
410  IF YP < YX(XP) THEN 350
420 YX(XP) = YP
430  IF FG = 0 THEN 460
440  IF F = 0 THEN HPLOT XP,YP:F = 1
450  HPLOT TO XP, YP
460  GOTO 350
]
```

FRONT COVER; LOWER LEFT

This image was developed to assist in describing some concepts of multi-variable calculus (partial derivative, directional derivative) and is used as part of an educational software package distributed by CONDUIT, Iowa City, Iowa. However, in addition to being instructive, the image is an interesting one.

Much of the program is similar to Program A6.2. The function which defines the surface is much more complex (see lines 70–110), but the point calculation and hidden line calculation is essentially the same. The program first draws the closer part of the surface, then the vertical plane, and finally the farther part of the surface. A separate projection subroutine is used for the plane, and the hidden line array update is handled differently than for the surface (line 340). The reason for the difference is that the array YX(I) does not need to be updated when the plane is being drawn.

Be patient; the program requires a substantial amount of time (approximately twenty-five minutes) to draw the image.

Program A6.3

```
1    REM PROGRAM A6.3  (SURFACE/PLANE)
2    REM DRAWS LOWER LEFT IMAGE ON FRONT COVER
10   HGR2 : HCOLOR= 5:CX = 140:CY = 96
20   RHO = 80:D = 750
30   THETA = .4:S1 =  SIN (TH):C1 =  COS (TH)
40   PHI = 1.25:S2 =  SIN (PH):C2 =  COS (PH)
50   DIM YN(280),YX(280)
60   FOR I = 0 TO 279:YN(I) = 191: NEXT I
70   DEF  FN W(X) = 3 *  EXP ( - .1 * ((Y + 10)
     ^2) - .02 * ((X + 10) ^2))
80   DEF  FN R(X) = 4 *  EXP ( - .1 * ((X + 10)
     ^2) - .3 * ((Y - 6) ^2))
90   DEF  FN S(X) = 3 *  EXP ( - .1 * ((Y + 8) ^
     2) - .02 * ((X - 10) ^2))
100  DEF  FN U(X) = - 6 *  EXP ( - .09 * (X - 5)
     ^2 - .09 * (Y - 7) ^2)
110  DEF  FN Z(X) =  FN U(X) +  FN R(X) +  FN
     W(X) +  FN S(X)
120  XS = 8:YS =  - 8:X2 =  - 9:Y2 = 8
130  SP = (Y2 - YS) / (X2 - XS)
140  HCOLOR= 5
150  REM CLOSER PART OF SURFACE
160  FOR X = 14 TO  - 18 STEP  - 1:FL = 0
```

```
170 YL = YS + (X - XS) * SP
180  FOR Y = YL TO 17 STEP .5
190 Z =   FN Z(X): GOSUB 490
200  NEXT Y,X
210  REM CURVE OF INTERSECTION
220 FL = 0
230  FOR X = 14 TO  - 18 STEP  - .4
240 Y = YS + (X - XS) * SP:Z =  FN Z(X): GOSUB
    490
250  NEXT X
260  REM PLANE
270  HCOLOR= 3
280  FOR X = 14 TO  - 18 STEP  - .4
290 Y = YS + (X - XS) * SP:Z = 5
300 FL = 0: GOSUB 780
310  IF SX < 0 OR SX > 279 THEN 390
320  IF SY < 0 THEN SY = 0
330  HPLOT SX,SY TO SX,YN(SX) - 2
340  FOR I = PX TO SX:YN(I) = SY: NEXT I
350 Z =  - 7:FL = 1: GOSUB 780
360  IF SY > 191 THEN SY = 191
370  IF SY > YX(SX) + 2 THEN  HPLOT SX,SY TO
    SX,YX(SX) + 2
380 PX = SX
390  NEXT X
400  REM FARTHER PART OF SURFACE
410  HCOLOR= 5
420  FOR X =  - 5 TO  - 18 STEP  - 1
430 FL = 0
440  FOR Y =  - 13 TO 0 STEP .5
450 Z =  FN Z(X): GOSUB 490
460  NEXT Y,X
470  END
480  REM PROJECTION AND HIDDEN LINES
490 XE =  - X * S1 + Y * C1
500 YE =  - X * C1 * C2 - Y * S1 * C2 + Z * S2
510 ZE =  - X * S2 * C1 - Y * S2 * S1 - Z * C2
    + RHO
520 SX = D * (XE / ZE) + CX
530 SY =  - D * (YE / ZE) + CY
540  IF FL = 0 THEN FL = 1:F = 0: GOTO 660
550 DX = OX - SX: IF DX = 0 THEN DX = 1
560 SL = (OY - SY) / DX:YP = OY
570  FOR XP =  INT (OX) + 1 TO SX
580 FG = 1
590 YP = YP + SL
```

(continued)

```
600   IF XP < 0 OR XP > 279 THEN FG = 0:F = 0:
      GOTO 650
610   IF YP > 191 OR YP < 0 THEN FG = 0:F = 0
620   IF YP <  = YN(XP) THEN 670
630   IF YP >  = YX(XP) THEN 720
640 F = 0
650   NEXT XP
660 OX = SX:OY = SY: RETURN
670 YN(XP) = YP
680   IF FG = 0 THEN 710
690   IF F = 0 THEN   HPLOT XP,YP:F = 1
700   HPLOT  TO XP,YP
710   IF YP < YX(XP) THEN 650
720   YX(XP) = YP
730   IF FG = 0 THEN 760
740   IF F = 0 THEN   HPLOT XP,YP:F = 1
750   HPLOT  TO XP,YP
760   GOTO 650
770   REM PROJECTION - FOR PLANE
780 XE =   - X * S1 + Y * C1
790 YE =   - X * C1 * C2 - Y * S1 * C2 + Z * S2
800 ZE =   - X * S2 * C1 - Y * S2 * S1 - Z * C2
      + RHO
810 SY =   - D * (YE / ZE) + CY
820   IF FL = 1 THEN   RETURN
830 SX = D * (XE / ZE) + CX
840   RETURN
]
]
```

FRONT COVER; LOWER RIGHT

This image, which resembles a Pennsylvania Dutch hex sign, combines boundary circles with a region defined by the polar coordinate equation $R = COS(2\theta)$. Polar coordinate equations are discussed briefly in Chapter 5. The points of the boundary circles are calculated by the recursive method, also discussed in Chapter 5.

Program A6.4

```
1   REM PROGRAM A6.4  (POLAR HEX SIGN)
2   REM DRAWS LOWER RIGHT IMAGE ON FRONT COVER
10   HGR2 :SC = 1.16
```

```
20 CX = 140:CY = 96
30 C =   COS (.1):S =   SIN (.1)
40  REM POLAR "ROSE"
50  FOR TH = 0 TO 6.3 STEP .05
60 R = 88 *  COS (2 * TH)
70  HCOLOR= 7: IF R < 0 THEN  HCOLOR= 5
80 X = CX + SC * R *  COS (TH)
90 Y = CY + R *  SIN (TH)
100  HPLOT 140,96 TO X,Y
110  NEXT TH
120  REM BOUNDARY CIRCLES
130  HCOLOR= 6
140  FOR R = 90 TO 95 STEP .8:X = R:Y = 0
150  FOR I = 0 TO 63
160 T = X * C - Y * S
170 Y = X * S + Y * C:X = T
180  IF I = 0 THEN  HPLOT CX + SC *
     X,CY - Y
190  HPLOT  TO CX + SC * X,CY - Y
200  NEXT I,R
```

BACK COVER; LEFT

This program makes use of the shape table alphabet and the subroutine which prints shape table text on the high resolution graphics screen (discussed in Chapter 3). The DATA statement of line 60 together with the total, TL, of these data elements (line 100) identifies the relative area of each of the five sectors of the pie chart. For example the area of the first sector is $20/TL = 20/135 \approx .14$ of the total area of the circle.

The DATA statement of line 70 identifies the consecutive colors to be used in drawing the sectors.

Lines 120, 170–190 arrange that the third sector stand out from the rest of the pie chart. If line 120 is changed to define $N = 2$, then the second sector will stand out from the rest of the pie chart. Any of the rest of the sectors could receive this treatment.

Lines 60–110 could be modified to accept user specified sector sizes and colors, so that a pie chart could be developed interactively. Such a program would work well, except for the assignment of labels. The variation in the length of labels makes it difficult to have a completely interactive program which properly positions labels; but you might try.

Program A6.5

```
1    REM PROGRAM A6.5   (PIE CHART)
2    REM DRAWS LEFT IMAGE ON BACK COVER
10   PRINT  CHR$ (4); "BLOAD SHAPE ALPHABET,
     A$6000"
20   POKE 232,0: POKE 233,96
30   SCALE= 1: ROT= 0:SC = 1.16
40   X = 0:Y =  - 75:PI = 3.14159266
50   C =  COS (.01):S =  SIN (.01)
60   DATA 20,50,30,10,25
70   DATA 3,6,5,2,1
80   FOR I = 1 TO 5
90   READ A(I)
100  TL = TL + A(I)
110   NEXT I
120   HGR2 :N = 3
130   FOR I = 1 TO 5
140  FI = (TL * FI + A(I)) / TL
150   READ K: HCOLOR= K
160  CX = 140:CY = 96
170   IF I < > N THEN 200
180  CX = CX + 11 *  SIN ((ST + FI) * PI)
190  CY = CY + 11 *  COS ((ST + FI) * PI)
200   FOR TH = ST * 628 TO FI * 628
210  T = X * C - Y * S:Y = X * S + Y * C:X = T
220   HPLOT CX,CY TO CX + SC * X,CY - Y
230   NEXT TH
240  ST = FI
250   NEXT I
260  HT = 25:VT = 22
270  ST$ = "MISCELLANEOUS": GOSUB 370
280  HT = 34:VT = 9
290  ST$ = "HOUSING": GOSUB 370
300  HT = 1:VT = 2
310  ST$ = "TRANSPORTATION": GOSUB 370
320  HT = 4:VT = 14
330  ST$ = "FOOD": GOSUB 370
340  VT = 21:HT = 5
350  ST$ = "CLOTHING": GOSUB 370
360   END
370  HT = 7 * (HT - 1):VT = 8 * VT - 1
380   FOR I = 1 TO  LEN (ST$)
390  CH =  ASC ( MID$ (ST$,I,1)) - 32
400   IF CH = 0 THEN 420
410   XDRAW CH AT HT,VT
```

```
420 HT = HT + 7
430   NEXT I
440   RETURN
```

BACK COVER; RIGHT

This program is the basis for Figure 7.1 which was drawn by a digital
plotter. The program which was used to draw Figure 7.1 differs from
this one only in that the graphics commands (HGR, HPLOT) used here
were replaced with corresponding plotter commands.

This program is long but simple. The coordinate of line endpoints
are provided through DATA statements, beginning at line 360. As these
are read, they are passed to one of several subroutines. Each uses the
perspective projection subroutine (lines 80–120). The subroutine which
begins at line 290 plots a sequence of N visible line segments. The subroutine beginning at line 140 handles hidden line elimination, using the
binary search method discussed in Chapter 7. The plotting of the sequence of lines which define a window is handled by the subroutine beginning at line 810 This subroutine assumes that the variables X, Y, Z
define the lower left corner of the window. Similarly, subroutine
920–1010 draws a garage door, assuming that X, Y, Z defines the lower
right corner of the door.

The data elements provided, and the hidden line technique used
(binary search) limit the selection of viewpoint. You might want to try
some other values for RHO, THETA, and PHI (lines 20, 30, 40), but be
careful; the range of choices is limited.

Program A6.6

```
1    REM PROGRAM A6.6 (HOUSE)
2    REM DRAWS RIGHT IMAGE ON BACK COVER
3    REM THIS IS ALSO FIGURE 7.1
10   HGR2 : HCOLOR= 3
20   RHO = 100:D = 390:CX = 100:CY = 150
30   THETA = .7:S1 =  SIN (TH):C1 =  COS (TH)
40   PHI = 1.3:S2 =  SIN (PH):C2 =  COS (PH)
50   GOTO 350
60   REM PERSPECTIVE PROJECTION
70   READ X,Y,Z
80 XE =  - X * S1 + Y * C1
```

(continued)

```
90 YE =  - X * C1 * C2 - Y * S1 * C2 + Z * S2
100 ZE =  - X * S2 * C1 - Y * S2 * S1 - Z * C2
    + RHO
110 SX = D * XE / ZE + CX
120 SY = CY - D * YE / ZE: RETURN
130  REM HIDDEN LINE ROUTINE
140  GOSUB 70:XP = SX:YP = SY
150  GOSUB 70:XQ = SX:YQ = SY
160  GOSUB 70:XV = SX:YV = SY
170  GOSUB 70:XH = SX:YH = SY
180 V1 = (XH - XV) / 2:V2 = (YH - YV) / 2
190 U1 = XP - XQ:U2 = YP - YQ
200 XT = XV + V1:YT = YV + V2
210  FOR I = 2 TO 7
220 VI =  SGN ((U2 * (XV - XQ) - U1 * (YV - YQ))
    * (U2 * (XT - XQ) - U1 * (YT - YQ)))
230 V1 = V1 / 2:V2 = V2 / 2
240 XT = XT + VI * V1:YT = YT + VI * V2
250  NEXT I
260  HPLOT XV,YV TO XT,YT
270  RETURN
280  REM VISIBLE LINE ROUTINE
290  FOR I = 1 TO N
300  GOSUB 70
310  IF I = 1 THEN  HPLOT SX,SY
320  HPLOT  TO SX,SY
330  NEXT I: RETURN
340  REM DATA FOR HOUSE
350 N = 11: GOSUB 290
360  DATA -11,-20,23,  6,-20,9,  6,-20,0
370  DATA 6,32,0,  0,32,0,  0,32,20
380  DATA 0,0,20,  0,0,13,  0,32,13
390  DATA 6,32,9,  6,-20,9
400 N = 2: GOSUB 290
410  DATA 6,32,0,  6,32,9
420 N = 2: GOSUB 290
430  DATA 6,0,0,  6,0,9
440 N = 3: GOSUB 290
450  DATA 0,32,0,  0,0,0,  6,0,0
460 N = 5: GOSUB 290
470  DATA 0,32,0,  -11.5,32,0,  -11.5,33.5,0
480  DATA -11.5,33.5,33,  -11.5,32,33
490  GOSUB 140: HPLOT XP,YP TO XQ,YQ
500  DATA -11.5,32,33,  -11.5,32,0
510  DATA 0,32,20,  -14,32,31.5
520  GOSUB 160
```

```
530    DATA -14,0,31.5,   -14,32,31.5
540    GOSUB 140: HPLOT XP,YP TO XQ,YQ
550    DATA 0,0,20,   -14,0,31.5
560    DATA -11,-20,23,   -11,0,23
570  N = 2: GOSUB 290
580    DATA -11.5,33.5,0,   -16.5,33.5,0
590  N = 2: GOSUB 290
600    DATA -11.5,33.5,33,   -16.5,33.5,33
610    GOSUB 140: HPLOT XP,YP TO XQ,YQ
620    DATA -16.5,33.5,0,   -16.5,33.5,33
630    DATA -28,32,0,   -16.5,32,0
640    GOSUB 160
650    DATA -28,32,20,   -14,32,33
660  N = 2: GOSUB 290
670    DATA -28,32,20,   -28,32,0
680    GOSUB 140
690    DATA 6,-20,9,  6,32,9
700    DATA 0,0,0,  0,0,10
710    FOR I = 1 TO 5: READ X,Y,Z: GOSUB 810:
       NEXT I
720    DATA 0,5,13.5,   0,14,13.5,   0,23,13.5
730    DATA 0,14,2,  0,23,2
740    FOR I = 1 TO 2: READ X,Y,Z: GOSUB 920:
       NEXT I
750    DATA 6,-11,0,  6,-1.5,0
760  N = 4: GOSUB 290
770    DATA 0,6,0,  0,6,6.5
780    DATA 0,9,6.5,  0,9,0
790    END
800    REM WINDOWS SUBROUTINE
810    GOSUB 80: HPLOT SX,SY
820  Y = Y + 4: GOSUB 80: HPLOT  TO SX,SY
830  Z = Z + 5.5: GOSUB 80: HPLOT  TO SX,SY
840  Y = Y - 4: GOSUB 80: HPLOT  TO SX,SY
850  Z = Z - 5.5: GOSUB 80: HPLOT  TO SX,SY
860  Y = Y + 2: GOSUB 80: HPLOT SX,SY
870  Z = Z + 5.5: GOSUB 80: HPLOT  TO SX,SY
880  Y = Y - 2:Z = Z - 2.75: GOSUB 80: HPLOT
     SX,SY
890  Y = Y + 4: GOSUB 80: HPLOT  TO SX,SY
900    RETURN
910    REM GARAGE DOOR SUBROUTINE
920    GOSUB 80: HPLOT SX,SY
930  Z = Z + 7: GOSUB 80: HPLOT  TO SX,SY
940  Y = Y - 7.5: GOSUB 80: HPLOT  TO SX,SY
```

(continued)

```
950 Z = Z - 7: GOSUB 80: HPLOT   TO SX,SY
960 Z = Z + 5:Y = Y + 1: GOSUB 80: HPLOT SX,SY
970 Z = Z + 1: GOSUB 80: HPLOT   TO SX,SY
980 Y = Y + 5.5: GOSUB 80: HPLOT   TO SX,SY
990 Z = Z - 1: GOSUB 80: HPLOT   TO SX,SY
1000 Y = Y - 5.5: GOSUB 80: HPLOT   TO SX,SY
1010   RETURN
```

FIGURE 5.1

The microcomputer cannot directly draw a curve. We have achieved curves as a result of drawing sequences of short straight line segments. This program shows how a sequence of curves (circles) can approximate another curve (cardioid).

The program draws nineteen individual circles. The center of each is located on a reference, or base, circle. Further, each of the nineteen circles passes through a common point P on the base circle. The twenty points (P and the nineteen centers) are spaced at equal intervals around the base circle. The base circle is not drawn.

In the program the identification of the nineteen centers (CX, CY) is handled by lines 60–120, using the recursive method of calculating points on a circle. For each center, lines 140–210 draw the associated circle through point P, again using the recursive method of calculating points on a circle.

Figure 5.1 was drawn by a slightly different program than this one. The figure was drawn by a digital plotter, requiring the graphics commands to be replaced with corresponding plotter commands. Otherwise the program is essentially the same as this one.

Program A6.7

```
1   REM PROGRAM A6.7  (FIGURE 5.1)
2   REM DRAWS A CARDIOID AS THE
3   REM ENVELOPE OF CIRCLES
10  PI = 3.14159266
20  XO = 25:YO = 0:XN = XO:YN = YO
30  C =  COS (.1):S =  SIN (.1):N = 64
40  C1 =  COS (PI / 10):S1 =  SIN (PI / 10)
50   HGR2 : HCOLOR= 3
60   FOR I = 1 TO 19
70  T = XN * C1 - YN * S1
```

```
80 YN = XN * S1 + YN * C1:XN = T
90 CX = 140 + XN:CY = 96 - YN
100 X = XO - XN:Y = YO - YN
110  GOSUB 140
120  NEXT I
130  END
140  FOR J = 1 TO N
150 T = X * C - Y * S
160 Y = Y * C + X * S:X = T
170 SX = X + CX:SY = CY - Y
180  IF FL = 0 THEN  HPLOT SX,SY
190  HPLOT  TO SX,SY:FL = 1
200  NEXT J
210  RETURN
```

Index

Books in the Microcomputer Books Series, available from your local computer store or bookstore. For more information write:

General Books Division
Addison-Wesley Publishing Company, Inc.
Reading, Massachusetts 01867
(617)944-3700